AMERICAN ARCHITECTURE OF THE 1980s

AMERICAN ARCHITECTURE OF THE 1980s

Foreword by Donald Canty
Introduction by Andrea Oppenheimer Dean

THE AMERICAN INSTITUTE OF ARCHITECTS PRESS
WASHINGTON, D.C.

CONTENTS

94 93 92 91 90   5 4 3 2 1

The American Institute of Architects Press
1735 New York Avenue, N.W.
Washington, D.C. 20006

Library of Congress Cataloging-in-Publication Data
American architecture of the 1980s
Selection of articles from Architecture, the monthly magazine of the Ameri-
can Institute of Architects.
1. Architecture, Modern—20th century—United States—Themes, motives.
2. Architecture—United States—Themes, motives. I. Architecture (Wash-
ington, D.C.).
NA712.A64   1990   720′.973′09048   89–18461
ISBN 1–55835–056–X
ISBN 1–55835–064–0 (pbk.)

Cover: Illustrations by Brian McCall, Alexandria, Virginia. Clockwise from
top right: Battery Park City, Cesar Pelli & Associates; Monterey Bay Aquarium, Esherick, Homsey, Dodge & Davis; Portland Public Services Building,
Michael Graves; Thorncrown Chapel, E. Fay Jones.

Permissions and photography coordination by Kim Vencill
Book design by Carole J. Palmer; cover design by The AIA Press
Prepress by Applied Graphic Technologies, Inc., Washington, D.C.
Printed by Everbest Printing Co., Ltd., Hong Kong, through Four Colour
Imports, Ltd., Louisville

PHOTO CREDITS

The publisher wishes to acknowledge the assistance of the following photographers, whose cooperation made it possible to republish *Architecture*'s original photographic coverage for most of the projects included in this book.

Peter Aaron • Jaime Ardiles-Arce • Thomas Bernard
Bruce Boehner • Henry Bowles • Richard Bryant
Lucy Capehart • Lucy Chen • Michael J. Crosbie
Mark Darley • Paul Ferrino • Wayne Fujii
Allen Freeman • John Gollings • F. Harlan Hambright
Jim Hedrich • Paul Hester • Hickey-Robertson
Evelyn Hofer • Wolfgang Hoyt • R. Greg Hursley
Timothy Hursley • D. J. Johnson • Howard N. Kaplan
Barbara Karant • H. Carleton Knight III • Robert Lautman
Jane Lidz • Norman McGrath • Joseph W. Molitor
Michael Moran • Peter Paige • Richard Payne
Jock Pottle • Steve Proehl • Cervin Robinson
Brian Rose • Steve Rosenthal • Nicolas Sapieha
Mark Segal • Ezra Stoller • Tim Street-Porter
Peter Vanderwarker • Matt Wargo • Tony Weissgarber

FOREWORD

By Donald Canty, Hon. AIA

The articles that follow come from the pages of *Architecture*, the monthly magazine of the American Institute of Architects, of which I was editor in chief from December 1973 to August 1989. I and Executive Editor Andrea Oppenheimer Dean chose the buildings shown here from the hundreds published in the magazine during the 1980s.

Over the decade covered by this volume every day a dozen or more buildings were submitted to the magazine by architects for consideration. The magazine's contributing editors in all areas of the country and its staff editors also proposed material. Probably one in twenty of the buildings considered was eventually published.

While *Architecture* is the AIA's official magazine it is editorially independent of the AIA. The selection you will see here was not influenced by any AIA board or committee. The magazine had no policy of seeking first or exclusive publication commitments to buildings, so none were excluded because of publication in other architectural magazines.

Since architecture is an art the choices are in part subjective and intuitive. But since architecture is the art of human habitation, each of the buildings shown here was visited and examined while under construction to see how well it meets the requirements set forth in its program, how well it serves the wants and needs of its clients and users. Each was examined for other things as well: How well it expresses the way in which it is built; how it relates to its site; how economical it is in expenditure of energy; how respectful it is of its neighbors.

To call this selection the best of the decade would be presumptuous. But we can claim with confidence that it is representative of the best and of the trends which Andrea Dean traces in her introduction.

Additional reflections on American architecture in the 1980s are contained in a set of essays that conclude the book. They were written by a group of distinguished architects, architectural historians, and critics.

The essayists respond to the following questions, put to them by *Architecture*'s editors: How would you characterize the architecture of the '80s? Have you discerned any trends, the beginnings or endings of any significant movements? What individual works have been most representative of the period?

Readers might consider what their responses will be after seeing the selection of buildings in this book.

INTRODUCTION

By Andrea Oppenheimer Dean

The best American architecture of the 1980s is arguably superior to that of any decade since World War II. As ever, most new construction of the period was not architecture at all; it was simply building. But the decade's best was superlative—more humane, emotionally accessible, and sensitive to physical and cultural setting than were comparable examples from other postwar decades.

If architecture is seen as reflecting the values of its times, the best 1980s design was an achievement that transcended its setting. Like the 1920s, the '80s were years of unrivaled prosperity and economic growth accompanied by conservatism and greed. The shadow of the stock market crash of 1929 hung over the roaring '80s, and a murderous drug trade recalled the massive lawlessness that accompanied Prohibition. There was a pervasive feeling of quiet before the storm, of being poised for a calamity that didn't occur. The stock market crashed, all right, in 1987, but the much-feared bust never came.

That seemed apt for a feel-good era, in which even the most disastrous events—potential or real—were, in the end, often reduced to mere spectacle, four-minute segments for the evening news, without palpable consequences or even existence beyond the nation's short attention span. Architecture, too, tended toward the theatrical, as in the '20s, and often toward the insubstantial and nostalgic. As government increasingly curtailed its responsibility for mounting social problems, individuals also tended to retreat from unpleasant realities and fears for the future into a private, make-believe world where the consumer was king.

Architecture, along with almost everything else, became a marketplace commodity with a short shelf life. In fact, architecture became a marketing tool as developers learned that, much as Calvin Klein's name sells jeans, the names of prominent architects can help lease buildings. "Architecture has taken its hyped-up place on the world stage of celebrity journalism," wrote Ada Louise Huxtable in 1985. The adage form follows function seemed often to give way to form follows form, or, more insidiously, fashion.

The design of the '80s was neither new nor revolutionary. Intellectual conservatism enjoyed a respectability absent since the 1920s as '80s fragmented pluralism and eclecticism mirrored a society frayed by private hubris. Daunted by the future, most architects sought inspiration from the past. As historic preservation became a money-maker, designers redeemed styles from every 20th-century decade before the '60s. There was neorationalism, neoclassicism, neodeco, neomodernism. What made eclecticism so appealing was precisely its lack of dogma and ideology. There was a pervasive disillusionment with the causes that had informed and shaped the architecture of every decade after the '20s. Perhaps modernism as a style wasn't dead, but its animating idealism and belief in human progress now seemed naive. Architecture reverted to being first and foremost a fine art—and a business.

The preeminent building type of the '80s, as of the '20s, was the commercial office building. Some corporations built new headquarters buildings, some private and especially cultural institutions expanded, and the Gatsbys of the period built lavish, architect-designed houses. But architecture's bailiwick shrank. It lost its place as a vehicle for social betterment, in practical as well as moral terms. And, as commercial projects grew in size and complexity, architects often were supplanted by specialists in such disciplines as construction management and programming. Design architects increasingly were used more as decorators of facades and lobbies than as the master builders they had been in the modernist decades.

A major explanation for the superior quality of the best 1980s design lies in some of the very characteristics that made the decade seem culturally anemic and politically and socially regressive. For accompanying a loss of belief in single or simple answers was a disillusionment with the crusader mentality of modern architecture: modernism's defiant, brave-new-world emphasis on the universal, the new, and the heroic was replaced by increased concern with the particular, the familiar, and the humane. Years of macho brashness in design gave way to a new restraint, respect, and responsiveness. A softening of hard edges coincided with a shedding of inflexible and austere theoretic positions.

The architecture of the 1980s sought to retrieve and regroup by restoring interest in such bogeymen of modern architecture as the past and cultural continuity, the everyday, the vernacular, and the regional. And, because the first wave of postmodernism emphasized surface manipulation, it had the effect of refocusing attention on ornament, craftsmanship, materials, the use of color and texture. The '80s produced some of the most exquisite detailing since the '20s. Taste replaced dogma; sophisticated finishes replaced raw-looking materials.

Overall, the greatest benefactors of 1980s architecture were America's downtowns. Victims for years of modernism's emphasis on buildings as independent objects, the downtowns breathed new life under postmodernism's view that a "great city is not a loose conglomeration of high-profile buildings but a densely woven fabric in which buildings are part of the whole," as Robert Geddes put it. Landscape architecture gained new importance as a way of making the connection between individual buildings and the rest of the world.

True to their decade, however, the new downtowns were built around consumption, frequently around so-called festival marketplaces, the progeny of developer James Rouse and architect Benjamin Thompson, who, along with less talented followers, went on to seed downtowns from coast to coast with old-timey-looking shopping complexes. These rapidly became standardized with slightly abstracted historicism, all-alike retail chain stores, and a quality of theater. They are "a theatrical representation of street life," wrote Robert Campbell in *Architecture*. He added that festival marketplaces cater to the affluent, underscore the schism in American cities between the monied and the poor, and thereby mirror the priorities of their time. The revived, carefully groomed and elegant downtowns were stranded in a bog of neglect, as ghettos grew more ragged and more violent.

Nineteen eighties architecture, as we know it, didn't really begin until about 1983, when the economy began to rally after years of recession and high inflation. The first three years of the decade now look like leftovers from the '70s, when President Jimmy Carter proclaimed the energy crisis "the moral equivalent of war" and architects believed energy concerns and a new austerity would serve as form-givers for the design of the 1980s. Instead, as the price of oil fell and the Sunbelt went bust, measures to assure energy efficiency were absorbed in standard architectural practice but failed to appreciably affect form.

With hindsight, however, we can see benchmarks for the decade's prevailing trends as early as 1980. There was, for example, the American entry in the 1980 Venice Biennale, entitled "The Presence of the Past." It hoped to do for postmodernism what the International Style exhibition of 1932 at the Museum of Modern Art had done for modern architecture—confer legitimacy and move it into the mainstream. "La Strada Novissima," as the American contribution was called, consisted of a row of facades by Robert A.M. Stern, Robert Venturi, Stanley Tigerman, and others. It was just facades, as so much '80s architecture was just facades. It looked thin, more like stage sets than real buildings, but La Strada Novissima did serve to refocus attention on decoration, composition, color, and diversity of expression.

The most talked about building in 1980 was the Crystal Cathedral in Orange County, Calif. Its architects were Philip Johnson and John Burgee. Its patron was television evangelist Robert Schuller, whose general message, appropriate to the '80s, was that the road to riches, as exemplified by Schuller himself, is paved with self-satisfaction. The dedication of Schuller's huge, $18 million, glass tent-cum-church headquarters building was pure Reagan razzmatazz. The President sent greetings, and a Goodyear blimp hovered overhead while Schuller delivered a sermon entitled "Why Did God Want the Crystal Cathedral to Be Built?" Nine years after completion of his church, Schuller would deliver the keynote address, on the inspirational value of architecture, at the last AIA convention of the decade.

A very different kind of religious building dominated the architectural stage in 1981. It was the highly personal, handcrafted Thorncrown Chapel by E. Fay Jones, a modest wood structure, gently set into the edge of a forest near Eureka Springs, Ark. If the Crystal Cathedral is a TV-Disney-corporate church, Thorncrown is a timeless, modest, and quiet meditation center. Both buildings fall outside postmodernism. The Crystal Cathedral is slick, late-modern, while Thorncrown (and its sibling, the Cooper Memorial Chapel of 1988 in Bella Vista, Ark.) has no identifiable style, though it is deeply indebted to Frank Lloyd Wright.

If the '80s were, in fact, the decade of postmodern corporate architecture—and to a large extent they were—two buildings were pivotal. The first was New York City's AT&T building, designed in the late '70s by the architects of Schuller's church and finished in 1983. It was a first in restoring to skyscraper design the classical tripartite division into base, middle, and top—in this case a Chippendale top. AT&T became a media event, as *Time* magazine ran a picture of Philip Johnson as a caped impresario holding a model of AT&T. The age of the celebrity-architect was upon us. But the completed building proved anticlimactic. As Paul Goldberger wrote in the *New York Times* in 1983, "Mr. Johnson and Mr. Burgee's commitment to classical architecture, which seemed so daring in 1978, now seems, oddly, not to go far enough."

The second benchmark building was Michael Graves's Portland Public Services Corporation Building in Portland, Ore. Officially dedicated in 1982, it caused at least as much stir as AT&T, in part because Johnson, as professional adviser in the city of Portland's competition to choose an architect, intervened on Graves's behalf. He wanted to give his favorite "kid" a chance to realize ideas until then restricted to paper. Though modern in its boxy shape, the vividly colored, classically ornamented Portland building was otherwise postmodern and the first large-scale commercial building by a member of the Venturi-Graves-Stern generation. As such, it ushered in a new crop of urban towers. It was also roundly criticized. Pietro Belluschi, during hearings on the competition design, called it "an enlarged jukebox, an oversized beribboned Christmas package." Wolf von Eckardt, in the *Washington Post,* proclaimed it "dangerous" to other architects.

Graves's second skyscraper, the Humana tower in Louisville, Ky., received a more benign reception.

Graves himself became the preeminent "starchitect." He was featured in the pages of *People* magazine, mobbed by autograph seekers at the dedication of the Portland Building, interviewed on network television news, and asked to design fabrics, furniture, and teapots. His drawings commanded prices in the thousands of dollars at a New York City gallery. Hundreds of architects at the 1982 AIA convention wore buttons proclaiming, "We Don't Dig Graves," which only confirmed Graves's celebrity.

The most eloquent and perhaps most influential urban achievement of 1980s postmodernism was Cesar Pelli's World Financial Center at Battery Park City in Lower Manhattan. The largest urban design project since Rockefeller Center, Battery Park City was a combined effort of state, city, and private investment and management. Its first accomplishment was as a masterpiece of planning by Cooper, Eckstut. The planning firm produced guidelines specifying the relationship of the complex to Manhattan's financial district, the placement of the project's buildings, their heights, massing, setbacks, circulation patterns, and so on. Though Pelli devised a boldly contemporary, synthesizing style of skyscraper, featuring the towers' extraordinary, taut, and glistening skins, his complex evokes earlier New York skyscrapers in its setbacks, geometrical tops, and tripartite division. As a group, the towers became a new model of urbanism for showing that huge buildings can be related to a fine-grained, smaller-scaled, old part of a city, maintain the line of the street wall and the scale of the neighborhood, and create usable in-between spaces graced by public art and landscaping.

As large developers spread their purview to become national, a few architectural firms began dominating skyscraper design and changing the skylines of many American cities. In addition to Pelli they included Skidmore, Owings & Merrill; Johnson/Burgee; and Kohn Pedersen Fox. Concerning the last, Walter McQuade wrote in *Architecture* in May 1989, "The KPF approach to architecture is grounded in three tenets: first, a frank and literal connection with the historical past, sometimes in blunted reproduction; next, an emphasis on matching the building to its urban context, without relinquishing the impact of the new; finally, a certain confidence in intuition. They intend their towers to resonate, like Empire State, like Chrysler." That was equally true of Pelli, Burgee, SOM, and a few others.

One result, however, of the trend toward a small number of architects designing a large number of buildings in cities across the nation was homogenization of urban architecture and dissipation of the benefits of regionalism. (As the Southwest regionalist Anthony Predock said, "A regionalist is an architect with no commissions out of state.")

By far the greatest concentration of U.S. urban development in the '80s was in the suburbs and exurbs rather than in the downtowns. At thruway intersections everywhere, new pseudo-urban concentrations popped up with the vigor and logic of Topsy. They included vast, impersonal stretches of second- or third- generation, high-tech-looking office buildings organized around retail malls, which, in turn, served the '80s as combination cultural center and village square. These minicities, usually composed of strung-together, sealed megastructures surrounded by cars, were sometimes called "urban villages." But they had neither streets nor other vestiges of urbanity nor hints of village charm. They were an advanced stage of what Lewis Mumford, more than 25 years ago, called Roadtown: "an incoherent and purposeless urbanoid nonentity, which dribbles over the devastated landscape and destroys the coherent smaller centers of urban or village life that stand in its path."

The obverse of these soulless subcities were the small-town new towns, which packaged nostalgic versions of bygone American village life, adapted for the rich and cleansed of Babbittry, tedium, and toil. The model was the new resort town of Seaside in Florida, designed by Miami architects Andres Duany and Elizabeth Plater-Zyberk. Seaside had Victorian forms, detailing, and charm, porches to rock on and public squares to gossip in. At a time of mounting opposition to unlimited growth, it was a deliberately limited community fashioned by a single organizing vision rather than a commercial or social imperative. It spawned offspring from coast to coast. Many of the knockoffs were standard-setters of a new kitsch, cut off from the original sources of artistic creation and, thus, from insight and integrity.

Far more convincing as showcases for 1980s' architecture were museums. Among the gems were Richard Meier's High Museum in Atlanta and his Museum für Kunsthandwerk in Frankfurt, West Germany; Charles Moore's Hood Museum at Dartmouth College; Harry Cobb's art museum in Portland, Me.; I.M. Pei's pyramid for the Louvre in Paris; and Renzo Piano's Menil Collection in Houston. Museums became the cathedrals of the '80s.

As repositories of icons, symbols, and memories of days past and seemingly simpler, museums embodied that sense of permanence, continuity, and meaning so pervasively sought after in the '80s. They also responded to our impulse to conserve and cherish anything predating 1960. In part, the museum boom of the '80s was a reaction to the buildings of the last museum boom, that of the '60s. That decade's progeny usually resembled warehouses for art— anonymous, all-purpose, boxy. Eighties museums, by contrast, had great variety, admitted light and sun, and, like everything else during the decade, became increasingly commercial. Museum shops became important as income-producers, and some museums added office and even condominium space. The best-known example was Cesar Pelli's high-rise addition to the Museum of Modern Art.

As architecture gained celebrity status, publishing houses and magazines for the general public devoted more pages to it, while television acknowledged it with air time. The results were usually controversial, as when, in 1981, social critic and author Tom Wolfe attacked modern architecture in *From Bauhaus to Our House.* Wolfe impaled modern architecture as a plot foisted on an unwilling world by a group of European intellectuals. His book, which similarly criticized postmodernism as the product of another out-of-touch compound, was received with hostility by architects of all stripes. But even bad publicity is good, and architecture hadn't received this much attention in years. Only four years after publication of his book, Wolfe was asked to be keynote speaker at the 1985 AIA convention.

Robert A.M. Stern's eight-part series "Pride of Place" aired on public television in the spring of 1986. Advertised as a personal vision of American architecture, it echoed Wolfe's view of modern architecture as a lamentable break with the past but cast postmodernism as the redeemer. Largely a tour of opulent American premodern residences, "Pride of Place" was an abundantly 1980s view of American architectural history that traded on sentimental-

ity and made history appear to be a matter of packaging, decoration, and facades. It ended with Stern and architect Leon Krier—the Aldous Huxley of the '80s—riding the streets of Williamsburg, Va., in a horse-drawn carriage and agreeing that in many respects the reconstructed colonial town was—oh, brave new world—the best hope for the future of American architecture.

Architectural historian Spiro Kostof's public television series "America by Design" aired in 1987. More ambitious than "Pride of Place," it was less about architectural history, as such, than about the sociological, technological, and political forces that shaped the American built environment. The series was about ideas more than images, and the American public—even the public television American public—tuned the program out.

By the close of the decade, the stylistic battles, tiresome arguments, and factional infighting of the early '80s seemed as out of date as the Cold War. While much of the early built work had been ironical, two-dimensional, and cartoonish, by decade's end the best architects had become more genuinely comfortable with history and tended to abstract and transform their sources and to agree that anything goes but only quality counts. By the late '80s, even dyed-in-the-wool old modernists were designing retro buildings.

Not surprisingly, however, the pendulum had begun to swing back again. Throughout the decade, modernism had remained an influential presence, a foil against which to react, test, and measure ideas. By mid-decade there was a revival of interest in Mies; Frank Lloyd Wright, who had never been eclipsed, received abundant attention; and Le Corbusier's centenary was broadly and respectfully celebrated. At least two disciples of Le Corbusier, Richard Meier and Charles Gwathmey, were among the decade's most respected designers.

The single most appreciated talent of the '80s was, arguably, the highly individual, downright quirky Frank Gehry of Los Angeles, whose sensibilities, again, were primarily modern. By 1989, Gehry had been awarded six AIA national honor awards, most accrued in the latter years of the decade.

In fact, the decade opened with completion and publication of Gehry's own house in Santa Monica. Brash and startling at first glance, it was really a studied composition of restored and new construction. Oddly shaped and positioned openings in the new parts framed views of the existing structure, and there were ambiguous readings of interior-exterior relationships, colliding forms, and the use of crude materials—including chain link fence, which soon became Gehry's trademark. Architect Robert Frasca regards Gehry as "first and foremost a regionalist (some would say a microregionalist whose work thrives in areas with high levels of carbon monoxide)."

Gehry himself has suggested that his work is a commentary on Los Angeles as a banal environment with "bits and pieces of industrial buildings and freeways" and corrugated metal and stud framing. "I have just regurgitated it in another personal way." To *US News and World Report,* the architect spoke of the affinity of his work with Andy Warhol's soup can paintings, where the use of common cultural artifacts altered the way we looked at things. Gehry also said, "I want to be open-ended. There are no rules, no right or wrong." That could stand as the theme of the 1980s.

By the end of the decade, Gehry was collaborating on designs for mammoth downtown projects with Skidmore, Owings & Merrill, and his colliding, diagonal, asymmetric, free-flying forms had been given a name, deconstructivism. Philip Johnson inspired an exhibition of deconstructivist work at the Museum of Modern Art in the spring of 1988, which featured work by Gehry, Zaha Hadid, Peter Eisenman, Rem Koolhaas, Daniel Libeskind, Bernard Tschumi, and the Viennese firm Coop Himmelblau. Some thought it would be the most important such event since the 1932 International Style show. Mark Wigley, author of the catalog, said of deconstructivism's importance, "Nothing has happened for so long, we are all desperate to talk about something. . . . I guess in a way the show marks the forgetting of postmodernism. . . . It's a very small exhibition with a very narrow agenda about a tight set of ideas."

Well, it was a little more than that. To the extent that it was valid as more than a mind game, deconstructivism posed a direct challenge to the cozy-comfy historicism of the '80s. In January 1989, the top two annual *Progressive Architecture* design awards went to projects that could only be called deconstructivist.

In November 1989, the first large building by Peter Eisenman, the guru of deconstructivisim, was opened, and Eisenman had a number of other large commissions in progress.

Further, in 1989, Frank Gehry was awarded the 1989 Pritzker International Architecture award, architecture's closest thing to a Nobel. In commendation, the jury praised Gehry for "his restless spirit that has made his buildings a unique expression of contemporary society and its ambivalent values."

The Pritzker's first winner, in 1979, was Philip Johnson. Taken together, the work and attitudes of the first and latest Pritzker winners embodied the prevailing design approaches of the '80s. (Premiated between 1980 and 1989 were Luis Barragán of Mexico, '80; James Stirling of Great Britain, '81; Kevin Roche, '82; I.M. Pei, '83; Richard Meier, '84; Hans Hollein of Austria, '85; Gottfried Böhm of West Germany, '86; Kenzo Tange of Japan, '87; and Gordon Bunshaft and Oscar Niemeyer of Brazil, both in '88.)

Johnson, ever a weather vane for developing design trends, became a barometer of early- and mid-'80s sensibilities, with his wide-ranging eclecticism and historicism. Gehry, by contrast, in remaining aloof from movements and working in a mostly ahistorical, abstract idiom, represented attitudes gaining dominance at decade's end. As different as these two architects were, however, they shared a view of architecture as first and last a fine art. The result has been a fertile decade that has embraced and refined a range of expression from literal historicism to minimalist abstraction, from regionalism to corporate internationalism, from organic architecture to cool high-tech. □

1980

The Atheneum

Gehry House

A Vision Continued

Richard Meier's Atheneum, New Harmony, Ind.
By Stanley Abercrombie, AIA

Anyone visiting Richard Meier's office in the last couple of years couldn't have missed it: the astonishingly detailed model of his design for the Atheneum in New Harmony, Ind. And anyone seeing it might have been forgiven for wondering: Had Meier finally overstepped his limits as a designer; had his fascination with complex parts overwhelmed his control of the total composition; had his work become overly complicated, overly mannered, overwrought?

Now that the Atheneum is built, these worries can be forgotten. The building is an exhilarating beauty, establishing a new and even higher level of achievement in Meier's work. Here and there it may seem, like the model, to be a bit esthetically muscle-bound, but there is no doubt that it is a superb work of architecture. The features that seemed fussy at one-sixteenth-inch scale are bold and clear at full size; the elaborate interior and exterior circulation system, which might have been suspected of being merely decorative, is seen to be a well-reasoned and fully used accommodation of public movement, and the complexities that might have been overbearing in a tighter context are welcome delights on the building's actual site—a broad, bare field sloping gently down to the wooded banks of the Wabash River.

It is a beautiful site in a fascinating community, and the building's purpose is to inform visitors about the town. It houses a giant model of the original settlement, a number of other exhibits and a theater in which a brief film is shown. At the end of the tour through the building, visitors climb (in good weather) to the roof for a view of the town, then descend a stair and a long ramp to visit a series of the town's restored buildings.

New Harmony was founded in the wilderness in 1814 by the Harmonists, a group of less than a thousand Lutheran Church dissenters from Würtemberg, Germany. We all might not have been at home there: The keystones of community life were hard work and celibacy. This life, however, produced an impressive number of sturdily built dormitories, mills and factories, a handsome cruciform brick church and two thousand cultivated acres. In 1825, seeking a location closer to the markets for its goods, the sect sold the entire town and moved to Pennsylvania. But New Harmony's experimentation was not ended: The buyer was the Welsh reformer Robert Owen, who imported a boatload of noted scholars in an attempt to found an "empire of good sense." One of Owen's changes was to convert the Harmonists' church into an Atheneum (a center of learning). Within two years, Owen admitted his experiment a failure, but many of his imported scholars remained, and New Harmony continued to be exceptional. It claims to have produced the first kindergarten, the first trade school, the first free public school system and the first free library. In 1960 Philip Johnson's well-known "roofless church" was built in New Harmony, and later and nearby, the Pottery, a

A restored 19th century farmhouse is one of the sights that Meier's gleaming new visitors' center explains. Next page, Evelyn Hofer's photo of the complex facade facing the curving banks of the Wabash.

Evelyn Hofer

'The white is not just white but shiny white.'

little-known Meier building housing a ceramics school, was built.

A distinction of New Harmony's character—in contrast to single-period communities like Williamsburg, Va.—is that it preserves elements from so many stages of its past. The addition of the new Atheneum, a building very clearly of the present, is thus a continuation of tradition, not an intrusion.

Meier's all-white palette is used to great advantage here, the only colored materials allowed being maple strip flooring and some dark gray industrial carpeting. In addition (unlike Meier's all-white houses), there is almost no freestanding furniture (an exception being a conference table and chair group similar to the one Meier designed for his library at the Guggenheim Museum). And, on the exterior, the white is not just white but shiny white, the skin formed from metal panels with a porcelain enamel finish. The result of this whiteness and emptiness is an inspiriting lack of clutter, and, here again, there is a remarkable difference between model and building. We are accustomed to seeing architects' models as all-white abstractions, no matter what the intended materials and colors. We are not accustomed to such an effect in a finished building of this size, and the effect is powerful.

The Atheneum's complexity, unprecedented in Meier's work, does not necessarily herald a continued escalation of complexity in that work, for the Atheneum is a specific response to its site and program. But the unprecedented *presence* of the Atheneum does herald a new degree of Meier's confidence as an artist. The Atheneum is at once the best and also the most uncompromisingly Meier-like of all Meier's work so far. □

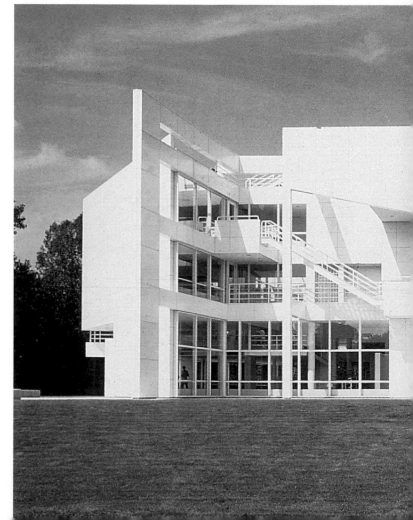

Three exterior views, with the building entrance visible in the top two. At bottom, the long ramp serves as an exit from the building and as the beginning guide for a tour of the restored town beyond.

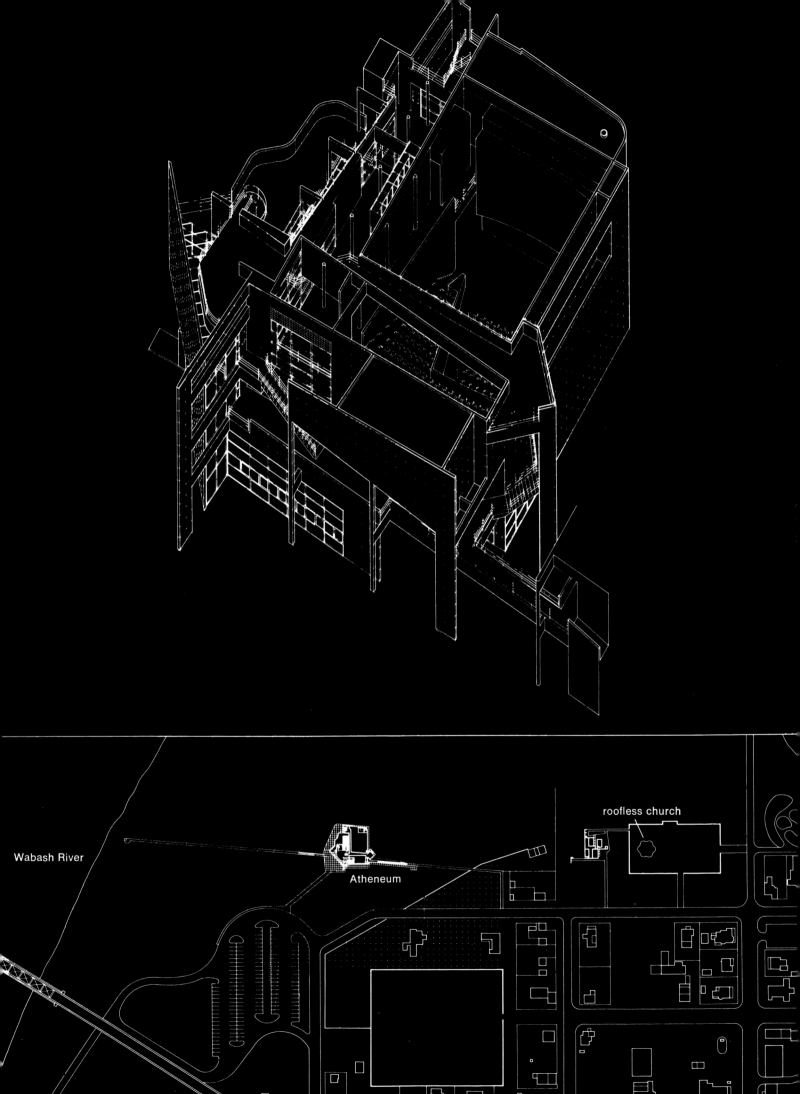

Wabash River

Atheneum

roofless church

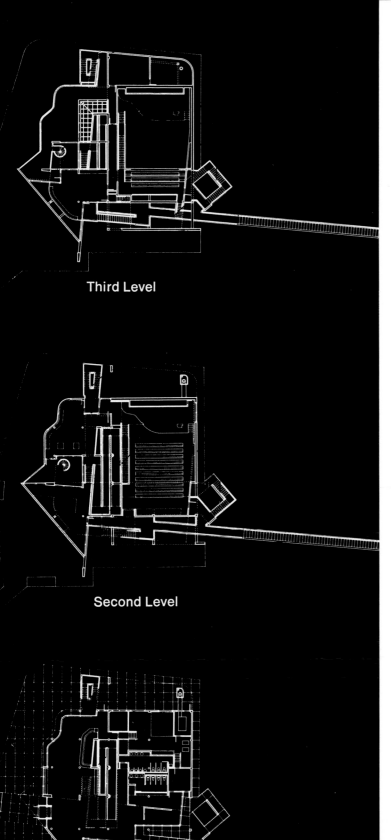

Third Level

Second Level

Ground Level

Axonometric, top left, and second and third floor plans, above, show the sequence of exhibit areas wrapped around the building's largest space, a simple gray and white auditorium. A brief film here ends the visitor's journey through the building; he then climbs to the roof for a view of the town, then descends the stairs and stepped ramp, right, for a closer look.

Evelyn Hofer

Left and left below, carpeted ramp climbs from lobby assembly area, its elaborate configuration heightening visitors' anticipation of the tour. The first exhibit seen on the second floor (bottom right, opposite page) is a scale model of the entire town in a large glass vitrine. Below, a low display case, like the glass wall behind it, undulates in response to the curving riverbank beyond.

Allen Freeman

The end of the tour: an open roof deck with a view of the river. A farther climb reveals a view, on the other side of the building, of the entire town of New Harmony. And, always close at hand, there is the fascinating play of the Atheneum's geometry and its immaculate porcelain surfaces.

Evelyn Hofer

12

Of Art, Self-Revelation and Iconoclasm

A house remade by Frank Gehry in Santa Monica, California. By John Pastier

Frank Lloyd Wright once said that America was tilted in such a way that everything loose eventually rolled into Southern California. Living in the land of Kosher burritos, drive-in churches, roller-skate disco, Rent-A-Wreck auto leasing and the Phantom Toenail Painter, its residents have learned to take most things in stride. Environmental calamities are borne as nonchalantly as cultural ones.

There comes a point, however, when enough is enough, and some of Frank Gehry's neighbors are sure that they don't like what he's done to his little pink house in Santa Monica. In fact, as you glance over these pages, you may even be forming similar opinions yourself.

That's understandable. Gehry's unconventional remodeling is a work of architecture that must be seen and wandered through if it is to be understood. Trying to convey its substance through photographs and words is an act of high futility on a par with alchemists' efforts to transmute lead into gold: The exercise may enlighten one who attempts it but will not produce the hoped-for results. People who know it only second hand, even if they are architects, tend to be unenthusiastic or even dislike the house actively. Those who have been through it become believers, because what the house is most about is what the flat photographic medium is least able to convey: tangible space, palpable scale, time, and a multiplicity of possible comparisons and interactions

between its elements. Once those qualities have been experienced, there can be no doubt that this is an extraordinarily original and deeply felt house, despite the somewhat self-conscious iconoclasm of its exterior.

It can be approached in several ways: as architecture, as a curiosity, as art, or as psychological revelation. The first three paths are well worn, for this house that defies successful publication has appeared in service magazines, newspaper real estate sections, airline magazines, alternative architectural tabloids and establishment architectural slicks. It has been presented as pure imagery, a West Coast cultural phenomenon, a local controversy involving an artist and his less than artistic neighbors and as an occasion for close architectural analysis. What remains is for someone adept in psychology and fluent in English to examine Gehry's house as a manifestation of nonlinear logic, visual symbolism and the Jungian collective unconscious.

Such an examination cannot take place here, but it is important to temper the architectural discussion with explicit recognition of the essential emotionally nature of this house. Some of Gehry's work has been conventionally disciplined and straightforward, but that is not his characteristic mode of design nor is it the one that stimulates him to his best efforts; if anything, it probably bores him. The ultimate basis of his work is nonverbal and visceral, and even with the advent of postmodernism, those are not

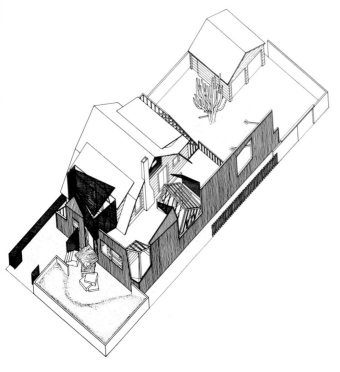

Photographs by Tim Street-Porter/ESTO

Wrapped around the existing house is a screen of plywood, aluminum siding, chain link fencing and other miscellany. Near right, the kitchen; far right the living area, with the original windows held in walls stripped to their studs.

More affinity to Watts Towers than postmodernism.

qualities that the architectural world has been able to deal with easily. Thus, Gehry's house continues to be discussed as though verbal constructs could always be equated with architectural ones, and as though linear thinking could somehow be applied, after the fact, to a work that evolved without significant reliance on that mechanism.

Frank Gehry's house is a major example of postmodern work, but not one arrived at through normal postmodern methods. Granted, it has one foot in the world of self-conscious and intellectualized architectural revisionism, but the other, the one to which more weight has been shifted, is in the world of intensely committed individual builders such as Simon Rodia, who worked out personal visions such as the Watts Towers intuitively and with their own hands. Many of Gehry's influences have clearly come from West Coast avant-garde art, but he has also absorbed the ethos of those tenacious craftsmen that the Walker Art Center has defined as "naives and visionaries."

Of course Gehry did not rebuild the house himself, but it looks as though he might have, and the design clearly benefitted from on-site decisions and feedback from the building process. Nor is he a *naif*, not after art studies and an architecture degree from the University of Southern California, a year of city planning at Harvard and more than 20 years of diversified practice. Yet he has

somehow managed to preserve, or resuscitate, the untrained artisan's capacity to see ordinary materials as wonderful and to use them in unexpected and poetic ways.

Simon Rodia used beer bottles, crockery and sea shells as cladding for his backyard castle, and Gehry has used chain link fencing, utility grade plywood and corrugated sheet metal for his. Like the neighbors, the local building departments looked askance at both creations.

But there the similarities end, and a critical difference arises: Rodia's spires, although built on an architectural scale, were sculpture. They provided no shelter from the elements and enclosed no useful space. Gehry's design not only encloses space, but plays with it, distributes it with a generous hand, and makes it the point of the whole effort. It is this focus on space that also distinguishes his house from the work of a group of New York City artists: By taking his house apart as well as putting it together, Gehry has invited comparison with SITE's disintegrating showrooms for Best Products. Within limits such comparisons are useful, particularly since both parties have ventured into the psychology of the unconscious with their paradoxical imagery. However, SITE's work is confined to facades and other external elements, while Gehry's exteriors are the lesser part of his accomplishment—the front elevation, in fact, is the one arguably unsuccessful episode in a complicated effort.

Perhaps unintendedly, the emphasis on interior space is a dou-

Incarnation of the houses of children's dreams.

bly potent metaphor. It represents the essence of shelter, of inhabiting, of the home as a family refuge and a private place. But it goes still further, suggesting that just as there's more to Gehry's house than the exterior meeting a skeptical neighbor's eye, so there may be more to his design than playing with unusual materials and distorted forms. Complex inner space, at least in this case, parallels complex inner meanings.

The house is a pink, asbestos shingled, gambrel roofed "Dutch colonial" affair in a desirable but environmentally nondescript part of northern Santa Monica. "It was just a dumb little house with charm," Gehry explains, "and I became interested in trying to make it more important. I became fascinated with creating a shell around it, one that allowed the old house to exist as an object, and, in a sense, defined the house by only showing parts. . . . It's very surreal, and I am interested in surrealism."

Gehry achieves that surrealism by direct visual reference—his use of diagonals to create illusions of sharp perspective recalls several of de Chirico's paintings—and by displacements such as transforming the old house exterior into an interior wall of the new kitchen and dining room, and then paving the floor of those added spaces with blacktop to represent a driveway that the original house never had. Stripping away some of the old finishes down to the wooden lath, or even the studs and joists, furthers the effect, as does the use of fine-mesh chain link fencing as flooring for a small, almost inaccessible upper walkway leading nowhere. One enters the house through a new door, only to find the old front door two steps beyond. The old windows look out on the new inside of the house, and the line between indoors and out is blurred in a far subtler fashion than ever effected by the old regional standby of sliding glass doors.

The original and added walls are counterposed in such a way that each questions and reassures the other. The new work echoes the old, the old seems to have awaited the new.

This is a splendid place for children—Frank and Berta Gehry have two young sons—for it is a timeless incarnation of all the houses that children have imagined in their dreaming and playing in attics, and even on the first visit it gives one the inexplicable feeling of having been there before. Through his preoccupation with the insides of a house, Gehry has discovered something about the inner mind, and in stripping away old shingles and plaster he has also laid bare part of his soul, and part of ours as well. □

Above, another window and stud composition.

1981

Thorncrown Chapel

The Crystal Cathedral

Immanuel Presbyterian Church

Gaffney House

'A Building of Great Integrity'

Fay Jones' Thorncrown Chapel, Eureka Springs, Ark. By Stanley Abercrombie, AIA

Thorncrown Chapel, winner of a 1981 AIA honor award, is more than a striking building. It may well be turning up 50 years from now in anthologies of 20th-century architecture, for it is an original. True, it owes something to Wrightian tradition (E. Fay Jones, AIA, was an apprentice at Taliesen in 1952), perhaps most apparently to the California "Wayfarers' Chapel" of 1951 by FLW's son Lloyd Wright; also true, it is closely related to Jones' earlier works. But it hews remarkably faithfully to the demands of its location, of its program and of Jones' personal vision, with not a glance toward any current design fashion. It is a building of great integrity.

Jones points out that Thorncrown reverses Gothic construction: Rather than being pushed together by outside masses in compression the building is pulled together by light interior members in tension. But there is also something here in common with Gothic structure and with so many works in which we find special poignancy: the use of the sparest means.

Also evident is a rare concern for fitting the Ozark Mountains site, a steep slope thick with oaks, maples and dogwoods. One might expect the chapel to point toward the valley view, but Jones' solution is less obvious. Lying along the slope, the building has one glass wall facing the valley, an opposite wall facing the rocky wooded hillside and an altar end opening to a small grove of trees, a rock outcropping and a steel cross. The cross is

Materials hand-carried through the woods.

placed a few feet off center of the otherwise symmetrical composition, and the unexpected placement gives it a visual interest it would otherwise lack. Nowhere, therefore, is the chapel thrust out into the open; except where a gravel path leads to the entrance, trees are close to it at all sides.

The desire to save as much adjacent growth as possible determined the construction technique. Heavy equipment was ruled out, and materials were limited to those two workers could carry through the woods. (Most members are pine 2x4s; the heaviest— in corner columns—are 2x12s.) Trusses were fabricated on top of the floor slab, not to one side. The necessary stacking of the completed trusses provided a check for the precise alignment of members that was desired. Beneath the wood structure are two long walls of stone, the one on the uphill side serving as a retaining wall, and both serving as duct work. Insulated cavities within the walls feed air into the space through hardly visible gaps in the mortar joints between the stones. The overhanging deciduous trees, of course, are great assets in temperature control, and the flooring of native flagstone beneath a large skylight provides an element of passive solar heating in winter.

But it is the delicate web of overhead structure that most commands our attention. Jones and his office did their own engineer-

R. Greg Hursley

An 'eye' at the crossing of the connectors.

ing, as is their custom whenever possible, aided in this case by a half-inch-scale model that was tested for reaction to applied loads. The result is a remarkable array of minimal elements. Some of these are frankly decorative, but the decoration is derived from the nature of the construction, and some vertical elements that may appear nonstructural do serve the function of stiffening slender diagonal members. A significant detail is the hardware at the central crossing: steel truss connectors made of four members that intersect like a slightly askew tic-tac-toe game. The felicitous touch is that the centers of these connectors have been left empty, providing unexpected sparkles of light at the heart of the structure. These connectors, as well as lecterns, pew supports, door pulls and the exterior cross, are painted an icy blue; the wood is tinted and preserved by a gray stain.

R. Greg Hursley

A caring and sparing touch on details.

Furnishings echo the structure's repetition of thin elements. Lecterns screw into plugs recessed into the stone floor and can therefore be used in several different locations. Two tall wood cabinets at the altar end hold music equipment and speakers. The blue speaker cloth and pew upholstery provide a touch of strong color.

Jones, assisted by Maurice Jennings, AIA, one of his firm's two associates, has created a chapel that seems to inspire visitors. Whatever its purpose, it is a building that should inspire architects as well. □

Soaring Space Wrapped In Metal and Glass

Crystal Cathedral, Garden Grove, Calif., Johnson/Burgee. By John Pastier

We live in a time of resurgent Christianity, yet up to now there has been scant architectural testimony to that pervasive movement. The great churches of this neofundamentalist period may still be in the design stage, but it is also possible that current forms of belief are not conducive to worldly monuments of brick and mortar.

Our national religious experience is becoming increasingly an electronic one. Syndicated television programs that straddle the ground between variety hour, old-time singing and preaching, talk show and on-the-spot healing have become a familiar if not standard video format. Accordingly, the quintessential meeting place of God and mortals is no longer a cathedral, church or chapel, but a broadcast studio housing evangelistic and performing stars, an audience of the faithful and sophisticated equipment and technicians.

For an architect concerned with the expressive possibilities of structure and space, this is not a very promising building type. Nevertheless, the most generally celebrated American building of the past year grew out of nearly similar requirements. The Crystal Cathedral, centerpiece of the Garden Grove Community Church, serves as a shooting set and studio, but assumes the size and purpose of a traditional church as well. It is undoubtedly one of the high points of Philip Johnson's long and varied career, but, even more significantly, it owes its existence to a rare patron of seemingly boundless optimism and energy.

Robert H. Schuller, the church's senior pastor, is no novice at finding world-renowned designers for his buildings. He began his career preaching from the roof of a refreshment stand at a local drive-in theater, but when it came time to build a conventional structure in 1959, his choice of architect was no less than Richard Neutra. That conventional church turned out to be anything but— Schuller insisted that his drive-in congregation also be accommodated on the new premises and Neutra, always receptive to technology, responded with a building that allowed the young minister to part the church walls with the touch of a button and preach from a cantilevered balcony to an outdoor congregation neatly parked in concentric semicircular rows. As Schuller's ministry grew, so did the sanctuary, and structures were built, including a 14-story office "Tower of Hope," designed by Neutra (with his

Photos show the cathedral, sitting in a sea of parking like an unearthly visitor to a suburban shopping center, changing in the changing light.

'Please, can't you make it all glass?'

son Dion) and surmounted by a 75-foot-high neon cross.

Even with these additions to what Schuller has termed "a 22-acre shopping center for Jesus Christ," the Garden Grove Community Church's parishioners continued to be cramped in the several buildings and parking lots. In 1970, Schuller took a step that helped relieve the need for more space, but which also cultivated that need in the long run: He began broadcasting Sunday services on television. A congregation that could choose to worship indoors, outside on folding chairs or outside in vehicles (listening in on its dashboard radios), could now also choose to attend services in its living room or den.

According to conventional wisdom, one would think that Schuller's space problems had finally been solved. The "global village" of electronic communication is supposed to make physical proximity unnecessary, if not actually undesirable, yet the church's flesh-and-blood congregation kept growing. Television had made Robert Schuller an even bigger magnet for worshipers, and even as it provided an alternative to seeing him in person, it also stimulated the desire to do so. After embracing a new technology, Schuller's logical next step was to return to an old one—architecture.

When he did, it was not an act of mere necessity but a recognition of the creative and symbolic possibilities that a new building represented. Schuller wanted nothing less than the world's best architect, and upon seeing a magazine photograph of Philip Johnson's Fort Worth Water Gardens during a transcontinental flight, he became convinced that Johnson was that person. Landing in New York City, he sought an audience with the architect by telling the receptionist that he "had worked with Richard Neutra on

several projects." This message failed to bring Johnson out of his office, and Schuller now laughingly deduces that he was mistaken for a draftsman seeking work.

Soon after, however, better communication was established, and Johnson set about designing a major church. The client's wishes were clear and simple: The building should seat 4,000 people, be flooded with light and respect the older Neutra structures. A budget was not specified.

When Johnson's first design was unveiled, it was not greeted with applause. "He nearly threw us out of the room," chuckles the architect. "I was politely nonaffirmative," says the positive-thinking pastor, tongue obviously in cheek. The problem was sight. The church had a transparent roof but opaque walls, rather like Johnson's art gallery on the grounds of his Connecticut home, and this was too confining visually for Schuller's taste. Accordingly, he asked the architect, "Please, can't you make it all glass?" Johnson did; the church gained a catchy nickname, and a few years and $18 million later, network television and the weekly newsmagazines were there to cover its inaugural event. By now it has become a small part of our native folklore and an Orange County tourist attraction.

Connoisseurs may consider Johnson's own house as his finest design, and the new AT&T headquarters as his most controversial, but this will very likely be the one that is most widely remembered. Credit for that must go to Robert Schuller. His love of architecture for its own sake has not obscured his understanding of its value as a promotional device, and his disavowal of grandiose intentions did not keep him from taking out a full page ad in the *New York Daily News* to announce the telecast of its opening service. Beyond that, the building is an integral part of Schuller's weekly program, broadcast over nearly 200 stations

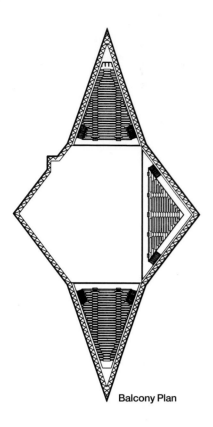

Balcony Plan

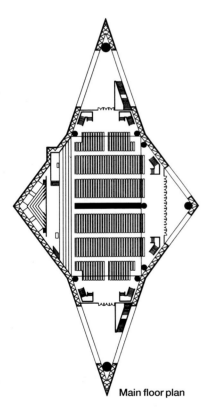

Main floor plan

Photo across page shows the giant organ enclosures. During services, Schuller reaches three audiences: those in the cathedral, those in the parking lot, to whom he turns through a tall slot in the wall, and millions of others through the television cameras, for whom the cathedral is a highly dramatic set.

The texture of the structure serves the space.

around the world. Here is one case where insufficient recognition of an architect's efforts is not a problem. It is also a rare instance of a building within the high modernist tradition that manages to please a significant portion of the lay public.

Viewed as architecture, however, the Crystal Cathedral is not such an unequivocal success. Like religion itself, it requires some faith on the part of the beholder, and it is vulnerable to the workings of a skeptical mind. The faith that it demands is not a blind one, just one willing to overlook certain lapses and inconsistencies. And even the most hardened skeptic should be able to appreciate its Apollonian fusion of light, space and structure. That triune quality pervades the interior, and is the essential proposition and achievement of Johnson's design.

The impact of the interior space is also due to its scale. Shaped like a distorted four-pointed star in plan, the building measures 207x415 feet along its two axes. Because of its unusual geometry, these dimensions are a bit misleading: The Crystal Cathedral's ground coverage is equivalent to that of a rectilinear building about 186 feet square. It is not, as has been repeatedly claimed, larger than Notre Dame Cathedral—in fact it is little more than half the size of the Parisian church. Nevertheless, it is a monumentally conceived structure, 128 feet tall at its high point and spanning as much as 200 feet without recourse to interior columns.

This is accomplished by space frames of welded steel tubing that comprise the walls and roof. The latter is made up of three sloping planes plus a vertical clerestory element, arranged asymmetrically above the symmetrical plan. That syncopated configuration produces a soaring, raked space that is given added dynamism by slanting triangular balcony sections in three points of the star.

Although this space is elaborately inflected and hierarchical, the structure that bounds it is surprisingly uniform. The three-dimensional, white painted trusswork is modular and continuous, and repeats its basic pattern so many times over that it assumes the nature of filigree rather than of a distinctive structural assemblage. Since it reads as undifferentiated texture rather than a more dominant framing pattern, it serves the space by granting it visual pre-eminence. It also underscores the sensation of light inside on clear days when the sun plays over its latticework.

But the pairing of space and structure also has some drawbacks. It is visually busy, and since the basic geometry of the interior space is already quite complicated, one might prefer a slightly more serene ensemble. Unlike most other such structural tours-de-force, this space frame is made subservient to a rather arbitrary volumetric conception; its own inherent properties were not used to give discipline to the process of planning the space. Johnson has cited Norman Foster's Sainsbury Centre as an influence on his design, yet that building is at an opposite pole of logic and rigor. Its uniform structure is used to generate a classical and regular space.

Foster's building also frames an important view by leaving two glass walls free of primary structural elements. This benefit of a simple trabeated space frame was not available in Johnson's picturesque application of a similar technology—the Crystal Cathedral has 15 bounding planes, typically intersecting at odd angles, and there is no distinction possible between bearing and nonbearing surfaces.

One can argue that a view was not as important in Garden Grove. The setting is flat and suburbanized, with neither the pastoral quality of an open landscape nor the built drama of a real cityscape. Still, view was essential to Schuller's vision of what the building should be. He wanted to see God's creation around him, yet it is the architect's handiwork that dominates the scene, especially on the main floor where most of the seats and standing room are found. What one sees there is the usually cloudless Southern California sky, with welcome light and sun flooding the sanctuary, but not Schuller's hoped-for vision of nature as a reminder of the Garden of Eden.

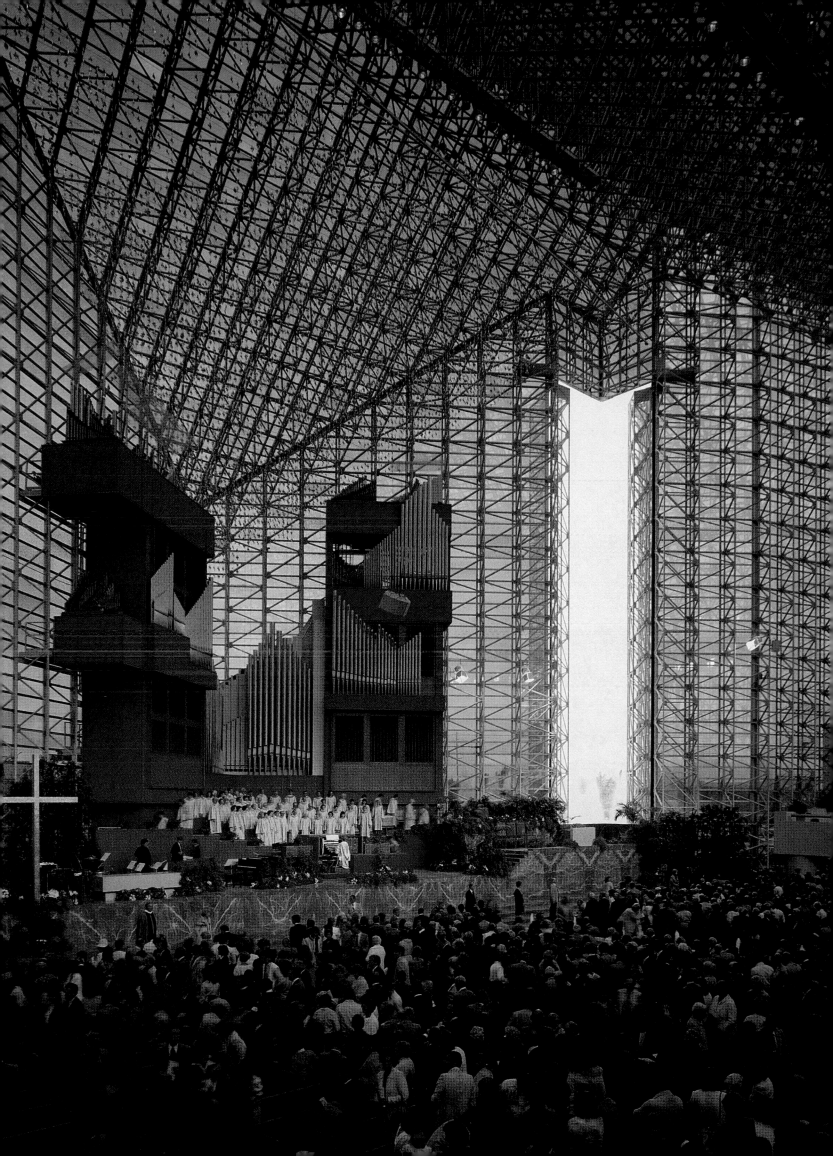

Eclecticism on the part of client and architect.

The effect of light and space is undeniably awesome and even inspiring, but in a curiously secular sort of way. Its gestalt is not mysterious but matter-of-fact and physical, almost as though the building were a splendid gymnasium for an enlightened band of 1920s European naturopaths devoted to sunbathing and hydrotherapy. (Pools and fountains abound in and around the structure.) These associations should not be seen as miscalculated architectural imagery, but as appropriate symbolism for Schuller's particular form of religion. It is a modern faith in that it seems based more on psychology than upon traditional Christianity. It is ego-centered and motivationally directed, practical and focused on the here-and-now. Getting things done constitutes one of Schuller's prime messages, and his own technological bent is demonstrated by his recent Sunday-morning advocacy of nuclear power. Schuller's vigorous pragmatism can perhaps best be summarized by two of his book titles: *Move Ahead with Possibility Thinking*, and *Self-Love, the Dynamic Force of Success*. His eclecticism is illustrated by the churchmen that he cites as his greatest influences: Norman Vincent Peale, Billy Graham and Bishop Fulton J. Sheen.

In designing the Crystal Cathedral, Philip Johnson appears to have been equally eclectic in his choice of models. In addition to the Sainsbury Centre, he also identifies Mies van der Rohe's angular and faceted Friedrichstrasse office project of 1919 as a subliminal influence. But, for a student of architectural history as informed as Johnson, there could have been many others. The lattice structures of Buckminster Fuller and Konrad Wachsmann come readily to mind, as does Bruce Goff's 1950 project for a "Crystal Chapel" and student religious center for the University of Oklahoma. This last design anticipated Johnson's work to a remarkable degree, not just in its nickname but in its exclusive use of glass for walls and roof, complicated nonrectilinear geometry, sparkling pendants suspended over the sanctuary, indoor and outdoor fountains and pools of water, its method of ventilation and even in the basic arrangement of its site plan.

This, of course, is speculative. Johnson characterizes the design process as one of solving specific problems rather than looking for convenient precedents. When asked teasingly whether the Crystal Cathedral was his last modern building, he laughed before answering: "I've never stopped being a modern architect in the sense that modern architecture starts with structure and with function. That is, we find out what the purpose of the building is, we find out what the best way of building it is and we suit things to that purpose."

A functional discussion of the church would therefore be very much in order. Some advantages and drawbacks of the structural system have already been touched upon. The planning of the sanctuary is decidedly odd for a church, since the chancel is placed on the long dimension of the building, and since Schuller's pulpit is about 50 feet off the central axis of the nave. This produces some very uncomfortable sight lines for several hundred parishioners on the west half of the main floor, and puts the congregation in the west balcony a hundred feet more distant from the pastor than their east balcony counterparts. The extremely broad shape of the nave, expressionistic though it may be, defies functional logic and generally places worshipers farther away from the services than a plan predicated on comfortable seating and viewing patterns. Even with viewing distances as long as 220 feet the designers fell 1,134 seats short of their goal of 4,000. And, because of bends in the wall planes, Schuller cannot be seen from certain east balcony seats—this in a column-free space!

Of course, people in poor seats can console themselves by looking at a spectacular building when seeing the pastor proves difficult. The ears, however, are not as lucky as the eyes, for the only way to characterize the cathedral's acoustics is hellish. In this ultrareverberant room the spoken word is not distinct and even some forms of music suffer badly. When Beverly Sills gave a fund-raising recital prior to the building's dedication, the

$1,500 ticket holders and the soprano were assaulted by cacophanous echoes that would have driven a less secure performer to tears. On a television talk show a few days later, she joked that her voice is probably still ricocheting from one glass wall to another, trying to find a way out.

Johnson says that he is not surprised by the problem, since the church was not planned as a concert hall. Music, however, has long been essential to Schuller's services, and continues to be so. The architect explains that the space was not designed for acoustics, but for electro-acoustics. In essence, this means using amplified sound to augment or to override the natural sonic properties of the structure. Even with this palliative, Schuller's words are not always intelligible. Installation work is now underway for a million-dollar organ of 12,688 pipes, which may benefit from the cathedral's highly reverberant space.

Structural integrity is especially important in earthquake-prone California. The triangulated framing is designed to withstand a major quake of 8.0 Richter scale magnitude, but the glass would begin to break well before that point. This problem is not really avoidable, but it has been mitigated by allowing for play in the glazing joints and by the use of tempered glass.

Because of the region's mild winters and dry summers, the Crystal Cathedral's main space has no heating or cooling plant. Winter temperatures can be kept above outdoor levels through solar gain, the greenhouse effect, and the body heat of the congregation. Mirror glass with an 8 percent transmission factor will reflect most of the summer sun, and operable windows at the balcony lines and in the roof clerestory, along with open banks of entrance doors, will create a chimney-like draft that should prevent any build-up of heat beyond ambient shade temperatures. Since some of the congregation used to sit in the sun on folding chairs, Schuller reasons that these comfort conditions will be acceptable. Further ventilation is provided when a pair of wall sections swing open to create a 20-foot-wide opening, 90 feet tall, that allows the minister to metaphorically part the Red Sea and be seen intermittently by people in their parked cars. These doors are oriented to catch the notorious Santa Ana winds that roar out of the desert, and their use on gusty days has created difficulties.

The operable windows create an esthetic effect that is quite marvelous. Seen from outside, the mirrored skin is not executed with the skill that one would expect from an architect of Johnson's caliber. Although it can be made to appear interesting by a good photographer, its awkward detailing (aluminum cover plates as wide as a foot, and obtrusive metal trim pieces at every opening and edge) combined with a paucity of interesting reflected objects make the church's exterior seem dull and ponderous, particularly on cloudy days. Its accommodation of the cathedral's central and corner entrances is especially ill-considered. But when the awning windows are open, their strong pattern of diagonally rising horizontal stripes gives life and functional expression to walls that are otherwise anonymous and curiously similar to those of recent midrise office buildings a few blocks away.

Evaluating Johnson's design by his own functionalist yardstick, it is more a failure than it is a success. Responding to its esthetics, one must lament many of the interior details as well as the blank exterior that hides the dazzling interplay of space, light and structure taking place within. By ordinary logic, this costly effort (over $250 per square foot for a building that has half its space in the basement) is a problematic piece of architecture.

But ordinary logic is not really the most appropriate form of judgment in this case. The Crystal Cathedral's essential idea—its soul, if you will—its mystic union of elements to form a great central space, is sufficient to outweigh whatever went wrong in its execution. The point is not whether another architect (or even Johnson himself) might have devised a better church, but rather that this evangelistic vision came to earth in tangible form. The Crystal Cathedral is a parable. It is the word made flesh; its virtues redeem its sins. □

Across page: the cathedral, with Richard and Dion Neutra's "Tower of Hope."

Pert and Plainspoken Sanctuary

Hartman-Cox's addition to the Immanuel Presbyterian Church, McLean, Va.
By Andrea Oppenheimer Dean

Like a proper but classy lady, this church addition in suburban Washington, D.C., has a decorous sense of quality and grace because of its simplicity. Architect Hartman-Cox used forms and materials comfortably familiar to the local landscape and put them together inexpensively ($302,000 for 4,500 square feet) to create vernacular architecture with smart and spiffy ideas. "Designing with both hands, one contextual, the other moderne," as Warren Cox, FAIA, describes it, has, in fact, become the firm's trademark.

The six-acre site in McLean, Va., is a rolling, partially wooded area that had on it an expendable, twice-appended farmhouse that had housed sanctuary, fellowship hall and school. The most nota-

ble asset stood behind the ramshackle structure, namely a pair of old linden trees, perfect, it would seem, as centerpieces for an outdoor courtyard, or so the architect thought. In fact, the trees, plus George Hartman's recent six-month study of contextual architecture in Rome, conspired as formgivers for the project. Parishioners were split between wanting a Georgian addition and a spanking modern one, but Hartman persuaded them to accept something that would give them both continuity and a degree of change.

The new addition consists of a white, wood-framed, barn-like building parallel and south of the existing structure. A U-shaped, covered arcade links it to the original building while tying togeth-

Photographs by Robert Lautman

41

Robert Lautman

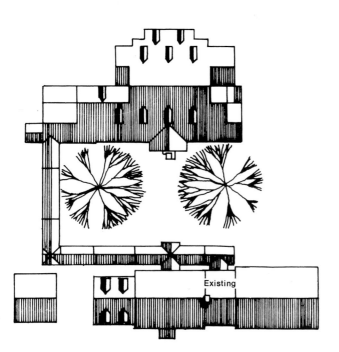

An arcade joins new to old and creates a court.

er the old structure's disparate parts and creating a courtyard around the linden trees. Hartman also relocated the entrance from the north side of the old farmhouse to the east edge of the arcade. In effect, now, the original building and its accretions have become ancillary space; the new addition is "the church." Its central focus is the outdoor courtyard where parishioners congregate after services or social events in the fellowship hall.

"Normally, when you talk about contextual work you think of starting with a good context," says Hartman. "Here we began with a not very good context and a very bad building and we didn't follow the dictum of one of our office wits: 'When you have a bad context, you do a bad building.'"

On its north side (above), where it faces the old structure, the addition looks much like a Southern farmhouse. Dominating its ground floor is the mullioned window wall of the fellowship hall, which could be an enclosed porch but for the chimney bisecting it. Above are dormers that admit light to the back of the sanctuary. The building's south face is all windowless wall except for high dormers. Hartman reduced its large space to residential scale by stepping the pitched roofline first from its central and highest point, where it contains the sanctuary, down a notch to the narthex and then down again to form a low structure housing coatrooms and lavatories near the entrance.

The division into discrete spaces is continued on the interior, despite the fact that it is in principle a large barn or hayloft. "The whole thing started in a hayloft, so we thought, why change it?" quips Hartman, adding, more seriously, "It's the easiest way to build cheap, big space." In the sanctuary, the chancel faces south, on the west is the choir, balconies are ranged along north

42

Robert Lautman

Allen Freeman

Allen Freeman

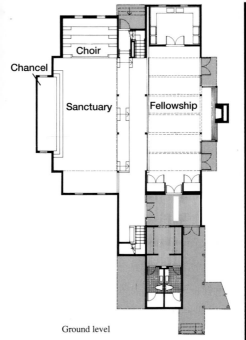

Chancel

Choir

Sanctuary

Fellowship

Ground level

Allen Freeman

A hall behind a sliding wall handles overflow.

and east walls. Separating sanctuary from fellowship hall is a mullioned window wall, which can be completely opened to make out of two rooms one huge space, transforming the sanctuary's plan from Greek to Latin cross. The feeling in the fellowship hall is old Virginia, cozy and warm. The scale is purposefully intimate with low, heavy overhead beams containing lighting. The ceiling above is gabled and there's a fireplace with brick seating on the north wall. It is intended to contrast to the cooler, more formal tone of the sanctuary with its much higher ceilings, wide open spaces and cooler colors.

In the 1971 chapel for Mt. Vernon College in Washington, Hartman-Cox used long spans and heavy screens to wall areas off from one another. In the McLean church, only reminders of screens remain (in the form of encased columns) to separate balconies from the central sanctuary area, and long beams have given way to braced and tied timber framing—a less expensive, simpler way of building. The idea was to make the job as easy as possible for the contractor, because money was tight. The dia-

The fellowship hall viewed from the sanctuary, across page above, and at closer range, left. The sanctuary looking toward the altar is shown above.

Timber framing, diffuse light entering from end and dormer windows and views into fellowship hall give the sanctuary an air of openness, yet formality (right). Across page, the sanctuary looking toward chancel and choir.

Allen Freeman

Dormers fill the sanctuary with soft, diffuse light.

mond-shaped large east and west windows that are fitted into the roofline were a consequence of the structure; the architect simply glazed what was left between the framing.

Although it is brighter in the sanctuary than outdoors on a cloudy day, there is remarkably little glass—the large diamonds east and west, five dormers on the south, three on the north. With exception of the two end openings, windows are all 2.5x5 feet. Because they are high, they provide ample light and because they are encased in dormers, light is bounced, diffuse and soft. Since openings are few and small and walls are eight inches thick and filled with insulation, the building is far more energy efficient than is required by codes.

The only uninterrupted vertical wall in the building is at the west, providing space for the choir, and looks somewhat incongruous and oddly proportioned with two low windows and a round one high up under the pediment. Explains Hartman, "The

choir is the single most important group in this congregation, so we felt we had to give it a throne."

Even when providing throne space the architect did the simplest thing throughout the building. He took stock windows and put them in the wall, put down drywall rails without wooden caps in most places, used standard columns and boxed them in with plywood and ordered the removable white and dark wood pews ready-to-go. When the contractor put ugly shoes on the base of the columns on the exterior arcade, the architect simply put a galosh, or box, over it, with somewhat mixed results.

The only really bad result of trying to build inexpensively and accommodate the contractor's mistakes is the roofing, which is an ugly, striped and cheap-looking, asphalt shingle. "It's an error," admits Hartman. "The builder got started with it and we couldn't bring ourselves to have them tear it off and start over. It would have caused a delay. When something would go wrong on this job, we redesigned rather than tearing it out. It's a scheme that doesn't hinge on the pickiness of detail." □

Robert Lautman

Simple But Sophisticated Farmhouse

Norman Gaffney Residence, Coatesville, Pa., Bohlin Powell Larkin Cywinski.
By Andrea Oppenheimer Dean

48

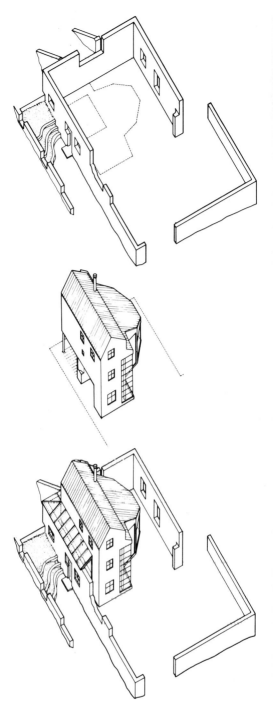

Photographs by Joseph W. Molitor

This small house for a man of modest needs is designed to revive and capture the owner's fond memories of time spent abroad in courtyard-style houses while he served in the Peace Corps and of his childhood on a Wisconsin farm. A simple residence filled with comforting allusions to delights of childhood, the house rests within the stone wall foundation of a barn that formerly occupied the site. It is perched on the southwest corner of a nine-acre plot overlooking rolling farmland in southwestern Pennsylvania not far from the timeless countryside of Chadds Ford conjured up in dream-like fashion by painter Andrew Wyeth. But where Wyeth's images are silver-point sharp, the Norman Gaffney house is purposefully soft-edged, as if unfocused; it is soothingly skewed and distorted, as is memory.

On first sight, from an unpaved road to the southeast, the building, its red shed roof tumbling in steps over grey wood siding, blends with neighboring farmhouses. At closer range, flat on, it looks far more singular. Set within the rough, low foundation walls, it rises smooth and narrow, a box with three small windows running down it, off center from the peak of the gabled roof. To the right (east), cutting into the edge of the box, is glazing, behind it a column, then off to the side, a pavilion-like living

area with angled corners. The entrance to the house is a rust-red door set into the west side of the stone wall; to either side of the entrance are small, low windows, one blue, one green. The scale is miniaturized and cozy, the impression a cross between a small farmhouse from southern Europe and an illustration from a children's tale, perhaps by Beatrix Potter.

Allusions to images from childhood continue on the interior, which reflects Gaffney's desire for openness without loss of privacy. The entranceway links the box of the house to the foundation wall via a plexiglass skylight. On its left and set at an angle to it is a single-counter kitchen, its chest-level window overlooking a small, raised garden. To the right of the entrance, a low-ceilinged dining area with round, small, stocky table and a low window opens onto a wide open living room. At its southwestern corner stands a two-story column, left exposed and unpainted as an allusion to the house's predecessors. The semicircular living room with high pitched ceiling is surrounded by glazing that masterfully manipulates views, which is one reason the building was selected for a 1981 AIA national honor award. Looking south, one sees the broad front courtyard and hills beyond. To east and north, the stone wall is only four feet away, giving a

The view framed by an opening in the foundation wall (above) is what one sees looking east from the living room. The north or back side of the house (across page top) nestles in a small hill. It gives the incongruous impression of a simple shed with high-tech, black ducts perched on a greenhouse.

Joseph W. Molitor

Nothing in the house is quite symmetrical.

feeling of enclosure and intimacy. But in the wall is a good-sized opening framing a view of meadowlands.

Furnishing is spare throughout. In its way, the little house is a completed artwork in which personal possessions would jarringly intrude. In the living room are only wicker chairs and a low, round white table with a bite-like chunk taken out of it to replicate a partial plan of the house. The table has three differently shaped legs.

Nothing in the house is symmetrical or four-square, mainly because of angled elements. One is the oak barn beam supporting the second floor between dining and living spaces. The beam and exposed framing beneath the second floor balcony are the house's only raw elements, left rough as reminders of what is beneath the building's skin. The stair leading up from the living room is also set at an angle. Just right of it is a cylindrical wood stove backed by a two-story, jagged edged, striped brick and block wall that acts as a heat sink. On it is a band of tiles with colored beasts and plants.

Color is one of the unalloyed pleasures of the house. The principal one is a soft gray; moldings are a darker shade. Muted rose, greens, and gray blues are used for pipe columns and rails.

A slick, gray steel pipe rail with rose trim wraps around the second story balcony overlooking the living room. On the second floor is a small bedroom and lavatory, on the third an attic-study, with exaggeratedly childlike proportions and images to recall memories of attics past. The stair punches through here with a Corbusian rail. As the architect, Peter Bohlin, AIA, says, "the style of the house is a soft stew." □

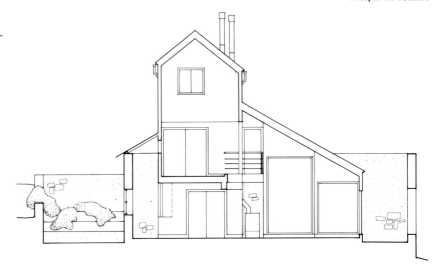

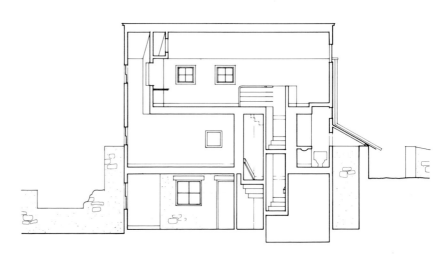

Joseph W. Molitor

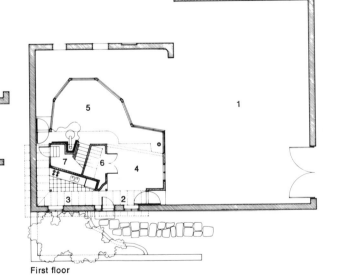

1 Courtyard
2 Entry
3 Kitchen
4 Dining room
5 Living room
6 Closet
7 Utility
8 Bedroom
9 Balcony
10 Den/Bedroom

First floor

Second floor

Third floor

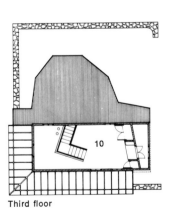

Above left are living and dining rooms with second story balcony. Slick, painted rail; old, raw barn beam, and corner concrete column contrast with one another. The living room table misses a bite-like chunk in the shape of a partial plan of the house. An expanded view of the living room, across page bottom, shows the wood stove and glimpses of the stone wall. From the southeast, across page top, the house looks much like neighboring farm structures.

Joseph W. Molitor

53

1982

American Academy of Arts and Sciences

Hartford Seminary

Steve Rosenthal

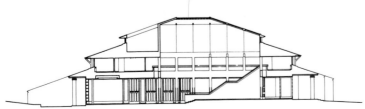

Arcadian House of the Intellect

Two views of Kallmann, McKinnell & Wood's headquarters of the American Academy of Arts and Sciences in Cambridge

Photographs by Steve Rosenthal

Robert Campbell: This is a series of personal footnotes to a building.

I can't do anything objective on the American Academy of Arts and Sciences because of my own involvement with it.

I should detail what that involvement was. Lawrence Anderson, former dean of architecture and planning at MIT, a member of the academy and its architectural adviser for the proposed new headquarters building, asked me to join a committee of four to choose an architect. After we had selected Kallmann, McKinnell & Wood, I continued as a part-time consultant to the academy to coordinate the process of design and construction.

From the beginning it seemed that all the stars were properly aligned for this new building. The academy was an architect's dream project. The Cambridge, Mass., site was a prize: five-and-one-half acres of wooded knoll within 10 minutes' walk of Harvard Square. The client had ample money, sensitivity and ambition. More than once, during the search for an architect and afterward, officers of the academy said they hoped for a "great" building or "a building that would be in the architectural history books."

Even the brief was almost a Beaux-Arts idealization, calling for a range of small and large spaces to be domestic in scale yet to possess a ceremonial character rare in our time.

The programmer was Dean Anderson. His program was and is a model of the art. It is short (12 pages) yet goes far beyond merely defining areas and functions into the trickier task of defining architectural character. Here are some excerpts:

"It is not necessary to assert a strongly visible presence in the community. Indeed a facade that 'claims' too much would be an affront to the conservative, well-kept houses nearby. . . . It would be as well not to be able to see the entire building at once. . . .

"Internally the general impression need not perhaps be so low-keyed as the external one, but the individual should feel at ease rather than in awe. Fruitful conversation is the academy's stock in trade, and the word implies small groups even if multitudes are present . . . .

"The academy does not want to become the vehicle for a personal or trendy stylistic statement. It should not be too obviously 1977."

Dean Anderson continued as a member of the group that met regularly to review the progress of the design by Gerhard Kallmann and Michael McKinnell. Only one specific restraint was offered to the architects, most of whose previous buildings are celebrations of reinforced concrete. This rule was that there be no

exposed concrete inside or out. "Of course not, we never would have considered it," Kallmann replied.

The academy, like most owners, came with several heads. The most influential one belonged to Dr. Edwin Land, chairman of the Polaroid Corporation, former president of the academy and the true begetter of its new building.

Land appeared only two or three times during the design stage but always with terrific impact. He expressed complete disdain for committees and groups of all kinds, although many such groups are sponsored by the academy. Instead he seemed to conceive of the academy as a maze of private nooks, off-stream backwaters where thinkers from different disciplines would meet casually to generate new ideas or, as he put it, places "where two great minds copulate."

"You need trysting places," he once said. "All I want is an even break for individualists. No group ever found the meaning of life." A physicist himself, he saw the academy as divided between physical scientists and social scientists, the former being individualists and the latter being natural group-formers. He wanted "secretive" access to private rooms, so that when two or three friends came to the new academy "they need not be confronted by huge symposia. You don't get a lot done in symposia."

Once Land delivered a memorable crit of the Ford Foundation headquarters in New York City. I've forgotten the words, but the gist was that everything is too harmonious at Ford. The real world, Land said, is a discord that is resolved only occasionally by talent. He felt that any attempt to create a world of apparent harmony was false and amounted to an affront to the creative spirit.

The layered, mazelike character of the academy ground floor plan, especially in the area of the so-called living rooms, is a direct response to this worthy client who knew what he liked and who clearly touched a sympathetic chord in the architects. Later, when Henry Millon, a member of the academy who is director of the Center for Advanced Study at the National Gallery of Art, saw the design, he said it looked like the plan of a Mycenaean palace. When I passed this on to Kallmann he was delighted and

quoted with relish an earlier comment by someone on Boston City Hall: "Not since Knossos have bureaucrats worked in such labyrinthine surroundings."

If Edwin Land was one major design determinant, the neighbors were another. The academy's lovely site was heir to a bitter history.

A house called Shady Hill once stood where the academy now stands, a house that was easily one of the half-dozen finest in Cambridge. In a remarkable act of cultural vandalism, Harvard abruptly demolished Shady Hill in August 1955 with the intention of redeveloping the site for dormitories. Outraged, the neighbors shot down a long series of Harvard schemes. Eventually the university gave up and offered the site to the academy.

To build at all, the academy needed a zoning variance, and in Cambridge this is obtainable only in the absence of serious opposition from neighbors. And at the start of its efforts the academy was faced with a petition of several hundred signatures opposing any construction on the site.

The process of persuading these people not to oppose the academy influenced its design dramatically. Their mere existence ensured that the building would be as polite as possible. More important, it was partly because of them that the building was moved from a shady, damp lower corner of the site—which was all Harvard originally offered—up to the top of the knoll. This

Exterior walls are of red brick trimmed in red granite, alternating with expanses of square glass panes framed in mahogany behind a procession of brick piers on the south and west. The project included restoration of the site as a park, partly for public use.

move caused a metamorphosis in the building.

On the lower site the building had been conceived as a kind of precinct. Columns inside the building were echoed by others standing free in the landscape. Indoor and outdoor space were equally part of the academy "grounds." It was fascinating to watch as the power of the new site gradually transformed the design from a precinct into a pavilion. It grew grander, more self-contained, until finally it became very much an object in space—the last thing the architects had originally intended. Soon they were talking of "a light sketch of a Tuscan villa." The notion the building now suggests—that it once was a more complete, pyramidal form that has been sliced back and chewed away—was arrived at by a series of intuitive adaptations to the new site, with the ideogram coming only afterward.

Because of these and other changes, the academy as built retains within its fabric the ghosts and marks of many design ideas that were abandoned along the way. This is surely one of its virtues. Isn't the difference between an original design like the academy and a mere knock-off precisely in the presence or absence of these ghosts of lost ideas? They give the original a depth, a slight inexplicability, that are absent in the copy. Because of them the finished building is the expression of a process, not of a single set of decisions, and gives the sense that time and change have washed over it even when it's brand new.

Kallmann and McKinnell have written persuasively of pastoral imagery and the notion of the building as a romantic ruin. Creation is mysterious, though, and sources are endless. Books by or about Kahn, MacKintosh, Aalto, Greene & Greene, and Voysey, and Girouard's *Sweetness and Light*, were all to be seen around the architects' office during design. Wright too is an obvious presence. Less obvious is Scarpa. Two modest sources that I can't help seeing in the building were never mentioned. One is a former stable in a Boston suburb, converted long since into a home for Thomas Adams, the academy treasurer. Its large sloping roof and long arcade of brick piers look very much like elements that appeared in the academy about the time of McKinnell's first visit to Adams's house. The other source, if it is one, is a conventional but attractive Tudor revival athletics building, next door to the Harvard swimming pool where Kallmann swims three times a week. This has the academy's two-tiered roof, small-paned window-wall and, most strikingly, its frieze of large brackets beneath the eaves, here made of metal instead of wood.

I guess it's obvious, incidentally, that the academy's braces don't brace anything. Much of the building's visible structure, in fact, is rhetorical, a free variation on the underlying steel frame.

In my opinion, the academy is best on its exterior, especially in the marvelous grace with which its rides the roll of the land. The landscape architect, Carol Johnson, as it happens, was often at odds with the architects. The conflict shows in a powerful building that seems to wish to radiate lines of force into the site, and a landscape that is not willing to be bowled over. It's a confrontation that is rather pleasing. Of the whole exterior only the great chimney seems to me to be slightly out of key, slightly overworked. Everything else is a triumph.

Indoors, the generally high level of success is undercut by a sense that things are too high and too grand. The atrium is so bright and strong that its tends to relegate the rooms around it to the status of periphery. The rooms are superb in themselves.

The staff offices upstairs are generous but pointlessly isolated from the public spaces below. There's a slightly distasteful sense of class in this, as if the bailiffs above must be kept from distracting the dukes strolling below.

The architects' concept for the furnishings was to acquire pieces (the academy owned almost nothing) that would be neither modern nor antique but simply traditional. These pieces would be chosen so as not quite to match, suggesting, for example, a sofa inherited from a grandmother that doesn't quite fit but is too good not to use. This beguiling concept works only partially, however, because the scale of the rooms is large enough to jar

slightly with the domestic scale of the furnishings.

There have been practical problems—snow sliding off the roof, feedback in the audio, migrating upholstery in the lecture room—that have been very distracting to the owner but that perhaps don't amount to a great deal in the perspective of the building over time.

That perspective in any case is one I can't yet get into focus. The purpose of these notes is not to evaluate the architecture but only to offer fragments of one response and to keep alive some sense of the complexity and multiplicity of conditions that create any building in the last quarter of the 20th century.

To date, it appears the new academy is liked by everyone—by all the neighbors, who represent almost every social and cultural viewpoint, by the owner and by the architectural subculture itself—including the 1982 AIA jury, which gave it a national honor award. Given the moment in time at which it appeared, I think this breadth of appeal is its most difficult and important achievement. □

Donald Canty: Coming upon the academy building fresh, without having seen so much as a single photograph, it registers immediately as a place apart—which, of course, is one of the things it is intended to be. This serene pavilion on a wooded knoll could scarcely have less to do with the turbulent urban area in which, like it or not, it exists.

Its spiritual home might be Kyoto; or, more likely, the Adirondacks. In its luxuriant rusticity it would be quite at home in a millionaires' "camp" of other days. Gerhard Kallmann speaks of it in terms of "the idea of the country house" in England. But it is more like a lodge, a point curiously accentuated by the occasional use of bright green accents.

Moving from outside in, it quickly becomes apparent that the real apartness of this building is not spatial but temporal. It is a movement back into the 19th century—into rooms that might have been designed by the Greene brothers, the early Wright, any number of figures in what Kallmann terms the "premodern" period and mode.

This is historicism with a vengeance, but of a different sort than that associated with postmodernism. The latter's historical roots are sometimes classical, sometimes Corbusian, sometimes obscure, sometimes imaginary. Like modernism before it, postmodernism ignores or rejects the work of those remarkable architects of the last century who were crafting an architecture that was original, evocative and, in this country, particularly American. It was enticing, then, to hear of a major new work that set out to build upon these neglected beginnings, to reflect this rejected tradition.

It is a little disconcerting, however, to find that the academy's major rooms—a cluster of dining rooms, a pair of conference rooms, a drawing room, a library (using the term in the domestic sense rather than that of a place to store and dispense books)—are more recreations than reflections of the past. They do not

One of the dining rooms, typical of the interiors in its high ceilings, cove lighting, wood trim and use of 'grandmother's attic' furnishings. The dining rooms open to the atrium for extra capacity.

61

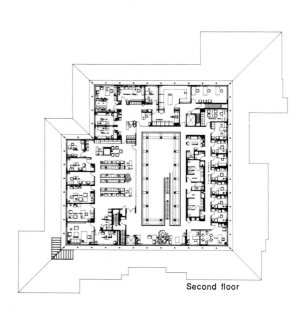

Second floor

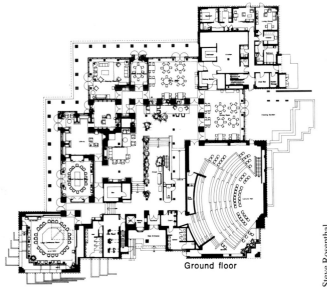

Ground floor

Steve Rosenthal

copy specific works, but except for a detail here and there they literally could have been done a century or so ago.

Let it be said, nevertheless, that these must be among the most beautiful rooms built anywhere in recent years. Ceilings rise to 14 feet, detailing is meticulous (and, as in the case of the fire-places, imaginative), the use of materials sure-handed to the point of being loving. In the architects' words, "There is a consistent language of wainscotings, picture rails and framing of Honduras mahogany, surrounding painted or linen-covered fields."

The architects seem to have adopted some of the language of the period from which they draw. They speak of the ground level of the building as "a suite of rooms, entered from a skylit hall and hearth area," rooms that are "invested with inglenooks and

Above, furniture plans by ISD Incorporated, the interior design consultants for the project, and one of the two conference rooms. Across page above, the central atrium, flanked by small parlors, with a draped skylight high overhead. At right, a second floor work space.

window alcoves conducive to private encounter." This suite is a place of warmth and quiet and obvious seriousness, kept from gloominess by the constant presence of the garden.

The "skylit hall" or atrium is the meeting place of past and present, and here things begin to fall apart. Several different light fixtures are in view, including some on the wall that can only be called quaint; large ceramic urns, profusely planted, are distributed around the floor; the grand stairway bears an almost industrial-looking metal railing.

The stairway, and the space itself, imply a linkage between the first and second floors that does not exist in any important way. Downstairs is the scholars' suite, upstairs is the domain of the staff, a set of pleasant but rather plain offices and auxiliary spaces, perhaps seeming plainer than they might elsewhere because of the contrast with the moments of magnificence below.

Likewise, if the building somehow disappoints it might be because of arriving at it with exaggerated expectations. After all, the architects have positively augmented the sensitive site, have given their clients exactly what they wanted—and there are those stirring moments in the 19th century rooms. □

*Across page, the secluded study, one of a series of quiet spaces
for casual encounter among scholars. Top, the larger of the two
conference rooms, perhaps the building's most successful single
space. Above, the swirling, Wrightian auditorium.*

Shining Vessel of Religious Thought

Richard Meier's Hartford, Conn., Seminary.
By Donald Canty

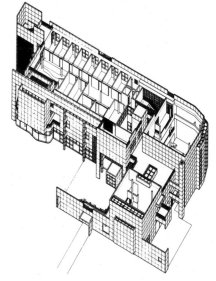

Photograph on pages 66-67 by Steve Rosenthal

Steve Rosenthal

All right, this is another gleaming, ship-like, enameled Richard Meier composition, a variation on a theme he has been plying for several years. But what's wrong with staying with and perfecting a consistent theme? Does every commission require invention of a new esthetic?

Also, this may be the most exhilarating variation yet: a highly rhythmic, even syncopated composition of forms and surfaces, light and shadow. And more is demanded of it than of such other recent variations as the Atheneum in New Harmony, Ind. (see pp. 2-13).

The Hartford Seminary was founded in 1834 by the Pastoral Union of Connecticut for the traditional purpose of preparing the young for the ministry in suitably traditional surroundings, first in East Windsor and more recently in Hartford itself. The seminary today serves other and more complicated purposes. It is partly a continuing education institution for clergy and lay people in midcareer, partly a research facility, partly a resource and con-

ference center for community as well as religious groups. There is a full-time faculty of 14 and support staff of 12.

The seminary is not lavishly endowed, and Meier had to serve these multiple purposes within a definitely finite budget. He responded by reducing the program to an essential duality and organizing the building around it. He expresses the duality as being between ''partly cloistered, inward-looking spaces'' and a reaching out to the world. In other words, he put the major public spaces on the ground floor perimeter and the offices and seminar rooms upstairs.

He did something else as well: He achieved high spatial drama unusual to his work (or anyone's) in the rooms most expressive of the seminary's fundamental functions.

Vertical volumes join the building's intricately interlocking spaces (see axonometric), often with views from one to the other. Front elevation (above and preceding pages) is the most complex.

Far right, the altar projects out from beneath the chapel's hooded roof. Right below, curving wall wraps around the adjacent meeting room. Below, the entry court viewed from the side.

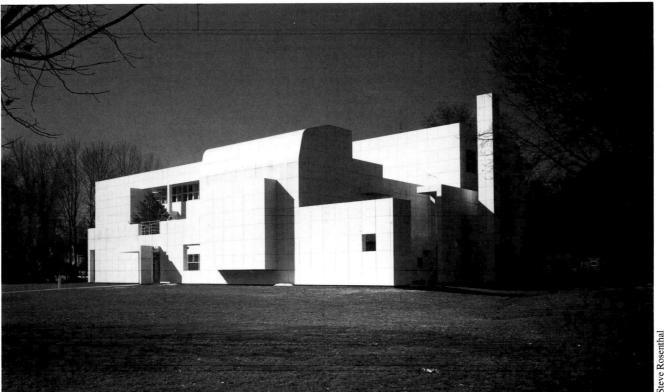

An enveloping welcome and changing faces.

For all of its functional and spatial achievements, what first catches one's breath about the seminary is, of course, its form. This is a remarkable sculptural object (with remarkable presence for a building of 27,000 square feet), and it changes constantly with the vantage point. No two elevations are alike.

Walls pop out to receive light through interstitial glass, the roof of the chapel arcs gently, a curving wall wraps around the meeting room that is the other major public space. The variations outside bespeak variations of use and space inside.

Once in a while, of course, there is a gesture for its own sake. And at the entry there is a kind of ceremony of planes. A screen wall passes across the face of the building at this point, penetrated by an opening on axis with the entry door, creating a transitional courtyard (entered also from a path from the parking lot to

the side). The entry door itself is projected outward in a small foyer. The building thus envelops you gradually as you walk in, then once in provides a generous gesture of volume and light (next page).

The seminary sits near the center of a four-acre greensward that nicely shows off its sculptural qualities and buffers it from the neighbors. These include, on one side, the seminary's former neo-Gothic campus (now the University of Connecticut's law school), and on two other rows of workaday New England houses, most of three stories, of the kind that gladdens hearts of asbestos shingle salesmen. There was little for Meier to relate to except for some neocolonial houses on the fourth side. Meier claims a relationship of the seminary to colonial New England, but one of feel rather than form: of crispness and whiteness. The fenestration, three-foot-square panes of glass used in various kinds of clusters, also contributes to this feel.

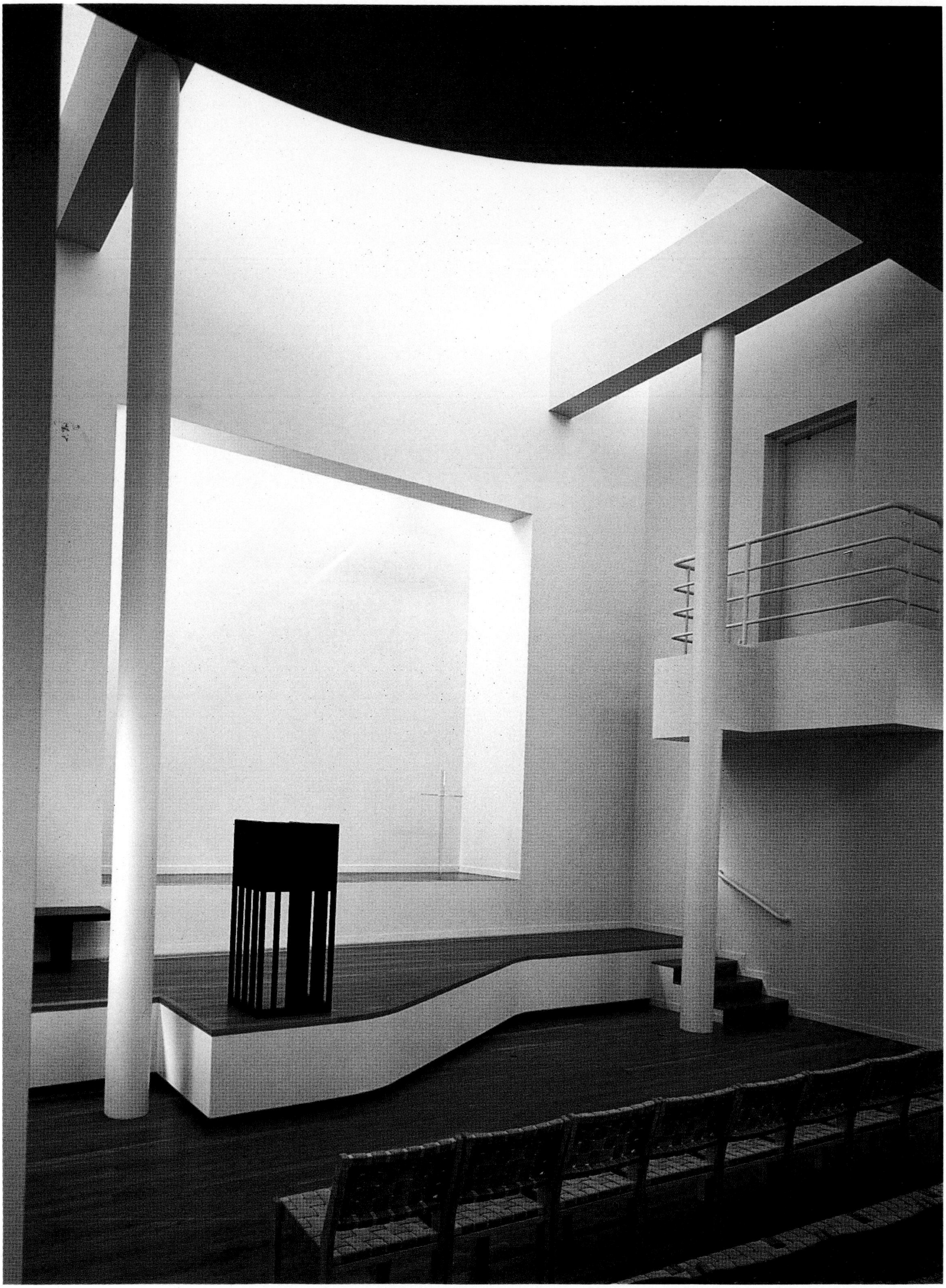

Steve Rosenthal

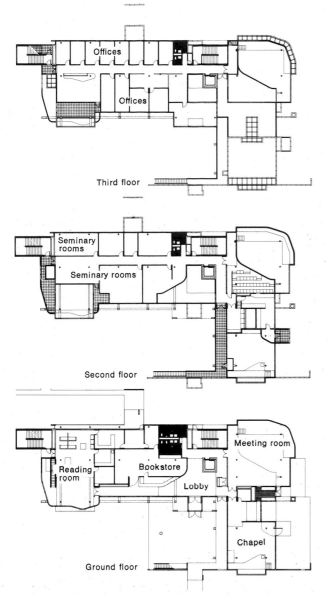

Third floor

Second floor

Ground floor

Vertical volumes that organize the plan.

Ezra Stoller © ESTO

Major volumes occur at the lobby and in the chapel and meeting room, the latter two aligned along the north side. These are soaring, emphatically vertical spaces. The chapel is a celebration of light, which enters through clerestories and bathes the altar almost theatrically. The light is such that the high, white ceiling all but curves out of sight, giving a sense of infinity to the volume. Meier designed an almost Wrightian bench and lecturn for the chapel. (A less fortunate detail is an industrial pipe communion rail, removable and happily removed in the picture at left.)

An unusual element of the chapel is the presence of four tiny balconies at the second level corners, each with its own entry door and each capable of accommodating no more than two or three people. They serve, says Meier, for people who want to drop in and out of services unobtrusively. They are also useful for all manner of musical, liturgical and oratorical special effects.

The chapel is the seminary's most spiritual space, in character as well as use, and also, on the outside, the most dramatic punctuation point of the form, making an L of what would have been a rectangle. Yet it was not in the program. The slightly strapped seminary was all for flexibility and multiple uses. Its thought was that a classroom could double as a chapel. Meier had to convince his clients that the combination was incompatible, and that a seminary without a chapel seemed an anomaly—"little more than an office building." Fortunately, he was persuasive.

The adjacent meeting room was always a key part of the program. It is very multiple in its uses—at various times a lecture hall, a concert hall, even a theater. There is access and seating at all three levels of the building.

This is a moving, almost swirling volume. Its plan closely echoes the arc of the chapel roof.

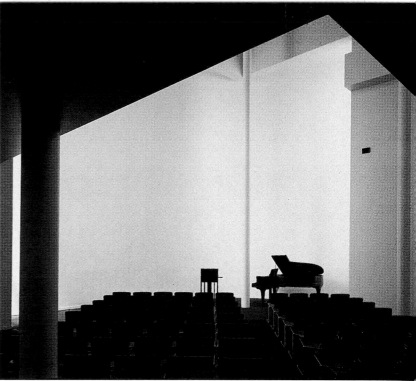

Ezra Stoller © ESTO

Across page, the soaring, luminous chapel, which protrudes to flank the entry court and give the plan its L shape. Top, the lobby looking toward the reading room. The bookstore is behind the reception desk. Above, the meeting room.

Top, the pleasingly sinuous space of the reading room. Above, a seminar room, whose pleasant but plainspoken treatment is typical of the building's working spaces. Also typical of these spaces is the fenestration, clustering four of the modular lights.

'Light is the dominating presence.'

Among other key program elements were a library and bookstore. These have not fared so well. The bookstore is an entirely enclosed internal space on the first floor. It is not a very pleasant place to be, perhaps seeming all the more dim and cramped because of the volume and light elsewhere. The library stacks are even more unhappily embowled, being in an absolutely undisguised basement. All in all, in a place of learning, it is a strange and shabby way to treat books.

In Meier's defense, the open stacks originally were intended to be closed. Now there is not even a librarian at the seminary. But the library is considerably redeemed by the first floor reading room, perhaps the building's most completely comfortable space. Volume, multiple light sources, curving walls, fenestration, appointments, all combine here in an architectural experience of a high order.

Meier had a knowledgeable client in Dr. John Dillenberger, president of the seminary, and left him an enthusiastic one. Says a descriptive flyer handed to seminary visitors: ''The different spaces [of the building] flow into each other while maintaining their own character. White and seemingly austere, the spaces highlight passage of color and, most importantly, the human ambiance of intimacy and openness. Light is the dominating presence, a single source serving multiple purposes, with new vistas meeting one at many turns.''

Amen. □

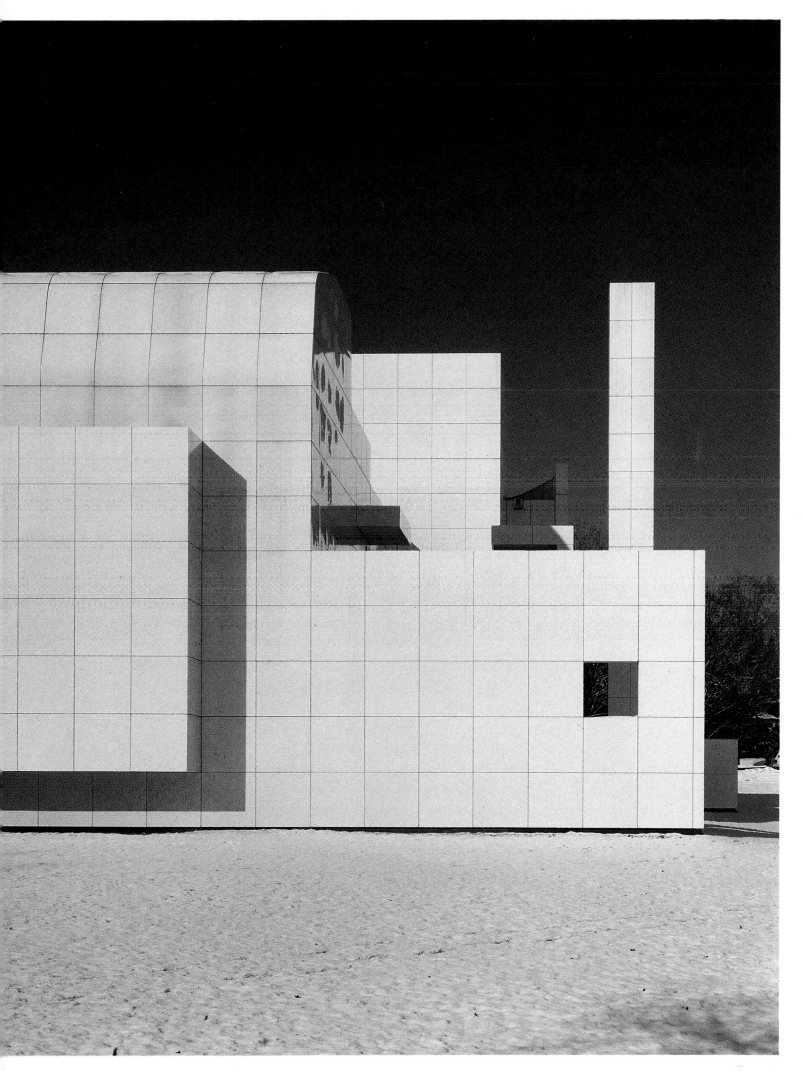

1983

Vietnam Veterans Memorial

Elliott House

Coxe/Hayden House

Portland Public Services Building

An Emotive Place Apart

By Robert Campbell

The Vietnam Veterans Memorial design by Maya Ying Lin was the winner of the most visible competition for a work of U.S. public art or architecture in the two decades since the F.D.R. Memorial competition. And, for a time, it seemed possible that the Vietnam Memorial, like the F.D.R., might collapse in a fiasco that would hurt the credibility of competitions and, still worse, lead to a bad compromise, crippling what many observers, including this one, felt was among the strongest designs for a war memorial ever conceived.

That didn't happen. The tide of opinion set firmly in favor of the memorial, it now seems clear, on Saturday, November 13, 1982, when tens of thousands of veterans and surviving relatives came to Washington to dedicate the new memorial. Families brought snapshots and flowers and laid them at the memorial's base, while faces and campfires and flags and sky could all be seen reflected in the long, mirror-black granite wall among the innumerable carved names of the dead, in an astonishing integration of almost everything a monument could say about a war. No one except the designer, perhaps, had fully realized how vividly the memorial would come to life through such interactions.

As everyone must know by now, the Vietnam Memorial is a retaining wall, 440 feet long, faced with black granite and inscribed with the names of the 57,939 American men and eight women who are listed as killed or missing in the Vietnam War. The top of the wall is horizontal and flush with the grassy lawn behind it. In front of the wall, the ground swales down gently to form a shallow amphitheater, thus exposing the wall's face. At either end the wall feathers into the rising earth and disappears. At the center, it's 10 feet high, and here it bends once, making an angle.

As you descend the path along the wall and reach this angle, you realize that one wing of the black wall points straight at the tall, white Washington Monument a quarter mile or so off, and the other at the Lincoln Memorial, visible through a screen of trees about 600 feet away. In making this descent you feel you're entering a cloistered space, set off from the busy surroundings. Streets and skylines disappear to leave you alone with the wall and its names. Then, as you pass the angle and begin to climb, you feel yourself emerging again into the world of noise and light after a meditative experience.

At close range, the names dominate everything. There are so unbelievably many of them, quirky and vivid as real names always are. The name of the first soldier who died is carved at the angle in the wall, and the names continue to the right in columns in chronological order of date of death, out to the east end where the wall fades into the earth. The names begin again, with the next soldier who died, at the west end, where the wall emerges from the earth. It is as if the wall, after sinking beneath the earth, has continued on around the world underground before emerging once more.

The names continue, remorselessly, to the name of the last soldier killed, which is carved on the wall at the angle, directly beneath the name of the first soldier. The angle here at the apex of the wall, between Washington and Lincoln, is thus a place of first

and last things, and there is a sense of closure, of a story completed. The wall is a huge book open at a place where it both begins and ends, and its text, its long march of names, has made it, you realize, a memorial to individual human beings rather than to any larger but vaguer concept of country or sacrifice or victory or heroism.

At some moment of your visit, probably not at first, you've noticed with a slight shock your own face reflected among the names of the dead, an effect that makes the granite mirror a kind of scrim set between past and present, between living and dead, integrating both on a single dark plane. Other images collect at special times. On some evenings, along the memorial's eastern wing, the image of the red sun setting among black trees is seen in reflection while, simultaneously, the same sun is casting the shadows of those trees directly onto the granite and lighting with pink the real trees rising behind the wall on the slope above. In such ways the memorial reaches out beyond itself to engage and transform its surrounding world.

The story of how this unlikely and wonderful design came into existence is one of the classic competition stories, too familiar to need much detailing. Maya Ying Lin was 21 and a senior at Yale, planning a career as an architect, when some students (she wasn't one) persuaded an instructor, Andrew Burr, to offer a design studio on funerary architecture. Lin enrolled. The Vietnam competition was Problem Number 3 in the Burr studio. The students visited Washington to reconnoiter the site. Maya Lin's chief impression then was one of living people enjoying a sunny open park that shouldn't be taken from them nor be trivialized into a mere setting for some big monument. A landscape solution seemed better.

"I thought about what death is, what a loss is," she remembers. "A sharp pain that lessens with time, but can never quite heal over. A scar. The idea occurred to me there on the site. Take a knife and cut open the earth, and with time the grass would heal it. As if you cut open the rock and polished it."

The notion of making the angle and aiming the wall at Washington and Lincoln came later, back in the studio. Last to occur was the unique arrangement of names. "Andy said, you have to make the angle mean something. And I wanted the names in chronological order because to honor the living as well as the dead it had to be a sequence in time."

These were powerful intuitions, and they led directly to a powerful design. The briefest talk with its creator makes it clear that nothing about the memorial is either casual or lucky.

Only Lin, from the Yale class, actually sent her proposal to Washington, in the form of two 30x40 inch boards onto which were glued, in a visually rather disorganized way, a few inept, scaleless drawings and a hand-lettered, very well-written statement. The jury saw through the crudeness of this student presentation to the great concept that lay beneath.

Detailing of the finished memorial was performed by the Cooper-Lecky Partnership, with Lin's collaboration. Most of it is excellent, but in light of the celebrated controversy over adding a flag and statue to the memorial it is interesting to note a couple of jarring elements not in the original design. A gutter along the base of the wall was demanded by the Park Service, which maintains the memorial, because power mowers can't cut grass against a vertical surface. The gutter is modest but clearly damages the design; this is one wall you want to see rise straight up out of the earth like a natural cliff.

A path of granite slabs of changing sizes and shapes is another alien presence in front of the wall, often too bright and always too obvious. And the contour of the earth as you read it against the wall is unnatural as a land form, part flat and part sloped. These are minor defects, but they should serve as a warning that Lin's conception was so complete and so delicate that any attempt at embellishing it hurts it. □

Sophisticated Fantasy in Three Parts

Elliott house, Pennsylvania. Architect: Jefferson Riley, Moore Grover Harper. By Andrea Oppenheimer Dean

Jefferson B. Riley, AIA, likes to design into his houses the qualities of ancient, walled villages: their legibility, mixture of ceremonial and secluded spaces, surprises, broad views and private peekholes, combinations of grand and cozily scaled buildings, formal and funkily shaped elements, "each different from the other, yet agreeing to disagree," as Riley puts it.

His Elliott house, in Ligonier, Pa., is three separate buildings—a sculptor's studio, a writer's cottage, and a main house—and a happy confabulation of mixed metaphors and odd shapes linked by what Riley calls the "fence-wall." With its crenelations and turrets and towers, the complex recalls Norman castles (sculptor Ann Elliott, who grew up on and inherited the land, says she always wanted to live in one after visiting St. Malo in France), while its balconies and peaked roofs are reminiscent of Victorian houses (favorites of writer Peter Gruen, Elliott's husband). Another source was the famed, nearby Rolling Rock Hunt Club's kennels, "the best of the local buildings," according to Riley. Despite its rampant eclecticism and nostalgia for things and times past, the Elliott house is modern in its open-plan first floor layout, it is a passive solar design with abundant glazing on the south and almost none facing north, and it is sensitive to the environmentalist concerns of its owners in blending unobtrusively with the landscape. Gruen's and Elliott's naturalist tendencies—and Riley's ideas of a village—are further reinforced by a layering that makes a gradual transition from spaces that are fully outdoors to outdoor-indoor areas and then to indoor-indoor rooms—Riley's language.

The setting is idyllic. Perched on a hilltop in green, rolling, Appalachian countryside, the Elliott house faces south overlooking a wheat field, and beyond it the Ligonier Valley. It is aligned with the edge of a dense woods, which still sports hunting trails for hounds and horsemen.

On arrival from the west, and in photographs, the complex looks far larger than it actually is. It stretches out in leisurely fashion some 192 feet, most of it tucked behind the "fence-wall" of cedar siding with redwood trim. With its arches and trellises, this wall lines a continuous path, which opens here and there to form little courtyards for a congeries of variously shaped and sized, mostly small buildings.

Disparate elements are linked by 'fence-wall.' From left: sculptor's studio, courtyard, writer's cottage, split rail fence, main living areas with bedroom tower, art gallery, and library.

Photographs © Norman McGrath 1983

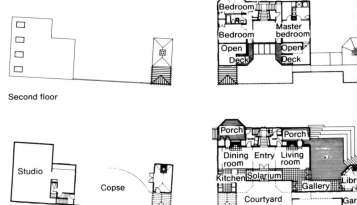

Second floor

First floor

A somewhat formal, yet cockeyed, entry.

First comes Ann Elliott's sculpture studio, with flat, slanting roof, the largest (21x31-foot) single space in the complex. Adjoining it, behind three trellised arches in the fence-wall, is a courtyard, then Gruen's tiny, peak-roofed writer's cottage. Next comes a break in the fence-wall that is bridged by a split rail fence, a favored spot from Ann Elliott's childhood, which was selected as "the symbolic, spiritual heart of the house," in Riley's words. The path behind the fence-wall continues to the main house, past its entrance, its three-story master bedroom cum campanile, its first story art gallery, to end at the edge of the last element in the complex—a small, pointy-roofed library.

The entrance to the main house is from a courtyard bounded by the fence-wall. It is symmetrical and somewhat formal, a sturdy anchor among wildly asymmetrical, odd-shaped building elements. But it is asymmetrically placed with relation to the fence-wall, peeking out rather cockeyed through one of its two south-facing archways.

The entry court, flanked by overhanging second story balconies, is conceived as an indoor-outdoor space, which Riley indicates in part by use of materials. The south of the house (and the cottage and the library) is faced with Dryvit, a Portland cement stucco, over rigid insulation board, to contrast to the outdoors material of the fence-wall. The glazed entranceway itself is framed in poplar, and the interior ceiling motif of 4x4-foot pine

Trellised fence-wall creates path with courtyards. Main entrance is from court, above, with overhanging balconies. Above half-arched door is sitting room, then high, light-filled bedroom.

The colors came out of a Hammett novel.

panels with poplar batons is introduced outside under the balconies. A slightly awkward, heavily framed glass door in a half arch to complete the arch begun in the fence-wall to the east of the entrance is painted white, again to connote that this is a partially interior space. Of all the elements in the complex, this door is singular for looking somewhat ungainly and unrelated visually to anything in view. There is something of a hodgepodge of riches in this attempt to differentiate outdoors from indoor-outdoor space at the entry court through different materials and shapes.

From the entry court, one passes through a small greenhouse with slate floor, which edges the south face of the first floor for purposes of solar heat storage. It also serves as another layering device to create a transition to indoor-outdoor spaces, and extends on the east side down two stairs to form a narrow art gallery, which, in turn, steps down to the six-sided, 14x15-foot, two-story, peak roofed library—a gem of a room. On its north wall is a soapstone-faced fireplace framed with curlicue cutouts carved by the architect himself. It also has a scoot-around bookshelf ladder, windows that face the woods, and a French door that looks onto a courtyard and through it to spectacular views framed by large cutouts in the fence-wall.

Returning to the main area, the living room, dining room, and kitchen are one flowing space, separated by a two-story central hallway, with balconies forming second-story corridors. It leads to a foreshortened stairway, whose walls angle inward as it rises. This stair is framed by a tall, narrow slot; at its top is a large window overlooking the woods. Bounding the north edge of the living and dining areas is a plastered masonry wall (again for solar storage), which has been carved with swirling forms by Ann Elliott and imprinted with leaves by Jeff Riley.

For purposes of heat distribution—and for fun—the kitchen area adjoining the dining area is two stories high. The young daughter's bedroom overlooks this space, and has windows that can be opened to admit warm air from below. Also double-storied is the area just in front of the living area, plus the gallery; overlooking the gallery is the parents' sitting room. These two-story spaces are painted white to reflect light and create, again, a psychological transition from the light of the fields to the cozy, woodsy look of the living areas with their pine and poplar paneled ceilings. The many double-hung windows in the double-level space have light blue sash and much lighter—almost white—blue frames.

The interior colors, deep green and light green for the stair, white and blues for the two-story spaces, red-rust and a taupe for the bedrooms, were chosen by Peter Gruen in a somewhat unconventional manner. He was reading Dashiell Hammett's *The Dain Curse*, where, he says, he found "a particularly luscious description of a house." From this house of Hammett's imaginings came the colors for the Elliott house.

Beyond color, the house has numerous fanciful touches: the cabinets over refrigerator and stove shaped as battlements and containing uplights; the medallions (squares within squares) dotting woodwork here and there; the child's hexagonal rooms with octagonal peaked roof; and, best of all, the two-story, small master bedroom with arched windows on all four sides.

"We wanted," says Ann Elliott, "a solar house, but something that looked funky, not like a farmhouse or a space machine." And that's what Jefferson B. Riley made for them.

The main entry, across page, is symmetrical, formal, an anchor for dissimilar elements. Inside, ceilings are high at the center, low in the living, right, and dining room. The space is enveloping and mood-filled. Above right, windows illuminating the gallery.

Above, the six-sided, peak-roofed, and paneled library with soapstone-faced fireplace, scoot-around bookcase ladder, and curlicues carved by Riley. In double-storied kitchen, right, canted, cren-elated cabinets are above refrigerator and stove. Across page, a plastered, masonry wall for solar storage was imprinted with leaves (by Riley) and flowing lines (by Elliott). The foreshortened stair is in a high, narrow slot. Second story balconies adjoin bedrooms. □

Thomas Bernard

Well Matched Couple

The design of the Coxe/Hayden house and studio on Block Island, R.I., is, as described by Robert Venturi, FAIA, an expression of "complex simplicity, new oldness, and a blending of individual expression within an established architectural vocabulary."

The programmatic requirements for the project were spelled out for Venturi, Rauch & Scott Brown in a written narrative: "Keep it simple, and make it architecture. . . . The living elements will best support the creative function if they are stimulating spaces, both within and without. I always feel stifled in boxy, rectangular rooms. Capture a beautiful view, change the loft of the ceiling, or vary the angle of the walls, and the space will feel different and more energizing for me. . . . Outside, I most want to feel a sense of community, not isolation. I don't like to feel physically alone. The proximity of other houses to the north and south is welcome."

The design fits these requirements to a "T." Instead of one vacation house, two smaller buildings that hug one another on the open meadow were chosen. The larger structure contains living, dining, and kitchen areas on the ground floor; bedroom and bath on the second; and writing studio in the gable. The smaller building has a garage-workshop below, with two guest rooms and bath above. To further develop the sense of community, the architectural language of countrified classic revival was used, a style typical of many 19th century buildings on the island. That style is

Northwest elevation of the two buildings—the larger one is the main house, the smaller the guest quarters, left.

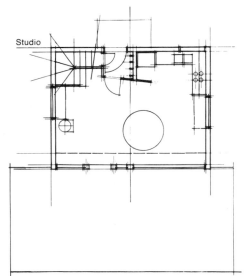

Studio

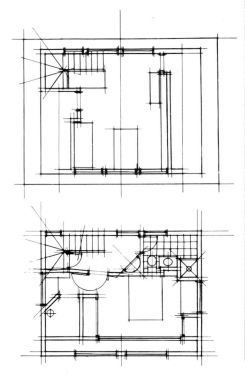

Photographs by Thomas Bernard

Playful gestures by the water.

exemplified by a temple front with symmetrical entrance, a simple profile with overscaled overhangs, windows, batterboards, and trim.

The front elevations of both buildings are embellished by symmetrically positioned windows, yet their shapes differ from the traditional and present a quiet, playful gesture. On the other elevations the playfulness becomes more explicit. For example, on the large building's rear facade the window placement loses its symmetry, with some of the balancing windows eliminated.

On the inside, great attention was paid to getting the "right" view, the "right" entrance, and the "right" feel, in Venturi's words. Careful details, such as the cupboard on the second floor landing and the kitchen cabinet edging in the main house, are meant to provide the extra touches needed to create "stimulating space," without sacrificing simplicity and ease of use.

"An immediate sense of warmth and human scaling are achieved, in part, by the buildings' charming simplicity, shingled exteriors, and orientation to views of the salt water pond below," the jury commented. "This is a contextual building suitable to its time and place." □

The main house's kitchen and bedroom, across page. The buildings' northeast elevation, above. The simplicity of the interiors as seen in floor plans: studio, across page, and guest house, right.

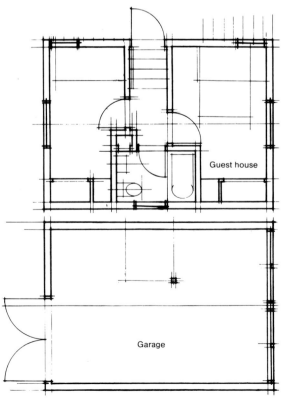

Guest house

Garage

'First Monument of a Loosely Defined Style'

Michael Graves' Portland Building. By John Pastier

Portland is the most traditional major city on the Pacific coast, but during the postwar era it has also been in the forefront of America's architectural and urban evolution. In 1948 it became home to Pietro Belluschi's Equitable Building, the first aluminum and glass skinned office structure in the country, and the winner, in 1982, of AIA's 25-year award. In the years since the Equitable opened, the city commissioned two of Lawrence Halprin's earliest and finest urban fountains and became a pioneer in providing free public transportation downtown and in replacing a riverfront freeway with a park. This is an impressive record for a city of 350,000, and it has gone largely unnoticed. Late in 1982, however, the completion of a single building generated what seemed to be as much attention as all those other events combined.

That building is, of course, Michael Graves' Portland Public Services Building. Just as Belluschi's work was the first American example of a modernist commercial genre that was later to become ubiquitous, Graves' is the nation's first executed monument of a loosely defined postmodern style. Whether it is the first of many is another question. If it is not, it will be seen as an architectural freak, but if it has credible offspring, it will be assured an important place in architectural history. Ours is a society that worships winners and forgets losers, and the Portland Building (which is one of its two official names) and its creator have advanced their argument with such insistence that black-and-white judgments are almost inevitable.

Its opponents, and there are many, find the building garish and without substance. The most concise statement of this position came at a city council hearing from Belluschi himself, when the courtly octogenarian called it "an enlarged jukebox" and "an oversized beribboned Christmas package" more suited to Las Vegas than to the city he has lived in since the 1920s. Its proponents, and there are some, fall into two groups. The more committed portion, found mainly in the geographic or philosophical vicinity of Princeton, declare it an unquestioned triumph of architectural humanism and symbolism. Its more realistic supporters concede the existence of flaws and compromises while finding it worthy on balance.

To address the issues raised by the building's friends and foes, a review of its complicated history is needed. In early 1979 the city decided to consolidate its various operating departments, scattered throughout 12 buildings, into a single new structure. Mayor Neil Goldschmidt, a mover behind Portland's Transitway Mall and later U.S. secretary of transportation, gave impetus to the project and declared his desire for a "high-tech building." (The irony of his request has gone unnoticed in the debate over the chosen design.) Concluding that a design/build competition would best meet its practical and esthetic needs, the city hired a

Across page, the Portland Building as seen from across Fifth Avenue. Entrance to the parking garage sits in the middle of the Fourth Avenue facade, above. Main entrance is at right.

© R. Greg Hursley

© Cervin Robinson

Entrance lobby, top, surrounded by public information and building security areas on the first floor, visual arts gallery on the second. Above, foyer through second floor elevator lobby.

A precompetition process of elimination.

consultant to prepare its program and budget, and advertised for entries. In June, a jury of five nonarchitects was selected—it was not an AIA-sanctioned competition—and Philip Johnson, FAIA, and John Burgee, FAIA, were appointed architectural advisers to the jury. This act would prove central to the controversy that later ensued over Graves' design, since the persuasive and esthetically mischievous Johnson was in effect the jury's sole source of design advice. He has been widely blamed for wielding undue influence in the selection of Graves from a field of three finalists, but the charge seems misplaced in light of the relative quality and cost of those designs. At that point—February 1980—Graves' team was proposing the most building for the least money, as well as the most interesting architecture, so that giving it the commission was the most practical as well as the most avant-garde thing to do.

But if Johnson's role in that final selection was beyond question, his earlier involvement was not. The crucial event occurred in July 1979, when the jury met in New York City to select three teams of finalists to compete from a field of 11 applicants, based on architectural design qualifications. The selection was to be based—to paraphrase the official document slightly—on the designer's potential and ability to respond to program requirements; to establish appropriate relationships between quality and form, function, and economy; to maximize efficiency of design; and to maximize energy conservation opportunities.

Given these criteria, Graves' inclusion was peculiar, for he was an academician whose building experience had been scant and at a small scale. At that point there was little concrete basis

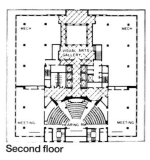

First floor

Second floor

Typical office floor

for concluding that Graves could meet the official criteria for design ability. The other two teams selected had as their architects Mitchell/Giurgola and Arthur Erickson. Both were less trendy designers than Graves but infinitely more experienced in dealing with a project of Portland's nature and scope.

If Johnson was exercising license to encourage a potentially provocative design, it is odd that he did not also choose the team that included Frank Gehry, FAIA, who is if anything more original than Graves and had a stronger record in urban-scale public design. (According to one observer of the selection process, Johnson literally tossed Gehry's application file away, calling him "a madman with a two-by-four.")

But the competition document was clearly seeking something other than provocative esthetics—it was aiming for responsible design in the fullest sense. Given that goal, Johnson's rejection of another team seems inexplicable. Van der Ryn, Calthorpe & Partners had under construction by then a governmental building that was everything the Portland building aspired to be. The firm's state office building in Sacramento, Calif., was predicated on energy efficiency, urban context, and a humane working environment, and it managed to integrate those qualities within a visually and spatially impressive design. Denying that firm a chance to compete in Portland was a blunder of the first order, and one that escaped the public scrutiny that was later focused on the Graves design.

As has already been said, the later selection of Graves' project over those of Erickson and Mitchell/Giurgola generated controversy that was not totally deserved. The furor was strong enough, however, to move the city council to ask that the Graves and Erickson teams modify and resubmit their designs. A month

Above, the open-office configurations and the four-foot-square windows on the 11th floor.

95

'A practical success and an esthetic failure.'

later, the council sought further changes from the Graves team, and a month after that awarded it the contract.

As a result of those mandated changes and other revisions the team made during construction, the building that stands today is not the one that was first submitted—it is simpler, starker, and more crude. Not much of this regression can be laid at the feet of the city, for many of the changes stemmed from miscalculation about what could be built within the budget, and others seemed to be a matter of purely esthetic revisions for the worse. The most satisfactory version of the scheme was achieved midway through the initial design period, and what was first submitted to the city already represented a decline in design quality. The later changes merely continued that decline.

The Portland Building is little more than one of Graves' Sunar showrooms blown up in scale and turned inside out. Its stylized garlands derive from Sunar's hanging fabric samples, its crudely abstracted "column capitals" are Sunar's lighting sconces magnified, and its undersized polka-dot windows correspond to the grids of brass studs that Graves uses to decorate Sunar's walls. (Originally, Graves designed three-foot-square windows 10 feet on center, but the city insisted that he enlarge them to 4x4. Some windows, however, remain less than two feet square.) As in the showrooms, much of Portland's design impact comes from color. Graves' strongest ability is as a colorist, but his usual subtlety is often lacking in this structure. As the revisions progressed, he opted for ever greater contrast, destroying what was once a balanced dialogue between solid mass and surface pattern.

Originally, a cluster of symbolic houses was to have crowned the roof, but they were eliminated by an admittedly stringent (yet also known from the start) $51 per square foot budget. All that remain of them are two trabeated frames that block the view from top-floor conference rooms. Symbolism figures often in the building's forms, sometimes obscurely (as in the remnants of the houses just cited), sometimes as caricature and mixed metaphor (as in the seven-story column "signifiers" that support a four-story keystone figure), and sometimes whimsically (as in the mechanically rendered ribbon garlands that make the building look as though it just won grand prize at the county fair). There is also inadvertent symbolism, including what is meant to be a seven-story representation of a window frame that reads equally strongly as a liturgical cross, and an entrance facing the park that leads only to the garage yet is far grander than any meant for people. The ground floor arcade carved into part of the perimeter is not especially pleasant: It is dark (Portland skies are not often sunny), has two dead ends, is narrowest at the main entrance to the building, and divorces the ground floor from the street. Under that arcade, however, there are several stores, a welcome touch for a governmental office.

There is a vast gulf between the exterior appearance of the finished building and that of Graves' early study models and witty first sketches. The models showed a rich three-dimensional expression, while the drawings humorously captured the anthropomorphic qualities that Graves claims for his design. The executed structure lacks these attributes: It is inert, essentially flat, and seems more an outsized object than a real building. On the evidence of this project, Graves is more an artist than an architect; his real media are the maquette and sketch pad rather than the full-sized edifice.

Inside, all but one of the public spaces are poor to mediocre. The two-story lobby, penetrated by four real columns and eight false ones, is poorly proportioned and self-consciously embellished by fat half-round sheet metal moldings that produce a hollow sound when tapped. The adjoining elevator is narrow and so

dismally dark that its peaked ceiling carries little visual weight. The rear lobby is larger but undistinguished, its stepped platforms leading to a view of the garage entrance. On the second floor an art gallery occupies the balcony of the front lobby, but it is so narrow that all it conveys is meanness. A hearing room on the same floor has a semicircular seating pattern that does not permit an effective view of the stage from a significant portion of the seats. The one exception to this dismal pattern of public spaces is the interior of the elevator cabs, where the architect's coloristic talents have transformed a normally banal space into a surprisingly pleasant one. In this instance, Graves has achieved an unqualified design success.

The working spaces upstairs were not designed by Graves, so his response to the problem of the building's large floors and small windows cannot be known. As occupied, the city's floors present (aside from their skimpy fenestration) an unmemorable image, but the two topmost floors leased by Multnomah County (the product of a different designer working with a better budget) are impressively elegant in a way that is sympathetic to Graves' building design while also transcending it.

If there is little doubt that in Portland Graves bit off more than he could manage, it must also be said that the structure has virtues beyond its elevator cabs and upper floor tenant improvements. In general ways it observes the context of downtown Portland. Its roughly cubic massing and approximate 200-foot height correspond to many of the district's older offices, and its use of strong color continues a polychrome tradition represented in dozens of restored Victorian commercial structures nearby.

The building also represents solid professionalism in areas beyond visual design. The design/build team included Pavarini Construction Co. of Greenwich, Conn., Hoffman Construction Co. of Portland, and the New York City architectural firm of Emery Roth & Sons, responsible for construction documents. In addition, the city retained Morse/Diesel of Chicago as project manager. These organizations were able to deliver a very economical, fast tracked building on time and on budget. The energy requirements of the structure are quite low (37,000 BTU per square foot per year), thanks in large part to its cubic form and its small, widely spaced windows. From the city's standpoint this building was its most trouble-free construction project in recent memory, and General Services Director Earl Bradfish is pleased with the effectiveness of the design/build process. Since Graves' client was the contractor, and since the contractor had to guarantee its bid figure and completion date, the design/build system also ensured strong coordination of design, cost, and timetable. Perhaps the strongest testimonial to the efficacy of the arrangement is that despite Graves' inexperience with large public projects, his team was able to meet its tough contractual obligations successfully.

The City of Portland proved to be an enlightened and courageous client. It opened the original bidding to all interested parties, heeded the advice of its professional consultants, and went ahead with the most controversial of the three designs despite the furor it caused. In doing so, it brought into being America's first large postmodern building, bearing a political and esthetic risk that government bodies usually do their best to avoid. The Portland Public Services Building is on the whole a practical success and an esthetic failure. Yet however badly one may be disappointed by the building, it seems fair to call the failure a worthy one: It fails not through timidity but through its very boldness, and not for lack of ideas but rather for retaining more of them than its designer could master. □

In the second floor, semicircular hearing room, grilled screens flank the rear entrance, right.

1984

PPG Place

San Juan Capistrano Library

Portland Museum of Art

House in East Hampton

Weekend House, Southwestern Michigan

St. Matthew's Church

Historicist, Spired 'City Of Glass' Around a Plaza

PPG Place, Pittsburgh. Architect: John Burgee Architects with Philip Johnson. By Donald Canty

On preceding two pages, the spires and tower of PPG Place as seen from Market Square.

It may be the most significant single large-scale addition to a major American city since Rockefeller Center. Philip Johnson and John Burgee have termed it, independently of each other, their best work, and they may very well be right.

It consists of a 40-story tower, a 14-story office building, and four six-story office buildings, arranged slightly irregularly around a paved plaza almost precisely the size of the tower in plan, joined by a brick-paved passageway to pre-existing Market Square 150 feet away. All of the buildings except the tower face the plaza with arcades that will be lined with shops, and hanging from them at second story level are large polygonal lanterns. At the center of the plaza is a Johnsonian version of an obelisk.

The buildings are sheathed in curtain walls of bluish gray reflective glass, but they are far from flat mirror walls. They are pleated by alternating rectangular and triangular bays reaching from the ground to continue as towers above the roof; the 40-story building also has turrets at corners and midpoints. The walls are overlaid with a delicate tracery of aluminum. Sixty-degree angles are highlights; 90-degree angles turn black, vertically striping the buildings.

The pleating has a great deal to do with the complex's success. Instead of presenting a literal reflection of what they face, these walls break up the images into an endless variety of visual experiences. They constantly change with the viewer's movement and with light. At times they can seem sparkling and bright, at other times as solid as stone. Inside, the pleating creates an effect not unlike a series of bay windows.

The towers and turrets end in pyramids. The result of all this, of course, can only be called Gothic. The architects neither deny nor apologize for their debt to history. In fact, they cite the Victoria Tower at Britain's Houses of Parliament and Pittsburgh's own Trinity Cathedral as antecedents. But they do point out that a pyramid is a very logical way to terminate angular towers.

All of this gives the complex a presence on the Pittsburgh skyline that is, to say the least, distinctive. It is an enriching presence, and makes the lopped-off tops of the modern towers on all sides look graceless and boring in comparison. From the square, the Gothic character of the complex gives it a pervasive sense of repose. Despite its size there is nothing threatening about the complex, partly because of the modulation in scale from the tower to the lower buildings. The latter make especially good neighbors to the rather funky shops and restaurants of Market Square. It's hard to imagine flat-out modern faces being so friendly in this situation.

There are three major interior spaces in the complex. One of the six-story buildings is punctured by a central skylit atrium for fast feeding. With round columns and flat glazing at its perimeter, the atrium is curiously out of character with the rest of the complex. At the rear of the tower three pointed arches project out to form a glazed, voluminous "winter garden" to be used as a kind of corporate and civic living room. It is a nice gesture toward the rest of the Golden Triangle urban renewal area, of which PPG's 5.5-acre site is part.

The third major space is the three-story lobby tower. It is entered through pointed arches that mirror those of the winter garden. The structural and elevator core is set back from the perimeter and sheathed in rich red opaque glass. Giant faceted constructions of metal and reflective glass proclaim the two elevator lobbies' entrance. These lobbies are sleek cabinets of stainless steel, and the elevators have walls of "fractured" glass.

PPG Industries occupies the first 14 and top 10 stories of the tower and two floors of the lower buildings to the west. A bridge links the PPG floors of the two buildings. Originally, there were to be more such bridges, which would have given the complex a far more self-contained quality, and they were wisely deleted. For one of the complex's happiest features is the way that its historicist imagery is woven into the fabric of the city.

bove, PPG's plaza. Passage between the two buildings at far right in photo joins this space to Market Square.

Brian Rose

© Richard Payne, AIA

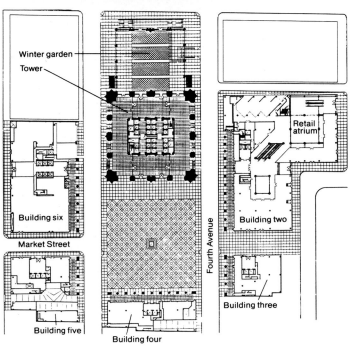

Winter garden

Tower

Building six

Market Street

Building five

Building four

Fourth Avenue

Retail atrium

Building two

Building three

The turreted tower from the river (right) and Fourth Avenue (left) where it bridges to one of the four six-story buildings (Nos. 2, 3, 4, and 5). In foreground of photo at right is the 14-story building (No. 6). In foreground of top photo is Market Square.

106

Mission Imagery, Introverted Spaces

San Juan Capistrano Library, San Juan Capistrano, Calif. Architect: Michael Graves
By John Pastier

For the second time in as many years, Michael Graves, FAIA, has completed a polychromed public building in the center of an older, tradition-conscious West Coast city. Each commission came about through a national competition in which three well-known architects were chosen from a longer list and asked to prepare designs for the final selection. These are the similarities, or more accurately, the coincidences, for otherwise the two buildings are remarkably different.

Few, if any, architects have been unaware of the Portland Public Services Building, and few have lacked an opinion about its design. The San Juan Capistrano Public Library will not go unnoticed, but it will have neither the renown nor the notoriety of its predecessor. It is a quiet and intimate structure that is also complicated and quirky. Portland's design was mainly externalized and boldly set out to express the pomp and power of municipal government through conscious architectural monumentality. Capistrano looks inward rather than outward, creating a series of internalized worlds and private experiences through carefully differentiated spaces of nicely gauged human scale. In an electronic age when reading is said to be in decline, it draws on the imagery and spatial sensibilities of earlier periods to create a setting that is an effective inducement to read, or at least browse. Judging from its heavy and enthusiastic patronage, the San Juan Capistrano is a runaway popular success.

The town itself, located halfway between Los Angeles and San Diego, is something of an anomaly. It dates back more than two centuries, making it virtually pre-Columbian by California standards. This antiquity is not much in evidence, save for the famous mission that is widely considered to be California's finest and that has attracted a flock of 20th-century souvenir shops as well as the legendary returning swallows. Most of the town's present character has resulted from its location in the path of Los Angeles' southward expansion and San Diego's northward growth. Being larger, Los Angeles has reached Capistrano first, and although the latter has a population of only 21,000 or so, its fivefold increase from 1970 to 1980 made it one of the fastest growing cities in the state. Topography and casual street patterns have spared it the gridiron form of a typical Orange County suburb, but it has still not managed to avoid the fate of a freeway town on the suburban fringe. Its most visible response to its own history had been, until lately, twofold: Its street signs bear rustic lettering not easily legible to motorists, and it has kept its fast-food outlets near the Interstate while ensuring that they are landscaped and that their signage is discreet.

About five years ago, however, San Juan Capistrano began a conscious effort of addressing the physical issues raised by its rapid expansion. It adopted a growth management ordinance limiting residential construction to 400 new units a year and retained

The elaborately articulated and complex library as seen from afar.

107

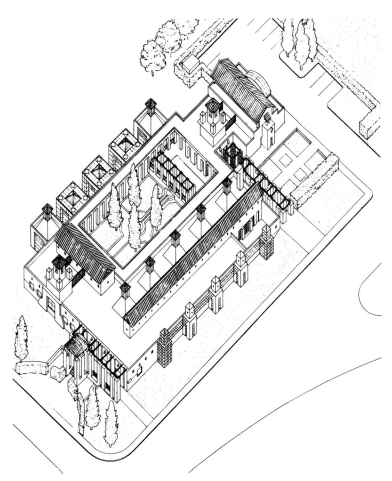

Accessible, intricate array of spaces.

Charles Moore's Los Angeles office to help develop architectural design guidelines for new nonresidential development in critical geographic zones. Moore Ruble Yudell's response was a sensitive but common-sense document that could be followed by the laypeople who would have to implement it. It defined the existing historic styles in the city as primarily California coastal and mission, identified their salient elements, and gave illustrated examples of their proper and improper use. Its goals were to foster intimacy, layering of views and spaces, arcades and small courtyards, richness of building surface, and a play of light and shadow.

Soon after these guidelines became official policy in 1980, they were put to use in the design competition for the library sponsored by the city and the Orange County Public Library system, on a site just a block north of the mission itself. Here too, the city showed considerable initiative, not only by holding a national competition for a relatively small building, but by funding the design process and augmenting the construction money provided by the county government. After screening 42 submissions of architectural qualifications and then interviewing five designers, the selection panel invited three to prepare designs for final judging 30 days later. The finalists were Robert A. M. Stern, FAIA, Moore Ruble Yudell, and Graves. Each responded consci-

entiously to the building program and the design guidelines, but Graves' scheme embodied the guidelines less literally than the others. Its plan was more like a monastery or mission with outbuildings than like a unitary structure, and its forms were clearly Gravesian rather than being directly referential to early California. Indeed, the building bears a strong kinship to the architect's earlier New Jersey Environmental Education Center, but the design seems more naturally at home in California than it does overlooking New York harbor. The Graves proposal quickly became the favorite of most of the six-person jury, although Moore's submission also had some support within that body and in the community. Ultimately, the jury endorsed the Graves design by a four-to-two margin.

Because of the complexity and elaborate articulation of the library plan, it was clear that its construction budget of $1.3 million would be exceeded. Once again the city of San Juan Capistrano showed its commitment to architectural quality by supplementing the original city and county budget to the tune of another $500,000 in order to keep the design intact. In the end, the library came in $200,000 under the revised budget, at about $115 per square foot.

The realized building is somewhat modified from the original competition entry, mainly in the disposition of functions near its entrance and in the treatment of its open atrium, but it is still an unusually complex entity for its 14,000-square-foot size. There

are roughly 60 separate indoor spaces, not counting those for storage and utilities, and another dozen outside. They fall into a supple and well worked out matrix that is most evident in plan or axonometric drawings. Every major element has at least one cognate in another part of the building, and what seems at first to be a casually picturesque building composition proves upon closer inspection to be a rigorously organized concept.

Almost all of the building's many spaces are accessible to the public, an arrangement that would be anathema to one school of library science that stresses large open floors, central control, and security. The competition program reflected some of this philosophy and certainly did not mandate the intricate breakdown of space that now exists, but the order and symbolism of the Graves design made converts of most of the jury members. On the one hand, the library has the comfortable scale and familiar quality of a private house; on the other, it is as rich in organization as a small city. There are at least 20 axes, indoors and out, that give the building a decidedly processional quality and an almost urban sense of order. At the same time, its colonnades and galleries are so agreeably scaled that this tour-de-force of planning is intriguing rather than intimidating.

Graves' civic metaphor was not originally confined to the library proper. He proposed virtual closure of the street that runs between his building and the mission property to the south, and a clear pedestrian connection to a new church on that site. (This

Above, the entrance canopy of lath atop a double colonnade, with overscaled window on its left. The interior spaces fall into a well worked out matrix, as seen in axonometric, above left.

structure is a steel-framed simulation, at somewhat enlarged scale, of a stone church that collapsed in an 1812 earthquake, and whose ruined apse still stands a few dozen yards from its copy.) The connective site work, which would have also included avenues of trees and other landscaping, was not undertaken.

As befits a Southern California building, the library forges a strong connection between indoors and out. On the east, three small, square, reading alcoves project streetward from the main bookstack area, flanked in the same row by two similarly sized and shaped wood lath gazebos attached to the building. On the west side, the sequence is reversed; there, two large enclosed pavilions form the ends of a row that also contains three equally large lath houses covered with flowering vines and intended for outdoor reading. A walled outdoor garden anchors the northeast corner of the building, while a colonnaded atrium lies at its center. There, an independently colonnaded raised deck, central fountain, and quartet of cypress trees give this main outdoor space the formal order of a monastic garden—more literally than first planned, for Graves' original and somewhat asymmetrical scheme of a symbolic stream and pool in a metaphoric landscape has become a rigid, foursquare arrangement with an off-the-shelf

Pyramidal light monitors and tiny clerestories.

imitation stone fountain placed dead center. The reasons for this change are threefold: The jury was put off by Graves' original courtyard design (which was one of the high points of his proposal), its detailed design was the work of a local landscape architect, and cost ruled out a Graves-designed fountain. Although the resulting space is banal when it could just as easily have been lively, it is nonetheless pleasant.

Two sides of the atrium colonnade shade windows and glass doors that bring softened light into the children's and adults' reading rooms. An unusual proportion of the daylighting, however, comes from above via 12 light monitors and perhaps six times that number of tiny glass-block clerestory windows. The latter are atmospheric devices, but the monitors are major design elements. Outside, they pop up above the roof line to give the building much of its external animation and character, while inside they create distinctive pyramidal ceilings and a soft, diffused illumination, artificial as well as natural, since the sloping monitor sides also distribute light from suspended pyramidal incandescent fixtures. The interiors are not bright, but neither are they dark, and the handling of light here reminds us that in a Mediterranean climate the time-honored architectural response to sun and heat is to introduce them indirectly and sparingly. There is little doubt that the library evolves from Mediterranean tradition. Its organization is strongly Roman, as are some of its specific forms. Graves was also deeply interested in Spanish colonial architecture at the time of Capistrano's design, and his competition presentation included reference sketches of Central American architecture of both Spanish and pre-Columbian origin that served as sources for many design elements.

Of course the library also has conventional windows, but they have been largely concentrated in the children's wing since bookshelves demand wall space. This last consideration points up the ingenuity of the light monitors, for they require no wall openings and introduce strong spatial character as well as illumination. The diversity of natural and artificial light adds a dimension to Graves' well-known abilities as a colorist. To date, most of his public work has not benefited from good natural light. His Sunar showrooms have been artificially lit, as are many of the public spaces in Portland. In the latter building, even the naturally illuminated spaces and the exteriors are usually dulled by the city's notoriously overcast climate. But in Caspistrano the sun is accommodating, and the design takes full advantage of that circumstance. The strongly three-dimensional wood and stucco forms are put in bold relief by the light, and the exterior colors are ones that are flattered by the warm illumination: The dominant tone is a light golden beige (the color of old paper, perhaps), and there are accents of lavender gray, red stripping, terra cotta tile, and lath painted charcoal gray. Additionally, there are stenciled decorative patterns painted on the atrium walls.

Inside, the colors are even richer and more varied, especially in the long, narrow galleria that forms the adult wing's ceremonial circulation spine. There, dark blue doors and niches combine with a puce wainscot, light blue trim, pale gold upper walls, and a warm natural wood ceiling to form what may be the building's strongest space. Some of that strength lies in its undiluted architectural quality—this is a pure circulation space with no bookshelves, magazine racks, microfilm readers, or reference tables to distract the eye. In the reading and reference rooms, where such paraphernalia abounds, the colors are generally lighter and simpler: pale gold walls, light blue-gray pyramid ceilings, some natural oak chairs and desks, and overstuffed blue camel-backed armchairs and sofas. Here, some of Graves' subtle effects are drowned out by the inevitable clutter of occupancy: Compared to his quiet order, it is surprising to see how motley and visually raucous a normally arranged wall of book spines really is.

In the children's wing, the proportion of books to wall space is lower, there are more windows, and the architecture is even freer, especially in the cylindrical story-telling tower that materializes unexpectedly in the midst of otherwise strictly rectilinear geometry. Graves calls his architecture "anthropomorphic," and his sketches often seem inclined to stroll off to another part of their page. This design walks a fine line between being solemnly ceremonial and good-naturedly tongue in cheek. In the children's wing, the balance seems tilted appropriately to the side of intimacy and whimsy.

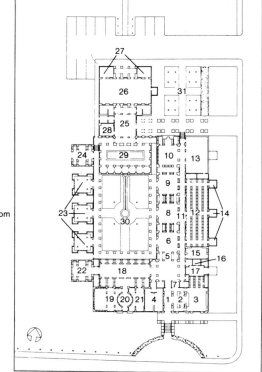

1 Foyer
2 Charge desk
3 Work room
4 Toilet
5 Information
6 Reference
7 Study carrel
8 Young adults
9 Spanish collection
10 Adults' lounge
11 Gallery
12 Stacks
13 Garden
14 Reading nook
15 Librarian
16 Kitchenette
17 Staff lounge
18 Children's lounge
19 Primary room
20 Storytelling
21 Conference
22 Children's fiction
23 Outdoor reading
24 Friends of the library room
25 Auditorium foyer
26 Auditorium
27 Storage
28 Kitchenette
29 Reflecting pool
30 Fountain
31 Orchard

Opposite page, the long, narrow galleria, the adult wing's ceremonial circulation spine. Right, the children's wing reading room.

Strong acceptance by the public—and librarians.

The feeling of ceremony is strongest in the gallery, in the repetitive colonnades and gazebos along the exterior, and at the entrance. In the last case, the ceremonial quality is contradicted by a segmental canopy of lath atop a double colonnade. Its awkwardness, which may be ironically intended, is obtrusive, but a lath pediment might have turned the trick. Similarly, an odd facade element to the left of the entrance, enframing an overscaled window and perhaps symbolizing a hearth, seems exaggeratedly prominent in the composition. This south facade is the most problematic passage in the library design.

Back inside—and it is inside where the building's principal achievements reside—there is a distinct sense that this is truly a community building. The semidetached auditorium at the rear, whose form and placement suggest a chapel in a monastery or royal compound, widens the library's purposes and constituency. Flat-floored and unencumbered by permanent seating, it is used for exhibits as well as films and lectures. The adult wing has the comfortable air of a small student lounge, or perhaps a private club. Much of this feeling is due to the intimate scale of the spaces, the lighting and colors, small touches such as brass table

Left, the periodical reading room with faux marble hearth. Clockwise from upper right: the reference room; the cylindrical children's story-telling tower; the flat-floored auditorium; and the auditorium's lobby.

lamps that look like nascent Graves skyscrapers, and the overstuffed living room seating in reading areas. (So comfortable is this furniture that one normally Philistine newspaperman became an advocate of the building after sitting in it.)

The periodical reading room even has a hearth of faux marble aligned with the central entrance axis. Originally this focal point was to have been visible anywhere along the string of reading rooms and even from the front door 170 feet away, but magazine shelving installed in a central passageway thwarted that intention. Despite this lost opportunity, there is a strongly hospitable ambiance in this wing, and consequently it is well used. Part of the phenomenon can be credited to operation—in addition to standard books, there are tempting displays of magazines, cassettes, and Spanish-language titles—but the lion's share is a product of Graves' unusual architecture.

The design of their workplace has made the librarians increasingly aware of appearance, and pains are taken to respect the structure's spirit in the countless acts of operation and housekeeping that have visual dimension. The library has been an extraordinary magnet for readers, and new cards are being issued at the rate of a thousand a month. (This in a town whose adult population is perhaps 12,000 to 15,000.) Worker morale is high, and the county library system has received many employee requests for transfer to Capistrano from other branches. Such strong popular acceptance is rare in the case of any new building, and more so when it is granted to one as unconventionally cast as the San Juan Capistrano library.

© Bruce Boehner

© Bruce Boehner

Above, the centrally located plaza with fountain and cyprus trees and surrounded by colonnaded arcades. Top, the eastern facade has three small reading alcoves flanked by two lath houses; the auditorium is to the right. Opposite page, a reading alcove. □

Modules Stacked Behind a 'Billboard'

Portland, Maine, Museum. Architect: I.M. Pei & Partners. By Robert Campbell

Like any museum, the new Portland Museum of Art, designed by Henry N. Cobb, FAIA, of I.M. Pei & Partners, is really three buildings superimposed.

First, as a work of architecture in the abstract, an experience of order and scale, of movement through light and space, it's marvelous.

Second, as a place for displaying and viewing works of art, it's also marvelous.

Third, as a piece of city-making, an element in an urban context, it's a responsible, intelligent attempt that perhaps falls a little short because it tries too hard.

Properly speaking, the new building is only a wing of the Portland Museum, although it's five times the size of the original museum. Officially, it is the Charles Shipman Payson Building. An offer by Payson of 17 paintings by Winslow Homer first led the museum to think of expanding. Further Payson gifts of money made the new wing possible. Four architects were interviewed. Harry Cobb's local connection—his great-grandfather once occupied a house on the site of the new wing—helped him nail down the job.

The museum is a regional one, concentrating heavily on works by Maine artists, many of them small in size and outdoorsy in subject. Natural light—Maine light—seemed critical, and so did the need for some relatively intimate galleries. Cobb responded with a concept that can be described as a stack of cubelike volumes, each cube being 20x20x12.5 feet high. Separating the cubes in plan are slots of interstitial space 7.5 feet wide.

One cube, in Cobb's view, is the proper size for the smallest desirable gallery. There are 26 cubes, stacked up on the site like children's blocks, each row higher and wider than the last. Thus, starting at the back of the site, first you get an element that is a single cube, then another that is two cubes wide, two cubes high, then three and three, and finally, at the entry front of the museum, a grand mass four cubes high and four wide.

It's an arrangement that allows Cobb to drop down at the back of his site to meet the scale of two historic houses that

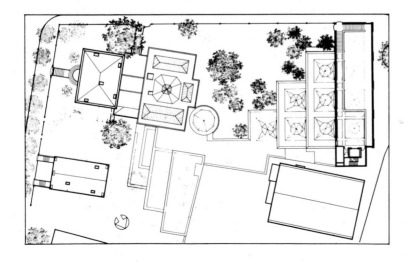

Above, the museum as it faces Congress Square, in the foreground. Behind the arched openings at the facade's top can be seen the first set of skylights that repeat on the other three levels.

This page, top, the rear of the museum steps down to relate to the smaller scale of the buildings behind, which are also part of the museum property. Above, detail of the rear of the museum showing bay windows, which occur at stair landings. Across page, top, three-quarter view of the front facade as it faces Congress Square; below, the museum as it links to the older museum building of 1911, distinguished by Palladian window.

Octagonal skylights atop descending roofs.

stand there, yet rise, at the front, to dominate a major intersection of the city. A seemingly compulsive, limiting geometric idea turns out to be the means of creating great variety of scale on the exterior.

Inside, the variety is even greater, and it's here that Portland really sings. Except for Louis Kahn's great Kimball Gallery, there can be no museum that creates richer configurations of space and light in so small a compass. The Portland interior is a wonderland of delicately skylit, subtly interpenetrating spaces, a sequence of unexpected vistas and overlooks alternating with intimate encounters. Wherever a space-cube meets the sky, it is topped with an octagonal lantern skylight. These are modeled, as Cobb notes, on those invented by Sir John Soane for the Dulwich Picture Gallery in London in 1811. The skylights are modulated only by fixed louvers. They lack entirely the paraphernalia of operable baffles, grids, and translucent screens that have become commonplace in recent museums. Yet the octagons work superbly to fill the museum with a light that seems very much alive but never glaring. On a normal day, you can turn off the electric lights and hardly notice a difference in the light levels of the top-lit galleries. As it is in Kahn's late museums, the light is almost a presence, a nearly visible gentle bright ether that fills the space, illumines the art, and models the architecture.

Some museums seem intended, by their architects, to be perceived as more important works of art than the paintings and sculptures they contain. Others seem meant to exhibit neither themselves nor their art but rather to be, primarily, places of public assembly. Portland belongs in neither category. It is a museum wholly devoted to the art it contains. The collection is not a great one, perhaps, but it is very good, and it has the virture of being quite different from all other collections. In too many American museums you can't tell, from the art, what part of the country

you're in, because the collection is trying to look like every other collection—to be a standard, approved sampler of the whole history of Western art, like a miniature, cloned Metropolitan Museum or National Gallery. Wisely, Portland has eschewed that approach and stuck pretty much to Maine artists, with the result that you come away impressed by how many good ones there are—not only the obvious Homers and Wyeths but many names less known. So well proportioned and roomlike are the various galleries, and so good is the quality of the light, that each artwork looks at home in its place and seems to glow with an inner radiance—many of them, indeed, probably look better than they really are. In this interior you are vividly aware of the architecture as the frame for your experience, but it isn't trying to be the experience.

The parti of space-cubes staggered in both plan and section leads to some curious problems of circulation. Some visitors find the museum confusing. Interior space is mazelike and complex, and you always seem to be turning a corner and happening onto a stair you didn't expect, or failing to find the one you were hoping for. The confusion is really a virtue, saving the building from the obviousness and predictability it might have suffered with its small size—only 63,000 gross square feet—and its rigorous modularity. There's a stair at the southwest corner of each floor, but since the corners never line up, you can't see one stair from another. After a while, you learn the ropes well enough to navigate, but you never lose your pleasant feeling of wandering, of exploration and discovery. The stairs have landings with curved glass viewing windows that orient you to the new museum garden (by Hanna-Olin Environmental Design and Planning) and, across the street, a fine federal house.

As an ordering concept the space-cubes work well. Galleries range from intimate nooks up to the great State of Maine gallery, four cubes wide and two high, which fills the front of the museum at its top under a row of octagonal skylights. This room is a

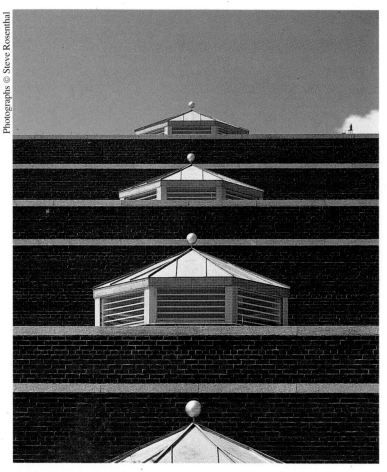

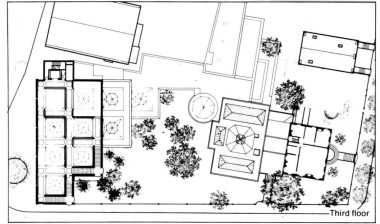

Third floor

Interior wonders, exterior puzzlement.

breathtaking space after the smaller scale of the rest of the museum. Some find it a little grand for the art it contains, most of which has obviously been created with parlors and breakfast rooms in mind, but if that's a drawback it's offset by the scale-giving modularity of the architecture and the simple pleasure of encountering so much art in one room.

The modules are expressed in plan on the floor, which is pine divided by strips of gray granite 20 inches wide. The strips demarcate the space-cubes from the interstitial slots, creating a plaid floor of pine and granite—two very Maine materials, although the granite in this case comes from Canada. Partitions are always located on the granite strips. Corridors, doors, and the like are placed at the interstitial slots. The system works to create a sense of order that isn't obvious. You sense the presence of intelligence and measure in this world without being able to see quite through to the underlying system.

Minor spaces work well, too. The best is the basement auditorium, a garden of blue seats in an arbor of white columns. The auditorium too is faithful to the modules: The seats occupy the space-cube, the aisles are the slots, the columns line up on the demarcation.

An octagonal conservatory, which connects the new wing to the older parts of the museum, is a sort of Victorian winter garden focused on an incredibly kitsch sculpture that would be at home in the Victoria and Albert: "Dead Pearl Diver" of 1858 by Benjamin Paul Akers, the museum's very first acquisition.

There is a kind of service blob of space that wanders along the museum's east side, outside the space-cube system, containing offices and the gift shop. The shop is the one real failure of the interior, arbitrarily cramped into an octagon shape that is inappropriate and inefficient.

Details are generally quiet and elegant, except perhaps for the idiosyncratic, capsule-shaped light fixtures in the stairwells.

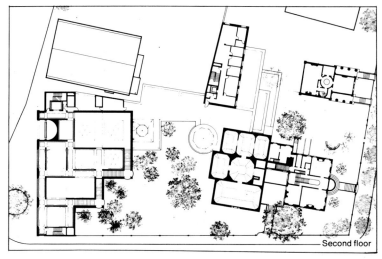

Second floor

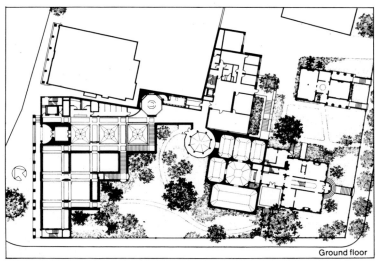

Ground floor

So much for the interior. It's wonderful. The exterior is something much more puzzling.

Most buildings planned as stacks of blocks end up looking like stacks of blocks—the works of Herman Hertzberger, for instance, or Moshe Safdie's Habitat complex in Montreal. They have no facades. Cobb's museum is just the opposite. Its facade, enormous and flat, bigger in fact than the building behind it, is a deliberately imposed abstraction of the hierarchical, ordered facade of an Italian Renaissance palazzo.

Everyone who mentions Portland talks of this astonishing entrance front. Both Cobb and the museum trustees admit that it was a source of much controversy throughout the design process. Not the least of its amazements is the fact that it gives not the slightest hint of the spatial delights within. It is a kind of giant brick billboard on which is inscribed a pattern of arches, squares, and circles that seem to have some occult, unfathomable meaning. The facade is a work of graphics rather than architecture, its flatness and thinness intentionally emphasized by the big cutouts at the top and by the fact that the parapet fails to turn the corner. It recalls the fake, two-story front of a one-story Western saloon.

The height and boldness are intended to help define Congress Square, the intersection onto which the museum faces, but the facade lacks the burly, space-containing strength of many more richly modeled older buildings around it. And it overscales some of its neighbors, especially the temple-fronted Chamber of Commerce next door. Nor do the big circles at the top meet the sky so interestingly as the gables, spires, and chimneys nearby.

The incised patterns are aligned, of course, with the modular division of cubes and slots behind, but the connection is a little academic. The patterns are notations, rather than expressions, of rich spatial system within.

Other things are wrong with this facade. At ground level, there is a continuous, elaborately vaulted arcade, meant to engage the building with the public realm of Congress Square. The arcade is much too shallow and much too blank to be of any interest or use, and it seems to attract only an occasional pot-smoking teenager. A grove of white paper birches in the plaza is extremely elegant as a foil, yet the trees fail to occupy or activate the space.

On the plus side, this facade has the virtue of being quite unforgettable once seen, and it has, more than any other element, made the building an instant landmark. And Cobb's willingness to be quirky, to doodle so freely on his building, to be a little inexplicable, is disarming. Perhaps with a little imagination one could also say that the facade's flatness and look of having been drawn on the building with compass and T-square is in character with the federal facades of many Portland houses.

At the back, the museum drops rapidly in size, meeting comfortably the two fine 19th-century houses, one federal and one Greek revival, that comprise the rest of the museum property, and shaping a pleasantly romantic if slightly residual garden and lawn.

To understand this extraordinary exterior you have to understand that for Cobb an architectural problem has to be solved in a way that exposes the problem rather than concealing it. Cobb never wants his solution to be so complete that the problem disappears. He is too much the pedagogue for that. His famous and beautiful John Hancock Tower in Boston, for instance, by its marvelous, absurd attempt to disappear into thin air, solves the problem of inserting a huge tower into a delicate historic fabric in a way that makes the predicament only the more vividly apparent. Portland is like that too.

What then is the "problem" at Portland? Cobb's own words, in a talk delivered at the Harvard design school, where he is chairman of architecture, define it:

"It will be immediately seen that the distinguishing feature of this design problem is the need to provide these extensive new facilities in a form that will respect and render eloquent the living presence of history on a constricted and awkwardly shaped urban

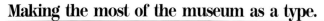

Making the most of the museum as a type.

site. Our solution proposes a stepped building form which, while presenting a bold, unified, large scale facade to Congress Square, nonetheless grants primacy to its smaller scale neighbors within the museum precinct. The new building must assert its autonomy—indeed its primacy—with respect to the public square, while remaining contingent in its relationship to the buildings and spaces within its own precinct."

The problem then is the need to be public at one end, private at the other, grand here, intimate there. The building exterior is the exposition, perhaps a little too diagrammatic, a little too teacherly, of this predicament.

Connecting this outside to its inside is an entry made of layer upon layer. You pass through a brick arch, a freestanding wood frame, a half-domed space, glass doors, and then a tight inner vestibule before emerging into the high, brightly daylit lobby or Great Hall. The layers are shallow but provide a strong sense of passage from public realm to very special interior place.

Left, top, second floor gallery behind arched windows of front facade; left bottom, ground floor gallery with typical overlook that shows the interpenetration and interlocking of spaces; above, the State of Maine gallery on the top floor with mezzanine.

Exterior materials are waterstruck local brick with gray granite string courses and trim. Originally, before costing, all was to have been granite.

Like the High Museum by Richard Meier in Atlanta, Portland as an art museum is an example of what has become probably the single most interesting architectural program our era offers. And it's an endlessly fascinating design. Though the main facade may not quite come off, Portland remains one of the most successful recent buildings in New England. □

Photographs © Norman McGrath 1983

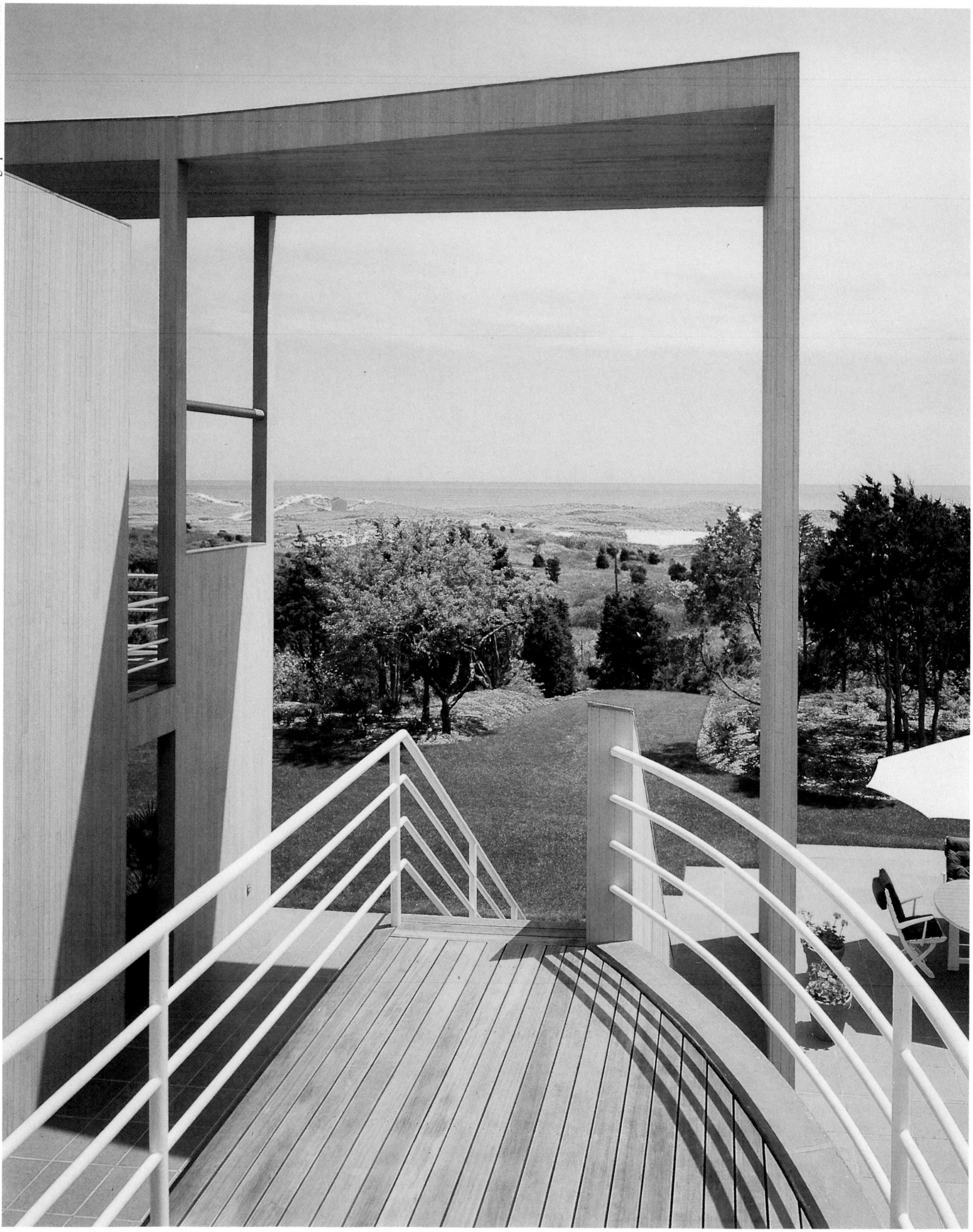

An Abstract Language Made Comprehensible and Comfortable

East Hampton residence. Architect: Gwathmey Siegel & Associates.
By Andrea Oppenheimer Dean

What many architects hope to achieve through decorative flourishes and facadism, use of vernacular shapes, historical allusion and quotation—namely a more emotionally accessible, "humanized," richer architecture—Charles Gwathmey, FAIA, has here accomplished through expansion of a modernist vocabulary that goes back to his first building of note, his parents' house in Amagansett, N.Y.

Eighteen years and 40 houses later, this new residence in neighboring East Hampton is by far his most complex, yet its first and lasting impression is one of serenity. And—despite its expense ($150/square foot) and expanse (11,000 square feet)—its comfortable scale, calm composition, layered spaces, use of wood, colors, and textures, and play of enclosed, open, predictable, and quirky spaces make this house as livable and snug as its conventional, older neighbors.

In fact, Gwathmey's attempt here is to bridge the gap between tried and traditional notions of house-as-haven—with a distinct sense of arrival and entry, and visibly separate, cozy rooms—and modern ideas of clarity in plan, modulation in section, and of designing with the sun, wind, and other site and programmatic constraints in mind.

So, like those of his colleagues who learn from Las Vegas and the Pantheon, Gwathmey looked to history and the vernacular, but for principles rather than quotations or allusions, to give a firm psychological anchor. And like the postmodernists, he uses layering, but in the service of volumetric space, to achieve a sense of density with transparency, rather than for surface effects.

Layering at the De Menil residence begins with the site, a narrow seven acres that you approach from the north and that ends in dunes and ocean, to the south. After emerging from a woods

From second story deck with curved Corbusian stair rails, framed view of dunes and ocean, left. Though a many-layered, abstract composition, from sea and dunes, above, the house holds its own in the tradition of conventional nearby dune houses.

Variegated volume 'held within a cage.'

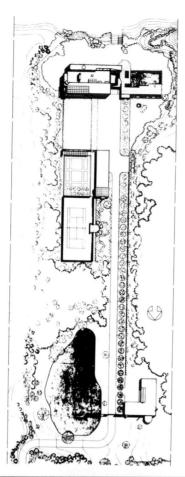

by car, you come upon a slightly surreal-looking pink stucco entry wall. The first association is to Luis Barrágan, whom Gwathmey admires for the stability and quiet of his work. At this entry wall, asphalt changes to cobblestones to denote "driveway," a quarter-mile-long driveway. Directly to the left is a satellite dish (speaking of surreal) and a manmade pond. Straight ahead is the first glimpse of the house, of its eastern-most edge, which forms a two-story, double frame for ocean, dunes, and sky. Marching down the right side of the driveway is a flank of linden trees, creating a firm edge to contrast to softer, more open elements on the left, a tennis court, a garden, an arbor, a stucco-faced guest house and garage, then to the left an auto court, and, finally, the first full view of the house.

It is divided roughly in half, a three-storied, peak-roofed greenhouse framed in cedar to the west, a more solid, cedar-clad volume to the east, and to the right of it a swimming pool, once again with stucco walls, "recalling," Gwathmey says, "both the entry wall and the guest house and garage." The south elevation, seen from the dunes, is a more variegated volume. Held within a cage formed by a brise-soleil, it is of a scale and heft to hold its own on the broad beachscape in the manner of neighboring dune houses.

The entry, back on the north facade, is a two-story cutout clad in cedar and has one curved glass block wall to gentle you into a

Left, from north to south are an entry gate-well, a quarter-mile drive, guest house and garage, then the house. The southwest portion of the house is seen below, and, across page, first from the pool, then looking toward it.

Photographs © Norman McGrath

The visitor's first view of the house is the double frame, on west, left. A view from the southeast is at top, and from the east, above.

Section through screen porch, living room, and greenhouse

Passages that reveal organizing principles.

wide Josef Hoffmannesque mahogany door. The sequence is an intimation of things to come: for instance, that this is a cedar-lined house full of Secessionist furniture.

The entry hall similarly serves not only as a point of passage but to reveal at a glance the organization and organizational principles of the whole building. Like the site, it is horizontally layered from north to south into greenhouse, circulation space, living areas, and brise-soleil-shaded screen porch overlooking the ocean. It is also varied in section, which transforms some potentially boxy rooms into intriguing, inflected spaces. Thus, the entry gallery begins as a low-ceilinged space; it is the cross axis of the hallway running east-west from which dining and living rooms extend as fingers. But a few paces ahead, just in front of a large painting by Clyfford Still, the entry gallery swoops up to the full height of the house, revealing a second story balcony and ending in a skylight.

This ordering system of plan and section is repeatedly echoed throughout the house. On the second floor, for example, a balcony overlooks the Still painting, then an odd-shaped study overlooks the greenhouse, and beyond it the entire site. The result of this "recall," as Gwathmey calls it, is to firmly fix even open spaces by anchoring them in a surround that almost instantly becomes familiar through multiple and varied exposures. "It's very important," says Gwathmey, "in a complex building like this to have not only primary references like the ocean, but to create internal references to remind you of where you are, to prevent a feeling of being on a big, moving ship, to make you perceptually comfortable."

In similar fashion, the green stucco chimney wall separating

Left, living area flows into corridors, one adjacent to green-house (right in photo), the other to porch facing the sea. Furniture includes screen and stool-like tables by Josef Hoffmann, one of twin, dark brown leather chairs by Emil Jacques Ruhlmann, and sofas by Gwathmey, intended to echo Ruhlmann.

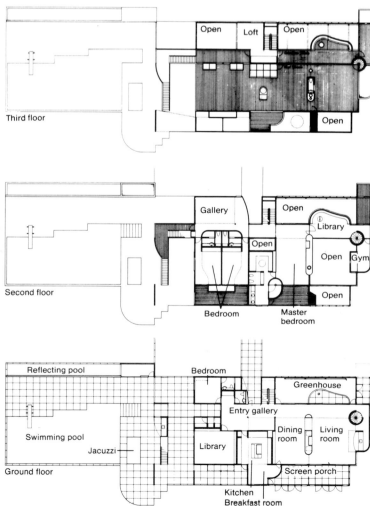

131

Spaces big and small and a 'new richness.'

dining and living areas recalls exterior walls—the pink stucco entry wall, the stucco-faced garage—and has a peephole to create a sense of connection and transparency. And, as at the entry hall, the nine-foot-high dining room ceiling sweeps up to almost 20 feet in the living room. The last is designed to feel like an ocean liner lounge, opened to the sea and sky, yet made secure by the sturdy stucco wall and the buffer provided by the brise-soleil-topped porch.

Though a far more closed space, a place with a door, the library, just right off the entry gallery, is similarly open to views of dunes and sea to the south, but defended from the elements by the brise-soleil-covered terrace. Lined on two sides with mahogany bookcases, the library houses Hoffmann's rather wild-looking Buenos Aires series consisting of a settee, table and armchairs. Next to the library is the kitchen/breakfast room, "the heart of the house," Gwathmey calls it, since it serves the library, library terrace, screened porch, and dining room.

At the top of the stairs on the second floor, a balcony overlooks the entry; to its left are two guest rooms with south-facing decks. Gwathmey uses a very rudimentary technique for distin-

guishing sleeping spaces: blinds that transform windows into walls. Just right of the balcony is the master bedroom, which is zoned into sitting and sleeping spaces through diagonal placement, almost at it center, of a built-in. One side serves as bookcase and console, the other as headboard. Next comes a curve in the balcony to form a study, and finally a game room. On the third floor are a study loft and kitchenette with splendid views into and beyond the greenhouse.

The interiors are furnished with plenty of built-ins, typical of Gwathmey Siegel's earlier houses and especially apt here as a surround for the De Menils' Secessionist furniture collection. The sumptuously crafted pieces prompted Gwathmey, for the first time, to use three types of wood—cedar, natural and finished mahogany—and a hierarchy of colors. "The furniture established a whole new richness that we had never explored before," he says.

Above, looking east from entry with Still painting to glass block partition gives glimpse of dining space, then stucco wall with opening into living area. High-polish materials—glass block, stone floors—are softened by cedar paneling. Across page: top, dining room, below, kitchen (left); bathroom (right).

Photographs © Norman McGrath

A continuous process of self-evaluation.

Gwathmey has called this a "summary house," and in 1982 when his office won the AIA firm award and this house was still a project, Stanley Abercrombie, AIA, wrote in *AIA Journal*: "The design addresses the formal issues that have concerned Gwathmey Siegel in all its best work at all scales, issues of arrival and procession, of circulation as an organizing element, of extension of building forms into the landscape, of separating public and private areas, and of giving appropriate importance to both overall compositions and to individual spaces and elements."

It is, however, also a departure, "a new way of looking at things," says Gwathmey, even from a 1981 honor award winning Cincinnati residence where the architect used many of the same elements as at East Hampton but in less complex, richly textured combinations. He says, "If you're pragmatic and you continually evaluate your own work, you come to see that you've run the gamut." Most artists and architects eventually reach this point, and then have only three choices: to abandon ship and join another, to settle for repetition and stay the course, or to chart a new and broader one that defeats previous limitations. Gwathmey, of course, chose the last. Some of the results are increased layering; increased use of color, varying materials, and textures; more complexity, especially in section; the making of rooms as well as open spaces; and an attempt to embrace traditional notions of house.

Most important, perhaps, Gwathmey has succeeded in translating the abstract language into an idiom that everyone can understand and feel comfortable with. □

A study and third floor gallery form curves invading the greenhouse, left. Below, the library; across page, a view from the north, through living area, to porch, lawn, dunes, and sea.

Sophisticated Use of Rural Vernacular

Weekend house in Michigan. Architect: Tigerman Fugman McCurry. By Nora Richter Greer

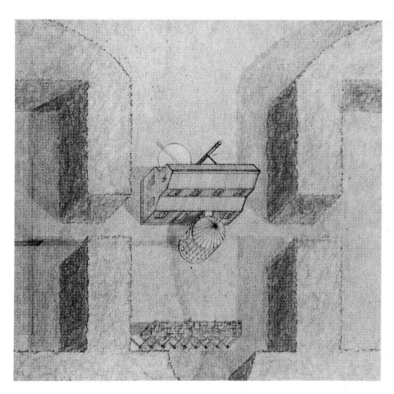

When two independently minded architects work together on a project it can often lead to disastrous results, but in the case of Stanley Tigerman, FAIA, and Margaret McCurry it resulted in a whimsically delightful vacation house that is also a more serious study of objects in space.

The house sits on a wooded lot about a block away from Lake Michigan in a sleepy southwestern Michigan town. For its design Tigerman and McCurry borrowed from the rural vernacular. It is straightforward in shape: a rectangular shed form with extended second story loft and attached cone-roofed screened-in porch. The materials are simple: corrugated metal siding and plywood, chosen largely because of a tight construction budget. Lattice decorates the two short sides of the house and the porch screening.

The east end of the house (seen in photograph right) will eventually become the ceremonial front, once the property is relandscaped. It is from this approach that one sees the dynamic interplay between the house and the porch, an image which evokes that of a barn and its granary. Tigerman also refers to this relationship in more allegorical terms: a basilica (house) and baptistery (porch). Eventually, the ceremonial front facade will be

Three views of the house reveal its vernacular imagery and the counterplay between it and the porch. The east end, right, will become the ceremonial 'front' when the property is relandscaped.

Photographs by Howard N. Kaplan

Inside, a feeling of friendly intimacy.

repeated, although in smaller scale, as a shed at the end of the driveway, and the porch's shape will be echoed in a pavilion at the rear of the property.

The 1,350-square-foot interior is symmetrically laid out. The focal point is a two-story living/dining room that sits as a square in the middle of the rectangular building. On two opposite ends of the central space are smaller rooms—a bedroom and sitting room on one side and a kitchen and a bath/utility room on the other. Each room is squarish in shape, and when doors are closed and shades drawn are very private places. Above these smaller rooms, again at two ends of the central space, are two identical lofts, each of which has two twin beds and drafting table and is entered via a very unusual staircase. Throughout the house, windows, doors, light fixtures, and ceiling fans are placed in a strict symmetrical configuration.

It is the staircases and lofts that most obviously signal that this is intended to be a lighthearted, playful design. Set into the wall as decoration, the stairs ascend steeply to witty cutouts over the lofts' Dutch doors. Most appreciative of the lofts are children who sit on the top step overlooking the adults' activities below. While the double-ceiling height affords a sense of volume (and, not incidentally, in combination with the two ceiling fans provides excellent ventilation), the overriding sensation is one of friendly intimacy, of being gently cuddled, a feeling that is reinforced by the interior's folk art and warm furnishings. Detailing is meticulous throughout. □

In the interior a strict symmetry is achieved by locating the living/dining space centrally, off of which are smaller rooms with lofts above, which are reached by specially designed stairs.

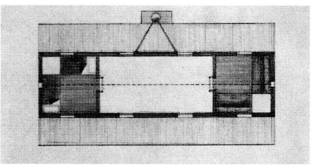

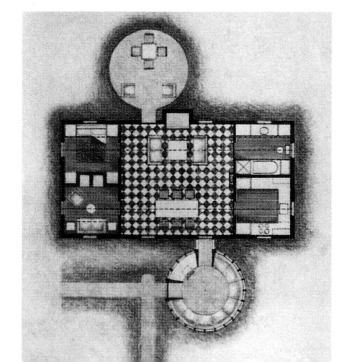

Built on Religious, Regional Traditions

St. Matthew's Church, Pacific Palisades, Calif. Architect:
Moore Ruble Yudell. By Carleton Knight III

"We didn't design the church, the congregation did," says Charles W. Moore, FAIA, of Moore Ruble Yudell's work on St. Matthew's Parish Church in Pacific Palisades, Calif. While Moore's remarks may be something of an oversimplification, the parishioners did play an unusually prominent role in the schematic design.

That role was the result of fortuitous coincidence. In October 1978, a raging forest fire roared down through the hills in Pacific Palisades, a choice residential area near the Pacific Ocean on the way to Malibu, incinerating everything in its path, including an A-frame church designed by Quincy Jones. The Rev. Peter G. Kreitler, associate rector of St. Matthew's, notes that with such a loss, a congregation thinks of the church's soul as having been destroyed and wants to participate in its reawakening.

In addition, a number of parishioners believed that they had, over time, been left out of the decision-making process of the church. As a result, the building committee's instructions from

the parish included a requirement that any new design be approved by a two-thirds majority.

When Moore Ruble Yudell was interviewed for the job, the firm told the parish that it wanted community participation in the design. It had experience in that kind of work and enjoyed the results. Moore, who says, "I don't want to be in the position of having to peddle a scheme," adds that the process "was the most exciting part of the design."

Moore Ruble Yudell asked planner Jim Burns, with whom the firm had worked previously, to assist in organizing a series of four workshops, held on Sundays about a month apart and attended by more than 200 parishioners. The format was especially designed to be loose, so as to inspire creativity. The architect's challenge was to synthesize the sharply divergent views of the congregation.

In general terms, says Moore, "many parishioners wanted, for acoustic and liturgical reasons, a lofty volumed symmetrical

Southwest elevation

From the exterior, St. Matthew's appears quite rustic, and, like its 19th-century counterparts, seems to grow out of the surrounding landscape. Bell tower marks the entrance.

church with a minimum of glass and wood. An equally vocal group spoke for a more informal and rustic building with intimate seating, views to the old prayer garden, extensive use of wood, and a close relationship to the benign outdoors of Southern California."

The first workshop was devoted to a tour of the rolling, partially wooded 34-acre estate owned by the church to settle on a site for the new building. To the second, the architects brought a kit of "church" parts—pews, altar, bell tower, arcades—for the parishioners to assemble.

Moore reports that he was amazed at the results. The parishioners attending had been divided into groups of 15 to 20, and each came up with roughly the same plan, a semielliptical arrangement

of pews. Such a plan allowed intimate participation in the church service—there is room for 350, but there are only seven rows of pews—and unlike a circular arrangement, members of the congregation are not forced to look at each other.

Moore and company then showed slides—the architect calls it his "Rorschach test"—of various church exteriors and interiors from around the world to see what the parishioners liked and disliked.

Later the architects returned with several building models that would fit over the semielliptical plan. The congregation chose what Moore describes as a modified Latin cross roof utilizing a gabled nave with long dormers acting as the transepts. To help the congregation understand the design, a full-size study model, using poles, banners, and ropes, was created on the site.

The approach seemed to please the congregation; the schematic design was approved by 83 percent at a special church meeting in January 1980. Design development, which was undertaken

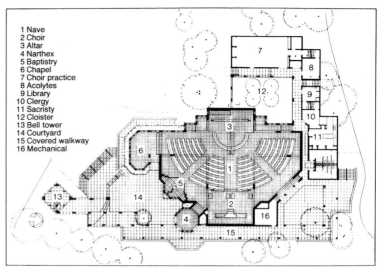

1 Nave
2 Choir
3 Altar
4 Narthex
5 Baptistry
6 Chapel
7 Choir practice
8 Acolytes
9 Library
10 Clergy
11 Sacristy
12 Cloister
13 Bell tower
14 Courtyard
15 Covered walkway
16 Mechanical

On the inside, a series of surprises.

with a 13-member building committee, would consume another year.

The result, completed in March 1983 at a cost of $2 million, is at once a contemporary building that evokes the past without resorting to mimickry and a fairly straightforward structure on the outside that is full of surprises on the inside. Architect John Ruble likens it to a Ming vase. "It's both subtle and complex," he says. "You can see as much as you want."

The 10,000-square-foot stucco and wood-beam structure is topped with a tile roof and appears to grow up through the trees on the site, much like buildings of the 19th century, Ruble notes. The varied roof planes undulate, as do the tops of the window frames—a typically "Moorish" stylistic touch—echoing the surrounding hills. The hipped roof slips down, creating low eaves at the perimeter. Sections are cut away to open vistas and preserve trees.

In plan, the semielliptical sanctuary is surrounded by such ancillary spaces as the chapel, baptistry, choir, and narthex. A separate building wraps around one side and the rear, creating courtyards for outdoor activities and containing a library, sacristy, rest rooms, choir practice area, and storage space.

The simple exterior, painted a light gray-green to pick up shades from the mottled bark of adjacent sycamore trees, belies a complex interior. After entering through a glazed, octagonal narthex, one is struck by a sense of mystery in the nave. There are few apparent windows, yet the space is filled with natural light. The transept windows, which utilize pastel-colored stained glass created by Jane Marquis, resemble the rose windows of old cathedrals. Roof-mounted skylights also open to permit natural ventilation, thus obviating the need for air conditioning.

The furnishings—lectern, altar, pews, light fixtures, and sconces—all were designed by the architects and show the same level of care and concern evidenced in the rest of the design. The AIA honor awards jury cited St. Matthew's as "an excellent example of how modern religious architecture can remain within the context of a proud historical tradition and blend harmoniously with its site. The imaginative use of stucco, exposed timbers, roof tiles, and other decorative elements, both inside and out, links this very contemporary church to the rich tradition of California architecture."

It may be, as Moore says, that it was the congregation that put the various parts together, but it was the architects who gave a sense of grace and style to the whole. □

The simple exterior belies a complex interior filled with natural light. Plan, above, shows semielliptical arrangement of pews surrounded by ancillary spaces.

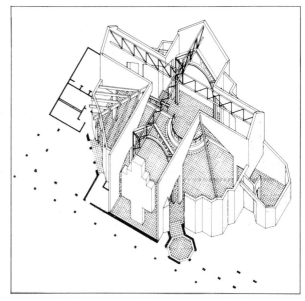

Opposite page, lofty sanctuary with open ceiling. Fanlike rafters at crossing stiffen trusses that support nave and transepts. Giant, pointed steel arches, 35 feet high, carry main truss in nave and are trimmed in wood attached with huge bolts. Architect-designed reredos mounted on wall at rear of altar interprets the Tree of Life. Battened walls evoke Gothic tracery, while floor of terra cotta tiles is reminiscent of California missions. Lighting, custom-designed by the architects, is suspended in curves over the pews. This page, chapel, bottom left corner of isometric, offers typical 'Moorish' detail in slanted line of window tops.

This page, top left, deep battens of natural wood give texture to wall. Sconces are aluminum with cutouts of religious images. Right, cutouts from Book of Kells on entry doors in the narthex. Below: the baptistry with artificial light, left; natural light, right. Opposite page, view to rear of sanctuary shows contemporary, unadorned cross suspended from interior structure. A 22-stop organ, designed by the late Charles Fisk of Massachusetts, is to be installed this year behind arch at rear. □

Photographs by Timothy Hursley © The Arkansas Office

1985

Procter & Gamble Headquarters

Loyola Law School

Herring Hall, Rice University

House in Delaware

House in Chilmark, Massachusetts

Public Housing, Charleston, South Carolina

Treehouse, Philadelphia Zoo

Monterey Bay Aquarium

Making a Nonentity Into a Landmark

Procter & Gamble headquarters addition, Cincinnati. Kohn Pederson Fox.
By Andrea Oppenheimer Dean

Proctor & Gamble's new headquarters signals a departure both for architects Kohn Pedersen Fox and for their client, a cautious old corporation known to some in its home city of Cincinnati as "Prim and Grim." According to the designers, P&G made only two stipulations for its new building: that it have a more public, less cloistered look than the existing headquarters—a dull and dour 11-story, 1956 limestone box with punched windows—and that the old be incorporated in the new complex.

P&G's headquarters has a sense of solid presence without appearing ponderous, is elegant without the flash and showiness of some KPF buildings. Moreover, it is KPF's first all stone building. The firm, known for taking design cues from nearby buildings, has until now created mainly collages that often juxtapose contrasting, sometimes jarringly dissimilar materials, shapes, and colors. The only consistent juxtaposition at P&G is of large volumes and contrasting linear decoration, granite and marble on the exterior, stainless steel banding within.

Partner in charge of design William Pedersen, AIA, explains, "Proctor & Gamble is a more homogeneous approach. It isn't an issue of taking one's personal style from place to place. The issue is one of drawing one's style from the place, to create a personality for a building that fits into but isn't distorted by the context. In this sense, this is a pivotal building, something of a departure." Senior designer Alex Ward adds, "P&G gave us the confidence to do all stone buildings. Previously, we thought it might not be modern enough."

KPF's starting point was urban design, and once they had settled on limestone as material and an L as basic shape, which generated the two rotated towers rising from the L's elbow, they had solved the basic urban design problem. It consisted of making the building a terminus for the eastern edge of Cincinnati's downtown grid, which unravels near the site into an amorphous riverside and spaghetti-like freeways. Because of the towers' diagonal placement, which aligns with the main artery into downtown from the northeast, the building, as Pedersen had wanted, has also become a gateway into the city. Limestone towers with setbacks were chosen for the simple and good reason that Cincinnati is a city of predominantly limestone buildings, many dating from the '30s, several having distinctive shaped tops. Without mimickry, whimsy, or irony, KPF thus adapted Cincinnati's typical building shapes and materials.

The L-shaped complex neatly incorporates the old headquarters by, in a sense, making it appear as an addition to the new, to which it is linked via a second story bridge. Like the old building, both new wings have punched windows, but of a special kind. These consist of four-foot-wide reflective glass panels flanked by two, one-foot clear panes set back six inches to reveal the thickness of the limestone skin. The effect is to enrich the wall surface with changing patterns of light and shade. Both new wings, like the old building, are colonnaded, and KPF performed superficial surgery on the 1956 arcade for purposes of adjusting old to new. Oddly, though, while in previous build-

ings KPF has tended to concentrate mass and ornament at the lower levels, at P&G the focus is on the jewel-like entry pavilion and the tower tops, leaving at street level a lusterless repetitive colonnade shielding a drab wall with false windows. Behind them is mostly shell space and mechanical equipment.

The L-shaped complex, including the old headquarters, embraces a two-block formal garden/piazza, which is aligned with Cincinnati's signature Fountain Plaza just two blocks away. In its last life the P&G plaza was a more casual backyard for the 1956 building. It was enlarged and landscaped with latticed pergolas and an entry drive when the decision was made to shift P&G's front door to its new three-story entry pavilion.

The last, popping out from the crook of the L, is the building's centerpiece and focus at street level. To underscore its special role, it is mostly clad in marble and has an octagonal window above the entry—a sort of medallion. Rising above the pavilion are P&G's two, 17-story, rotated, octagonal towers. Here again, KPF used white marble cladding just under the domes to call attention to these special elements and topped them with green tern-coated metal to echo the colors of nearby tower tops.

Asked what he likes best about the building, Pedersen responds, "The external volumetric relationships to the site were relatively predictable. But there are few buildings in modern architecture that can rival the interiors of this building. They

Center above, P&G towers in skyline. Left, with precursor.

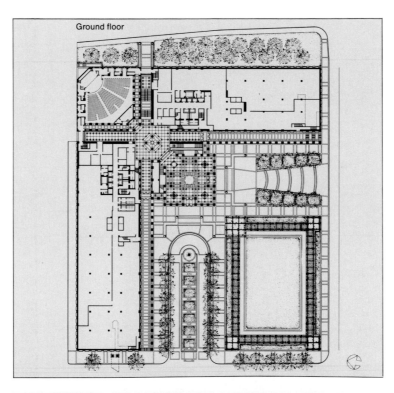

Ground floor

Left, with existing headquarters in foreground, the L shape with rotated spires at its knuckle embraces a formal garden and creates a terminus for the eastern edge of the downtown grid. Right, a view through trellis on precast tapered columns to neo-Greek Masonic Temple and newer towers.

have a high level of complexity, a layering that takes on an almost Piranesian quality." In truth, the interiors are splendid.

At the center of the entry pavilion is a marble fountain, artfully composed of curves and crooks, a lovely object and a damper for noise. Furnishings and fixtures—sconces, suspended light fixtures, flooring in several types of stone, plus corner seating—are all art deco motifs. And stainless steel banding is used not only for decoration but to conceal joints, sprinkler systems, air intake valves, and lighting.

Like the rest of the complex, the entry pavilion is sympathetic in scale and though richly, sometimes sumptuously, detailed never approaches that overly expansive, overly expensive yet impersonal look of "high corp."

From the entry a stair or escalator leads to the second floor wings whose corridors yield to dining, kitchen, and other service areas, and act as a public street to the old building. Four cores, two for each tower, service offices in the spires.

The higher reaches of the towers become not only smaller in floor area but "more domestic," in the architects' words, a euphemism for less expensive. But the principal motifs, such as stainless banding and deco sconces (albeit now in plastic), are constant throughout the building.

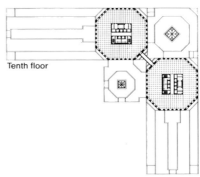

Tenth floor

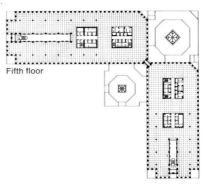

Fifth floor

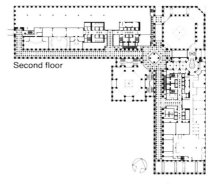

Second floor

In each wing above the second story is a large atrium with hanging light fixtures and clerestories (the architects acknowledge a debt to Wright's Larkin building), and ranged on either side are floors of open offices with views into the atria. Circulation is on the perimeter where all ducts have been enclosed in a dropped soffit that signals "corridor," in part to prevent the amoeba-like growth such plans are prone to.

Surprisingly, while other companies have forsaken office landscaping for conventional offices or some combination of closed and open spaces, all of P&G's work spaces are open plan. But before deciding on furniture systems, lighting, acoustic devices, and the like, the company researched almost all available equipment with all the thoroughness it would lavish on testing a new detergent or diaper, according to Patricia Conway, president of Kohn Pedersen Fox Conway, KPF's interior design arm.

Most office partitions are six feet high, the work floors are orderly and attractive, and, best of all, quiet—thanks, in part, to the electronic revolution. P&G's top brass, nonetheless, has elected to remain in splendid isolation in their closed offices in the old building, ostensibly to avoid making the original headquarters seem inferior to the new. □

Top, entry pavilion interior; above, second story 'street' to old building. Right, view from piazza/garden.

Distillation of a Paradoxical City

Loyola Law School, Los Angeles. Architect: Frank Gehry, FAIA. By John Pastier

As a city that first flourished through the efforts of real-estate promoters, and then through the rapid growth of the entertainment industry, Los Angeles owes much of its character to the remarkable human capacity for hope and imagination. Here people's dreams are projected upon a highly malleable reality. The results can be magical, surreal, frustrating, or merely banal. We hear mostly about the first two qualities and less often about the latter pair, for this is America's great illusionistic metropolis, and its myth is more easily perpetuated than confronted.

After four decades in the city, Frank Gehry, FAIA, understands all four aspects of the Los Angeles character. He rejects the obvious romanticism that makes up so much of the built environment and attempts a more difficult transformation of the banal into the poetic. This is a high-risk approach that has won him both unreasoning enemies and worshipful acolytes. It is a difficult way to work, especially since Gehry seems bent on confounding the expectations of the world with respect to virtually each new building, almost as though he is testing the steadfastness of his friends and his foes alike.

Loyola Law School is a vivid illustration of all these phenomena. Dedicated just a few weeks ago, it is profoundly contextual, not so much in the specific and literal way its designer suggests, but more as a distillation of the city's own paradoxical variety. It provides grist for supporters and detractors alike, as well as food for thought for those who would like to assess each Gehry project afresh and on its own merits.

The institution itself poses some interesting anomalies. It is part of Loyola Marymount University, a Jesuit body with a main campus on the posh west side of town. The law school, however, has a largely non-Catholic student body and a largely secular faculty and is located in a poor neighborhood on the fringes of downtown. Interestingly, when Gehry's family moved to Los Angeles in the 1940s, the family's first home was an apartment just three blocks away.

Until recently the law school was housed in two structures: a nondescript (but architect designed) 1964-vintage building that had been added onto once but was still too small for a growing student body that eventually reached 1,300 and, of equal necessity in Los Angeles, a somewhat newer above-ground parking structure. In 1977 the school decided to expand on adjoining property within the same block.

Its architect selection process was both methodical and astute. A faculty architectural selection committee made a list of all architects who had won design awards from the local AIA chapter in the previous three years, then boiled down the list to about a dozen, and then to about half that. Upon interviewing the finalists, the committee found that Gehry stood out from the others in several respects. His presentation was refreshingly informal, he was clearly used to dealing with restricted budgets, and the committee was impressed with his "creativity." (One member, Professor Robert Benson, still recalls a slide of a baby elephant standing atop a piece of Gehry-designed cardboard furniture.) In this outspoken advocate of "cheapskate architecture," Loyola saw a designer prepared to give it something that was both exceptional and within its means; accordingly, in 1978, the selection committee chose him by unanimous vote.

One of Gehry's prime goals was to create a place and therefore give the institution a physical identity. While not large, the site provided sufficient space for such a goal, and a basic design decision to separate long-span and short-span interior spaces led to a multibuilding design that permitted flexible definition of exterior spaces and also kept construction costs down. The program requirement of just under 57,000 square feet is accommodated in five separate buildings. Three lecture halls and a chapel

total a bit less than 8,000 square feet, while a four-story building housing faculty offices, administration, small classrooms, and
a bookstore contains the rest of the space. This arrangement
also permitted phased construction when funds materialized more
slowly than expected.

The largest building, named after donor Fritz B. Burns, was
built first and was completed in 1981. It seems a simple, straightforward volume, but in fact it is complex and filled with inci-
dent. Its Valencia Street side is plain and gray to the point of
drabness—Gehry says he did not want to upstage the neighborhood but now feels that he could have done a bit more on the
street side—while the inner facade is warmly colored and
brilliantly articulated. A loggia occupies most of the first floor,
its columns clad in unpainted galvanized steel that has weathered
to a splendid patina. The second floor has large, squarish windows on the same spacing as the smaller ones of the third and
fourth floors. The building is cracked open near its center by a
lightning-bolt grand staircase and a greenhouse aedicula that
serves as the top floor elevator lobby. Near the ends of this
210-foot-long wall, metal exit stairs are cantilevered from the
building in bold irregular zigzags. As a totality, this courtyard
elevation deftly walks a tightrope between being a backdrop,
which it is for the neighboring lecture halls and chapel, and
being a composition capable of standing alone esthetically, which
it was for several years before those smaller structures were built.

There is more to the Burns building than its facade, however.
Inside, it is quietly inventive. Natural lighting, brought in through
glass-enclosed wells, enlivens the corridors of the top two floors.
Muted green walls in the halls give the light an underwater quality. All the corridors also have exposed ductwork and ceiling

*Left, looking north into the campus with the Burns Building on
the left, the chapel in the middle, and the South Instructional
Hall on the right. Above, the large, central courtyard.*

structure, an arrangement that paradoxically proved too expensive for application in the offices and classrooms, as Gehry had
wished. Instead, those spaces have standard acoustic tile ceilings. The disarmingly simple greenhouse elevator lobby is a superb
space, possibly the best on the campus, which leads to small
adjoining outdoor terraces and to the central stair. There are
larger top floor terraces at the ends of the building, and these
also lead to exterior stairs. Thus, in one stroke repeated in trip-
licate, Gehry was able to provide usable outdoor space, legally
required exits, and bold sculptural elements.

When the Burns building was finished, it was easy to imagine
the eventual campus as a magical place. Since the backdrop
structure had such a clear poetry of its own, the smaller, more
fanciful little buildings that were to come would surely provide
a splendid conclusion to such a good start. Oddly and dis-
appointingly, that never quite happened. Those smaller buildings are more individualistic and more overtly symbolic than
the Burns building, and they are clearly more intimate in size,
yet their forms and placement don't quite coalesce into a fully
realized whole. This phenomenon must be observed directly,
since skillful photography can make the spaces created by these
buildings seem more convincing and eventful than they are .

It is easy to see what Gehry tried to accomplish. The campus was to be a little town with streets and squares and evocatively
shaped buildings and towers. The client had a leaning toward
classical forms, and, in the smaller buildings, the architect obvi-

157

ously tried to accommodate that predisposition within his own esthetic. Here, Gehry may have been too accommodating, for he is not only not a historicist designer, but is unusually outspoken in his condemnation of that movement. Although the chapel and lecture halls are unsentimental and free from the quasi-literalism of stock postmodern classicism, they are clearly not unfettered Gehry either. He is a deft reductivist working, on this occasion, in an idiom that relies on explicit detail that cannot be reduced very far without becoming arid. The north instructional hall is almost anonymous, while the south one strenuously seeks identity through insufficient architectural means. Compared to his best work, these forms are diagrammatic and underdeveloped.

There is an exception to this tendency. The chapel is a child's drawing of a church that has been built half size. It is clad in a glowing reddish-brown Finnish plywood, specially surfaced and normally used for concrete formwork but here polished to the luster of fine furniture. Its front and two sides of its adjacent square tower are faced with plexiglass, allowing the space of the former and the structure of the latter to be revealed clearly. The tower is built in five diagonally braced stages, each one taller than the one below. This is a worthy little building whose virtues are obscured by its siting, an issue that will be discussed shortly.

Merrifield Hall, the central building in the composition, was originally programmed to be a moot court where students would argue cases before judge and jury. Gehry therefore intended it to be Loyola's grand symbol of the law. The client found its interior insufficiently courtroom-like and therefore designated it as a lecture hall. The moot court was shifted to the third phase of

Above, the Burns Building acts as a backdrop to Merrifield Hall. Right, stairs lead to the Burns Building's glass atrium lobby.

the construction program, a remodeling of the original building, which is now underway. (In it, Gehry is providing a skylit library and a more conventional moot court. He has also been retained for phase four, which will involve an eastward expansion of the campus.)

The symbolic courthouse is a brick box that is gabled and colonnaded on the end that faces the main plaza, but which also happens to be its rear and contains only a half-hidden pair of exit doors with small windows above. Its front, far less architecturally ambitious, faces the old building and a secondary plaza. As the most overtly symbolic campus structure, Merrifield can only raise questions of what it represents. Its nearly blank walled "front" that cannot be entered suggests an inaccessible legal system worthy of Kafka rather than the idealistic and lucid vision that one would expect to find symbolized in a university. Its minimal colonnade, poorly finished and lacking entasis, base, capitals, entablature, and pediment, implies major deficiencies in traditional legal institutions.

Likewise, the chapel's siting, six steps below the level of the plaza and pushed deeply back into a pocket between two larger buildings, could easily be seen as a comment about the peripheral role of religion in a secular, legalistic society.

Are these really Gehry's thoughts on the subject? I doubt it. His architectural interests are not intellectual or symbolic, but tangible and experiential. His architecture derives principally from the physical world and the world of art, and as such is a matter of construction, light, space, materials, "moves," and carefully judged effects rather than any desire to express ideas or philosophies. At its best, his architecture communicates on a personal level rather than on a societal one. His work method is not to proceed methodically from a preconceived set of premises (as a lawyer might) but to work visually and intuitively, primarily with models, pulling them apart and putting them back together until he is satisfied. It is a serious and challenging game that he plays better than anyone else, but it is not inherently suited to social comment or rigorous symbolism.

That much said, what does Loyola's metaphorical townscape really signify? Four things, all interconnected: It is the reflection of the strengths and limitations of the clients; it is a manifestation of Gehry's art world values and of his need to be provocative; it is an Italian reverie that drifts in and out of surrealism; and it is a contextual statement about its city, not in the literal sense but in the psychic one.

As a client, the school was willing to take risks and set its sights high despite severely restricted resources. (The cost of the first five buildings has been under $5 million.) This gamble has produced a campus that is attracting unprecedented attention to the institution. Loyola's strengths come largely out of the specific challenges of the problem: a nondescript neighborhood, a somewhat encumbered site, a low budget, and a desire for excellence despite those constraints. Gehry was given a generally free hand—the client's principal concern was economy rather than esthetics—but there were also times when Loyola's conservatism had visible results, such as the freestanding classrooms that wear their semiclassical academic robes so uncomfortably. (Gehry was also largely prevented from siting those buildings at his customary irregular angles, a freedom that might have produced a more convincing ensemble.) Nevertheless, Loyola has proven itself an adventurous and enlightened patron; few other institutions have made such a commitment to avant-garde architecture. The law school also has instituted a vigorous art program that has resulted in the installation of many works of living local artists in the Burns building. It plans to commission three law-related murals for the side of Merrifield Hall, and, if

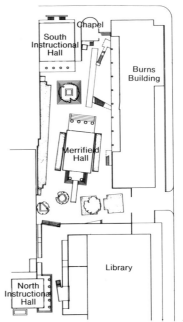

Right and below, the plexiglass and plywood chapel, a 'child's drawing of a church that has been built half size.' Far right, view of the courtyard looking toward the South Instructional Hall and chapel reveals the de Chirico spirit that permeates Gehry's design.

the money can be found, will acquire a Claes Oldenberg sculpture that will form an ironic sixth element in the colonnade.

Gehry has been an interested participant in the art program, for his architectural approach derives at least as much from artists as from his colleagues. In explaining the basis for his site plan, he cites an old photograph of Constantin Brancusi's sculpture-filled studio that served as his general inspiration for Loyola's building placement. How literally true this is is hard to tell, but the site plan does have arbitrary gestures that are difficult to explain in rational architectural terms. Gehry exhibits a frequent tendency to be rebellious and confound his audience, which, though usually counterproductive to an architectural

career, is almost conventional behavior in the world of contemporary art. This accounts for many of the misfires in his work and a good part of its brilliance and inventiveness as well. In Loyola, it produces the paradox of simple, decently budgeted buildings of interesting function (the small freestanding structures that were built for $143 a square foot) that are esthetically inferior to the programmatically dull, $76 a square foot Burns Hall, which steals the show.

Whatever Brancusi's role may be in Loyola, the artistic spirit that seems to permeate the design is that of Giorgio de Chirico. The exaggerated perspectives, the colonnades, the plazas, the oddly blank facades, the mysterious towers, and the muted sense

of the surreal that collectively permeate the painter's best work can all be found at Loyola. Of course, many of these features are found in nearly every older Italian city of decent size. Other Loyola elements that recall Italy are the Burns building facade, clearly descended from Aldo Rossi; its second floor piano nobile; and its ochre stucco, an old Roman standby. Gehry built the towers of the chapel and South Instructional Hall in response to downtown skyscrapers a mile away; medieval Italian clans practiced similar "contextualism" by matching the self-aggrandizing tower construction of their neighbors. Why is Loyola so much like Italy? Because its architect has been there and has become fascinated by what he has seen. It's that simple.

And that simplicity and directness of motivation is part of what makes the Loyola Law School such an authentic Los Angeles building. This city is home to virtually every style of building because people here are not afraid to act out their fantasies and are relatively unconcerned over what others may think. Beyond this, Gehry has achieved a contextualism that transcends the mere mimicking of adjacent physical fabric or regional building forms. He has taken the ultimate Southern California building tradition—illusion—and applied it to a profession that seeks to bring order and rationality to human affairs. This may not be the way that things are done in other places, but there's no law against it in Los Angeles. □

Combining Adventure and Respect

Herring Hall, Rice University.
Architect: Cesar Pelli & Associates.
By David Dillon

© R. Greg Hursley

The Rice University campus is an oasis of Beaux-Arts tranquility in a tangle of freeway loops. The main source of this calm is a 1910 master plan by Cram, Goodhue & Ferguson, which established the succession of greens and quadrangles that are among the institution's lasting glories. Any architect who builds here must somehow come to terms with this superb arrangement.

Many architects from the 1940s onward did so only in the loosest way, respecting the general scale of existing buildings but ignoring the underlying principles of balance and axial alignment, and deviating markedly from the overall detailing and imagery of the original campus. The result was a succession of dull, plodding buildings, often poorly sited, that turned their backs on the design opportunities provided by Cram's plan.

In the last few years, however, architects of Rice have been rediscovering the virtues of contextual design, with the most distinguished architects leading the way. James Stirling, Hon. FAIA, and Michael Wilford produced a discreet and self-effacing addition to Anderson Hall in 1981, in which from the outside it is virtually impossible to tell where their work starts and that of their predecessors leaves off. And now comes Cesar Pelli, FAIA, with a considerably sportier but no less thoughtful building for the Jesse Jones graduate school of administration.

Above, Herring Hall, right in photo, as seen across the green. Left, the north side opens onto a terrace and lawn. Right, from the southeast, the exterior is alive with decorative brickwork.

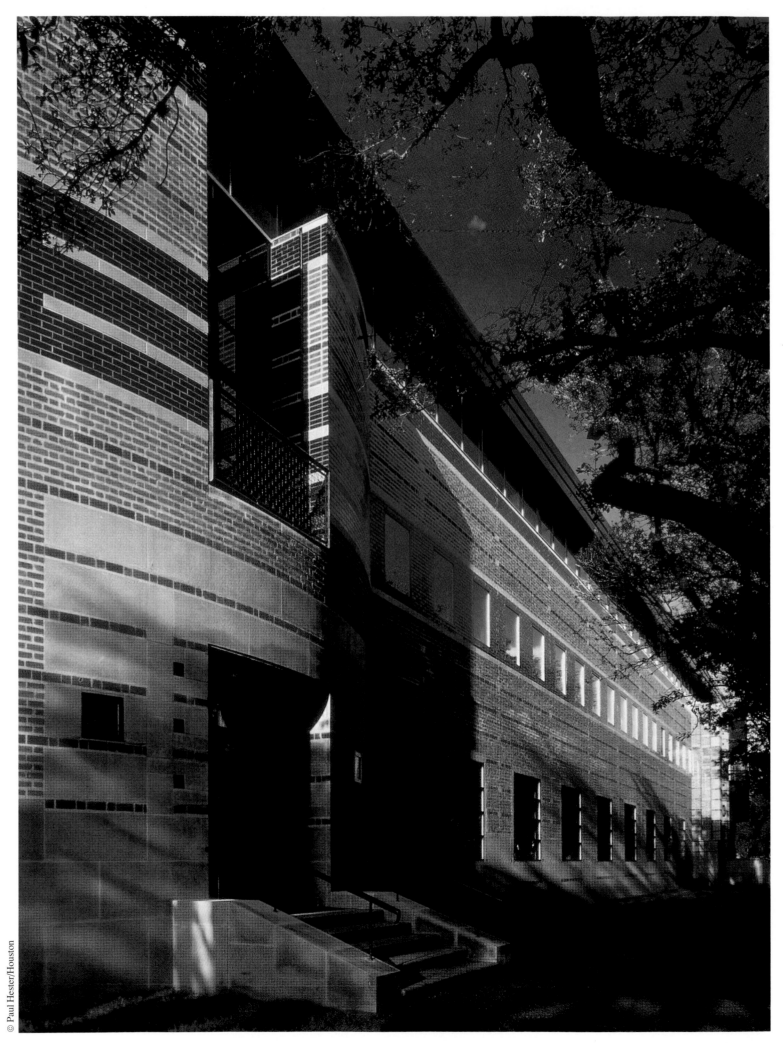

Herring Hall is a taut, three-story building containing class-rooms, faculty and administrative offices, a library, auditorium, computer lab, and related facilities. The south or public side of the building holds tight to the street, in the best Rice tradition, while the north side opens onto a terrace and broad, shaded lawn. In Cram's original plan this lawn would have formed the western end of the majestic main quadrangle, dominated by the ornate Lovett Hall, with buildings arranged along the edges in crisp linear fashion. Few of the proposed buildings were actually built, and in the mid-1940s the lawn was bisected by the university library. The undistinguished Rice Memorial Center, which Pelli is renovating, came a few years later, deepening the impression of unrealized potential that hovers over the space.

Herring Hall consists of two offset rectangular forms, one topped with a vault and the other with a pitched roof, connected by glass enclosed corridors. The offset rectangles recall the plan of Anderson Hall but are not typical of the campus as a whole, while the connecting corridors are reminiscent of the bold curtain walls on many Pelli buildings, including Four Leaf Towers in Houston. The gesture is repeated above the entrance on the south side of the building in the form of colorful steel and glass canopies that give the building a bolder public profile than is customary at Rice.

The exterior of the building is finished in Rice's ubiquitous "St. Joe" brick. On the long sides it is laid horizontally, interrupted by bands of raspberry-colored glazed brick that mark the divisions of floors. But on the blunt east and west facades the brick has been arranged in a distinctive crosshatch or diamond pattern. Hence the campus sobriquet "Herringbone" Hall.

In his efforts to deepen and intensify some of the traditional detailing of earlier Rice buildings, Pelli occasionally turned the decorative throttle up too high. The glass canopies and corridors, striking though they are, seem somewhat gratuitous, even polemical. But in most other respects Pelli has gone to commendable lengths to make Herring Hall fit in rather than take over.

Rice is a campus of loggias, arcades, colonnades, and terraces, a Mediterranean sort of place that is open to the elements yet in which the sense of protective enclosure is strong. Pelli has respected this tradition by designing a terrace and colonnade on the first level, with an interior arcade linking the east and west ends of the building. All of this is on axis with the entrance to Memorial Hall across the green, though in another of his "then and now" juxtapositions of materials, Pelli has clad his columns half in steel and half in brick and limestone. (Three

Across page, notched southwest entrance and the expanse of the south facade. Top, detail of the north facade. Right, faceted window over the southeast entrance.

165

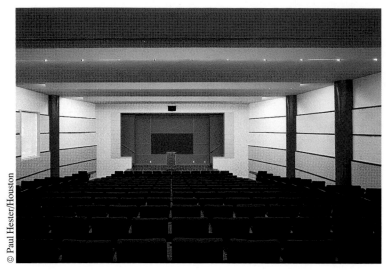

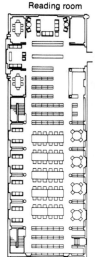

Reading room

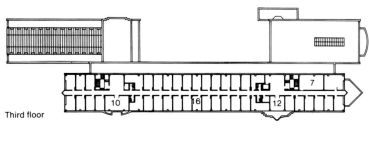

Third floor

Second floor

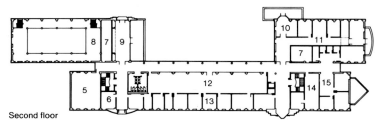

First floor

1 Reading room
2 Courtyard
3 Lecture hall
4 Arcade
5 Caseroom
6 Seminar
7 Mechanical room
8 Mezzanine
9 Student lounge
10 Conference
11 Dean's suite
12 Secretarial pool
13 Administrative offices
14 Computer lab
15 Admissions and placement
16 Faculty offices

Left, tranquil lecture hall on ground level. Above and right, two-story vaulted reading room with decorative patterning.

mature live oak trees, planted decades ago to mark the inner edge of the quadrangle, have been preserved as part of the terrace design.)

Though Herring Hall appears dense and solid on the outside, one experiences it as light and airy, with large windows and numerous small balconies and terraces that provide unexpected glimpses of the outside. There is a delightful serendipitous quality to the interiors that one doesn't ordinarily associate with high-powered business schools.

The first floor arcade is taken up mainly with lecture halls and small seminar rooms. On the second level it is lined with administrative offices, which have splendid views of the green. There are also large terraces at either end of the corridor that have a casual, relaxed, informal feeling.

This feeling of spaciousness extends throughout the building. The corridors are wide and generous; the stairwells, ordinarily the most neglected spaces, are also wide and brightly detailed, with windows, no less!

The one grand space is the library, a two-story vaulted room that is filled with comfortable traditional features: oak tables, brass lamps, even a metal grille on the landing and stairway that recalls the interiors of town libraries all over the country. It is a warm room, not just a huge repository for books.

The one disappointing space is the third floor, on which dozens of faculty offices have been jammed along a long narrow corridor. This space is unhappily reminiscent of some interiors in Anderson Hall, a niggardly and claustrophobic counterpoint to the openness and generosity of the rest of the building.

Much of Sterling's budget on Anderson Hall was eaten up trying to match existing exterior finishes, leaving him little to work with on the interiors. If he did as much as could be expected with wallboard and white paint, nobody would call the interiors distinguished. Pelli had a somewhat larger budget, reportedly around $5 million, and he spent it very wisely.

In 1983 Pelli presented his master plan for the Rice campus, which was actually an elaboration of his numerous planning studies for Herring Hall. It is a conservative document—in the best sense of the term—in that it calls for building upon Cram's original scheme. In practical terms, this means more trees, greens, and quadrangles, new buildings arranged in accordance with Beaux-Arts principles, a respect for order and proportion.

Among the many virtues of Herring Hall is that it shows how this can be accomplished without resorting to mindless copying of the past. In the materials, massing, and siting of the building, Pelli has deployed many of the traditional elements of the Rice campus in new and imaginative ways. It is not simply an isolated example of enlightened contextualism; it can serve as a paradigm for development in the decades ahead.

Top, left, arcade bordering the courtyard; top, right, view from ground floor corridor looking north to edge of northeast entrance porch, with courtyard at left in photo; above, courtyard from student lounge terrace; across page, view of the northeast entrance. □

Photographs by Matt Wargo

Friendly House Full of Surprises

Delaware house. Architect: Venturi, Rauch & Scott Brown. By Michael J. Crosbie

You might miss this house from the main road in that it sits way off, down at the end of a cornfield. The land in this part of Delaware is a blanket of rolling hills and shallow valleys, and the approach to the house is a geography lesson, a game of hide-and-seek. Starting down the half-mile-long gravel driveway, one sees the house almost entirely. Farther along it begins to sink, and around a curve it disappears altogether. Then its low roof pops up again, and the house rises to meet you.

Designed by Venturi, Rauch & Scott Brown, the house is in form a reference to the 18th century vernacular farm buildings of the region, explains Venturi. "In eastern Pennsylvania and northern Delaware, in the barns and to some extent in the houses too," he says, "there is a generous, low, stretched-out proportion. We didn't want to put a pert house in these gentle hills." Extending across the south side, a pent eave (a common vernacular element) underlines the horizontal theme and brings the broad roof down. The exterior materials restate at a smaller scale the farmhouse esthetic: a textured, wood shingle roof; multipaned, double-hung windows (with counterweights!); shiplap siding; and a buff-colored masonry base.

This is not really a farmhouse, of course. The family of three (a couple, Peter and Karen, and their son) are not farmers nor do they fancy themselves as such. But they enjoy the solitude and quiet of the rural setting, are not ostentatious, are attentive to the natural wonders beyond their doorstep. Thus, around an accommodating interior suited to their particular wants is a farmhouse

wrapper with just enough quirks to keep it interesting.

For example, the semicircular window screen on the east side's upper story, behind which is a large window, looks like a misplaced piece of Viennese pastry just floating there above the roof, hung on the house's sturdy steel frame. Venturi refers to it as a "lunette," and it has a baroque flourish. As it turns out, Karen studied music in Salzburg and performs in a baroque chamber group. What at first appears as an arcane classical reference is actually a little homage to the client.

The other side of the house has another surprise, this one in the form of three chubby Doric columns, seemingly paper thin, standing on guard for whatever might creep out of the woods nearby. Two of them (and a sliver of a third) support an arch (which, according to Karen, creates great patterns of moonlight), while the last holds up the end of the roof. The columns underwent a considerable metamorphosis. Venturi originally intended them to be fully round, which would have rendered the shallow porch behind them unusable and made them look like a row of Claes Oldenburg milk bottles. In a cardboard model they were simply cut out in profile for representation. Karen remembers Venturi looking at the columns in the model and then saying, "Let's do them flat." The effect is all at once humorous and troublesome, eccentric and endearing; they're like a funny old aunt in a George S. Kaufman play who comes for a visit and decides to settle in.

The clients say that they chose Venturi because they saw in his

Left, approach from the winding driveway; above, west side with its playful flat columns; below, east side with floating lunette.

Across page, the fanciful music room on the second floor with windows that open to dining hall below. Below left, dining hall with table, chandelier, and built-

in sideboard designed by Venturi. Below right, blue tile floor designates dining from living spaces and gives the feel of an entrance hall.

work a "lot of warmth, and the use of design that makes it friendly and comfortable." This sentiment aptly describes the interior. One enters through a wide, teal-colored door just under the pent eave. This is the "back door" and the first one you see. The front door is tucked around the other side of the house, hidden from view. This is the "trophy front door," as Karen calls it, and a small wooden arbor near the driveway labors to entice the visitor toward the unseen main entrance. More often than not visitors head straight for the back door instead, and, as Venturi points out, "That's the way it is with country homes in America; you usually go in the back door."

Inside, to the right is a small nook with a built-in bench and cabinets on either side. To the left is the kitchen with its large pantry, dining counter, and breakfast nook, which is surrounded on three sides with six-over-six double-hung windows. One of the family's favorite pastimes is birdwatching, and this house is filled with windows, most of them robustly mullioned, each light framing a view and lending a delicate texture.

A straight shot from the back door delivers you to the dining hall, with an unassuming living room at left, both with walls alive with yellow and white stenciled flowers. Above the dining table is a two-story space. This volume is light-filled from the lunette-hidden gable windows, directly across from which is found another set of windows on an interior wall. What's going on upstairs, behind those windows? As if overhearing the question, a grand staircase offers to help solve the mystery.

After ascent, we are under the broad, low roof whose ridge lines cross in a room alive with color, sunlight, and music. The music room seems like a prized possession from an earlier time, its decorative roof braces arching above your head, its wide-plank oak floors spreading beneath your feet. This is where they keep the "toys," fine instruments that require careful climate control. The windows across from the lunette can be opened to allow views and music down into the dining hall, while the whole room can be closed off with a wide pocket door. The music of preference performed here is baroque, and as Karen demonstrates the acoustics on the organ, the braces' jaunty and colorful stenciling seems to dance to the music.

To the south of this room is a backstair to the kitchen (without which no good farmhouse would be complete), an office with a large west-facing window low to the floor, and a bedroom that makes sensible use of the ample space under the roof with a loft. A large bedroom to the north of the music room seems top-heavy with "left over" space, but it's pleasant enough with a wide, built-in window seat and a broad band of windows for eyeing the wildlife (even the bathroom has two big windows for spying bluebirds).

The entire house, as well as its placement on the site, has a playful quality to it, but not at the expense of some very livable spaces that are tightly designed and function well. "We didn't want the house to be uncomfortable just for the sake of looking good," says Peter. It isn't and it does. □

Photographs by Matt Wargo

West elevation

Shingle Style Reinvented

Residence at Chilmark. Architect: Robert A.M. Stern. By Robert Campbell

Using history as a sourcebook for design has been the method of Robert A.M. Stern, FAIA, since this architect's work first became known in the early 1970s. In recent Stern works, however, like this summer home at Chilmark on the island of Martha's Vineyard, Mass., a change is apparent. History is being plundered as voraciously as ever, but you don't get any sense that the trophies are on display for their own sake. The architect is being neither self-conscious nor theatrically ironic. As a result, you can call the Chilmark house a shingle style house without feeling you have to put quotation marks around the term. The house isn't quoting a style of the past but matter-of-factly putting it to good use as living tradition, employing it with the kind of confident understanding that frees the architect to reinvent virtually every element of the style in his own idiom. The more closely you look at the Chilmark house, in fact, the more original it seems.

The first impression from the curving, rising approach drive is the great front gable with its oversized round window. Gable and window are a billboard-sized ideogram expressing the idea of "house." The centered gable gives you a sense of overall symmetry, but it's a sense that instantly starts to come unstuck as you notice that the entrance porch, itself elaborately symmetrical, is asymmetrically placed. The placement of the porch is one of the improbable inventions that make this house so beautiful a sculpture. Many further games with symmetry are played, as for ex-

ample by the two "chimneys," one of which is real, the other a bathroom skylight.

As were the 19th-century shingled houses of the New England coast, the Chilmark house is a metaphor of a seaside village, its dormers perched on the great shingled sloping roof like tiny cottages clinging to the face of a rocky cliff. It differs from such models, however, in not heaving up out of the ground on a craggy stone base meant to look like a natural form. Instead it hovers, in a more obviously crafted way, over its grassy dune site. In this it resembles the Low house in Rhode Island by McKim, Mead & White, and it recalls the Low also in its use of a wide, low profile that makes the house a long wall dividing the world into two zones. Passing through the house from the entry to the porches is like a cleansing passage through a ritual portal, taking you from a crowded world of cars and work to a quiet one of water and dunes and peaceful vistas. A screened porch and generous decks on the water side provide places for Zen contemplation of the vista, although the swimming pool they also overlook is a less magical element.

Indoors, the house is even more quirky and surprising than the outside leads you to expect. Opening the front door, you find

Across page: top, west side of house overlooking pool and ocean; bottom: entrance facade, with asymmetrically placed front entrance. Above: second-floor landing with dining area below.

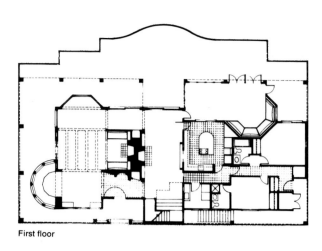

First floor

Photographs by Wayne Fujii/Retoria-Futugawa

Across page: Enclosed porch on house's northeast corner with built-in seating and access to open-air deck.

yourself face to face at close quarters with an angled wall containing a niche with a French stove in it. In a Lutyens-like way the wall baffles the path of circulation. The living room is to your left, the dining room to your right. The angle of the wall inflects you toward the living room, which is a simple rectangular volume with three appended space-blobs: a semicircular bay with seating, a semi-octagonal one without, and an inglenook. The dining room by contrast is as modern, spatially, and as unenclosed as a room by Breuer, with space flowing past it at both ends. The signature front gable turns out, unexpectedly, to contain a staircase at one end of the dining room, giving this room some of the feeling of an English great hall. Upstairs, a marvelous master bedroom with built-in his-and-hers desks for the owners opens into a bathroom (with his-and-hers sinks) that opens onto a splendid private balcony overlooking the ocean.

Materials on the exterior are white-painted wood and untreated white cedar shingles that have already, in the salt air, turned silver-gray. Much of the interior is paneled in beaded vertical boards of obeche wood from South America, a wood that is supposed to remain dimensionally stable in the dry winters and humid summers of the Vineyard. This wood has been stained with a bleaching stain that leaves it pale salmon-ochre in color, in harmony with the orange glazed ceramic tiles of the entry and inglenook and in contrast with the blue ones of the dining room. All the interiors are filled with light and feel breezy and salt-washed, with the sense any vacation house should have of a carefree lightness of touch.

Taken simply as a crafted object the Chilmark house is remarkable. Many details suggest the arts-and-crafts period, like the inglenook with its tile and S-profile art nouveau benches, or the staircase with its elegantly gridded railing and spherical newels washed with downlight from the round oculus window. Such detail isn't easily achieved. A great deal is demanded of a builder who is asked to create (for instance) a continuously curving soffit vent edging a round bay window. For the most part such details are both conceived and executed with satisfying skill, the only exceptions perhaps being a few unresolved conditions at places where wall, deck, and ground come together. Aside from that, the only reservation one has about this fine house is perhaps a nagging sense that an object so unitary, so well-made and self-contained, belongs rather on a manicured green lawn than on a ragged hillock of dune.

The Chilmark house reminds us that an architect who knows what he or she is doing can be just as inventive working within a strong tradition as starting from scratch. Perhaps more inventive, because the tradition provides a ground against which the architect's inventions figure all the more vividly. □

Gentle Infill in a Genteel City

Scattered site public housing, Charleston, S.C. By Michael J. Crosbie

The city of Charleston is ever conscious and proud of its history and vigilant in protecting the remnants of its past, notably its architecture. Settled more than 300 years ago, the South Carolina port adopted as its motto: "Charleston protects her buildings, customs, and laws." It is a city of "firsts," being one of the colonies' first planned cities and having America's first chamber of commerce, museum, Georgian theater, and municipal college. In the spirit of its motto, Charleston was also the first city to pass legislation designating a historic district in 1931. It is now the largest such district in the country, encompassing 1,000 acres in which more than 3,000 buildings have been restored.

Many of these buildings are especially distinctive in that their form was an invention (another "first") of Charleston's 18th century master builders, and one that has survived to this day. The Charleston "single house" is a long rectangle in plan with its short side facing the street. As the city grew at a brisk pace (in its first dozen years more than 100 houses were built), lots became scarce. They were soon subdivided into deep, narrow-faced parcels due to the local practice of taxing property according to street width. The building form also made sense climatically, because the single-room-wide houses were easier to ventilate. In this subtropical region, prevailing off-shore breezes were coveted, and single houses soon sported grand, high-ceilinged porches (dubbed "piazzas" by highfalutin British). These piazzas, which captured breezes while providing shade, were always placed on the longer side that faced west or south. So uniquely efficient was this building style that a French visitor in the late 1700s wrote that "in Charleston persons vie with one another, not who shall have the finest, but who the coolest house."

The single house proved quite adaptable to the resources of the occupant, and today it is found in every social strata; from the fine, extravagant mansions on East Battery, to the meager, ramshackled homes of Charleston's poor. Given this history and the architectural inventiveness of Charlestonians, it seems natural to find the single house style perpetuated in new construction, especially in the historic district. But it is downright amazing to find an enlightened city government and a committed housing authority building single houses with HUD funding as low-income housing, and doing it in such a way to revitalize neighborhoods.

Charleston's scattered infill housing, comprised of 113 units on 14 sites in five different neighborhoods, began in 1978 when the city was awarded new construction funds from HUD for the first time in a decade. An analysis of Charleston's housing needs by citizens that same year revealed vacant parcels where low-income rental units could best be developed using the scattered site approach. With HUD money and the survey in hand, the city and the housing authority began their search for the most appropriate sites on which to build. Donald J. Cameron, executive director of Charleston's housing authority who oversaw the projects through completion, remembers the search as a long, involved process but one guided by a clear set of criteria. "We wouldn't build on sites in which private redevelopment was possible," Cameron explains, "we wouldn't choose sites not zoned for multifamily housing, we'd use only vacant land zoned for residential use, we'd build no more than 22 units on a site, and what we built would be compatible with the existing neighborhood." During the process of looking at more than 100 sites, Charleston became

Across page, detail of Charleston's scattered infill housing on Reid Street; right (top and middle), single house form in grand and modest versions and (bottom), in public housing on Cannon Street.

Michael J. Crosbie

D. J. Johnson

Michael J. Crosbie

179

Top and above, Coming Street project, the first of single house units built, with a view from a second-story porch of the same project. The 113 units on 14 sites break down into nearly equal thirds of one-, two- and three-bedroom apartments. Across page, top, streetscape of units on Line Street.

eligible for another round of HUD funding in 1979, which was approved.

Originally, 139 units were planned. Some were cut because of small pockets of neighborhood resistance. Residents were concerned, says Cameron, "that we were going to build a traditional housing project with densities equal to what was permissible under zoning, which is 26 units per acre." Such an influx of low-income renters, they felt, would drive down property values and lessen their potential as homeowners to secure home improvement loans. Other units were dropped for unexpected reasons, such as the discovery of a cemetery on a site during excavation. "Being a public agency," says Cameron, sheepishly, "we can't build unless we relocate the cemetery intact, and that wasn't feasible. So now we own a cemetery."

Because funds were allocated for two separate projects the units were divided into two groups of 67 and 46 and given to two separate architects (Bradfield Associates of Atlanta and Middleton McMillan Architects of Charleston) who worked with two separate contractors. The strategy was to develop some friendly competition between the two, who worked under the same guidelines on projects that in some cases would be within sight of each other.

Both the architects and Cameron agree that the most difficult

phase was developing a scheme that met the housing authority's notion of appropriateness. During the two years of site selection, Cameron became aware of the generic qualities of the five neighborhoods. He was advised by Paul Reavis, who was then city architect. Reavis was "really in tune with what was going on," explains Cameron, and suggested careful consideration of the existing fabric, what the houses on either side of the lots were like, what the units would face, what was down the street.

At the outset of design, Cameron did not say that the projects should be like single houses. "We knew what we wanted conceptually," he says, "but we had no idea what the finished product would look like." There were some false starts, but slowly the ideas of the architects and the housing authority began to coalesce. Bradfield Associates had an especially hard time, being based in Atlanta and making numerous trips to Charleston. After one particularly discouraging public review, Richard Bradfield, AIA, remembers walking around the neighborhoods for the rest of the afternoon and then sitting up all night in a Holiday Inn, sketching single house schemes on the back of his blueprints. "The next day," says Bradfield, "Don and I went to the planning people and showed them the sketches. They said, 'Now you're on the right track.' "

Bradfield then sent two people from his office to Charleston, and they measured the single houses around the Coming Street site, from entire facades to the spacing of the balusters on the railings. The Coming Street project was the first to be built and the only one actually in the historic district. It thus served as a good prototype, because it had to meet the approval of the city's board of adjustment, zoning board, board of architectural review, the state archives review, and the president's advisory council on historic places. This would assure compliance of the other units as the historic district expands to include them.

Although based in Charleston, Edgar B. Gale, AIA, of Middleton McMillan is not a native and took a similar approach, walking the streets near his office and noting single house details and characteristics, such as color. "They're very pale and soft here," says Gale, "and very earthy." Since the architects did their field work in different parts of the city there are subtle differences between the two schemes—in the use of stairs, shutters, parapet walls, and materials—just as there would be differences between the works of two master builders centuries ago, even on the same street.

The architects also picked up tips from local builders. Bradfield consulted with a contractor who had restored many single houses. "Within a few hours he taught us some tricks where we could accomplish some of the character of the older details without actually using the molded pieces," says Bradfield. Railings are milled out of 2x4s, balusters are nominal 2x2s, and porch columns are champhered 4x4s. The architects even found S-curved shutter holdbacks manufactured right in Charleston. Although the original single houses were clad mostly in homegrown cyprus (now prohibitive in price), Bradfield chose California cedar, placing the finished side against the house so that the texture of the grain was revealed. Gale opted for a beaded masonite siding but had difficulty convincing the architectural review board to accept it because as large sheets it was often poorly installed and cracked. Clapboard-sized pieces were easier to install, however, and Gale specified nails to be driven to within 1/16 of an inch and then finished with a wood block, preventing the carpenters from cracking the material.

With the preliminary plans complete, the housing authority submitted them for HUD approval, and then things got complicated. "Each state develops its own standards," says Cameron, "and in South Carolina they have an eight-page list." One standard specified brick veneer; no other material was allowed. A second required all kitchen ranges to be placed on an outside wall. Another called for curbs and gutters along every drive and a four-foot-wide sidewalk. "When you're building in a small residential neighborhood and trying to be compatible," Cameron re-

marks, "curbs and gutters in a driveway aren't going to make it. The standards were written for complexes with 100 or 200 units, where you need all those things." The technical staff in the state HUD office reviewed the plans and then sat down with Cameron to discuss the variances. "They had two legal pages of things that didn't conform," says Cameron, smiling. "But the technical people helped us because they were in a funny position. Their job is to review designs in accordance to the standards, not to make judgments." When the plans were presented to HUD supervisor William Nixon, who had final approval, the technical staff gave the pros and cons of each variance, explains Cameron. "They told him, 'It doesn't fit the standards, but then the standards don't fit this site, or this problem, or this project.' They supported almost everything we wanted."

Bid as two projects, the first 67 units came in at 4 percent under budget and the second 46 units came in at 8 percent under. "I would love to say the reason was that we were super efficient," says Cameron, but he admits that when the projects were bid in late 1981, early 1982, the construction industry was in a slump and contractors were bidding low to compete for work.

As built, the number of units per site ranges from two to 22, with an average density of 13 ½ units per acre. (The density for the older residential districts is 23 units per acre.) Single houses occupy all but four sites (which are garden apartments outside the old section) with a fifth site having "freeman's houses": one-story versions of the single house, named for the house type built for freed slaves. An inventory of unit sizes breaks down in nearly equal thirds of one-, two-, and three-bedroom apartments, and there are three four-bedroom units. Of the sites I visited, the buildings and yards are neatly kept. According to Hewitt Dominick,

who is housing manager, most residents take the initiative to repair their own units and have planted flowers and shrubs. The single house style allows efficient ventilation and cooling of these unair-conditioned houses, and porches are a welcomed outdoor amenity in this urban context. One resident told me that her only complaint about her house was that she couldn't own it. "It should be mine," she laughed. "I take care of it!"

The initial resistance by some in the neighborhoods has completely disappeared. In fact, many homeowners have reacted with a flourish of repair and paint since the projects have been completed. "They don't want their own houses looking worse than the low-income projects," says Dominick, wryly, and in some areas new private construction has occurred. Charleston's achievement has also attracted about a dozen inquiries from other cities, Cameron reports, which are seeking to revitalize neighborhoods through sympathetically designed public housing on scattered sites.

And there are awards. Charleston's scattered infill housing has won a HUD recognition award in the category of innovation (prompting one HUD administrator to comment: "Pretty good for government work; break all the rules and you win a prize."), an award from the National Endowment for the Arts, a federal design achievement award for meritorious design, and, most recently, a 1984 Presidential award for design excellence.

Coming full circle, Charleston may now be a city of firsts *and* lasts in respect to this last laurel. "It's sort of ironic that President Reagan, first to recognize a public housing project with such an award," says Richard Bradfield, with 30 years' experience in public housing, "has done more to dismember the program than any other President in our history." ☐

Photographs by F. Harlan Hambright

The Making of a 'Magical Place'

Treehouse, Philadelphia Zoo, Venturi, Rauch & Scott Brown. By Michael J. Crosbie

" 'How nice it would be if we could get through into Looking-glass House! Let's pretend the glass has got all soft like gauze so that we can get through.' And certainly the glass *was* beginning to melt away, just like a bright silvery mist. In another moment Alice was through the glass, and had jumped lightly down . . ."
Lewis Carroll, *Through the Looking Glass*

Pass through the door of the Treehouse at the Philadelphia Zoo and you will step, much as Alice did, into a world where you can become a frog or a honeybee, where you can hatch from an egg or a cocoon, where you can spy fish beneath the water or nocturnal animals beneath the ground, where you can make crickets sing or a dinosaur roar. It's a magical space within a century-old structure, created by a team of architects, zoologists, sculptors, painters, and inventors, all coordinated by Venturi, Rauch & Scott Brown. The result of nearly four years of design and con-

Left, visitor astride the hadrosaur in the primordial swamp. Above, another emerges from a bird's egg in the everglade.

struction, the Treehouse is a place for children to learn about the natural environment through play.

"I was searching for a way to create a setting in which kids would feel some awe or empathy for nature," says Mary-Scott Cebul, the zoo's director of planning, who developed the concept of the Treehouse. "The idea came to me that if you can pretend to be an animal, maybe you'd feel something about the animal. So why not create contexts in which kids' imaginations can take off, which would immediately transport people when they opened the door."

Cebul determined that the best way to the imagination is through the senses. Six separate environments are found in the Treehouse—a primordial swamp, a milkweed meadow, a beaver pond, a honeycomb, a ficus tree, and an everglade—and each invites the visitor to sensually explore the special qualities of the environment. Our sensory experiences of the world shape our understanding of it, so each environment is designed to be perceived by the visitor in a way similar to the way its inhabitants do—having a bee's-eye-view of a honeycomb, for example.

Photographs by F. Harlan Hambright

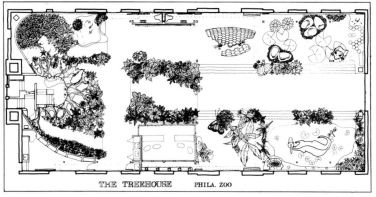

THE TREEHOUSE   PHILA. ZOO

"Having gigantic things immediately changes the scale," says Cebul, "and gets you out of your own skin." The sensory experiences are more than just visual. The photographs on these pages cannot convey the sounds of the Treehouse—squeaking birds, croaking frogs, rainfall, bats and rats, howling monkeys—all amid screams and yelps of delight from the visitors. And there are scents, too. Crawl inside the beehive and there is the smell of honey. Poke your head up into that of the hadrosaur for a prehistoric view of the world and you will smell the grass that he holds in his mouth.

To translate Cebul's ideas into reality (or illusion) Steven Izenour, associate-in-charge of the project, assembled a collection of artisans and technicians—about a dozen in all—through whom the Treehouse took form. The setting for their work was the zoo's Antelope House of 1876, designed by George Hewitt (one-time partner of Frank Furness), home of the zoo's hoofed stock until the mid-1970s. The zoo considered demolishing the Antelope House and replacing it with a Butler building to serve as a "black box" for the Treehouse illusions within. That's the classic Disneyland approach to the design of such environments—the interior architecture is subdued so not to detract from the illusion being created "on stage." But the concept of the Treehouse was different from Disneyland in that the visitors would be invited to physically become part of the illusion. Besides, it would have been criminal to destroy Hewitt's marvelous interior. The building's neo-Gothic style (which, as Izenour points out, borders on art nouveau) is also appropriate because its architecture is an idealization of the natural world and creates a child's storybook setting for the six environments. Many of the more than 200 meetings of the design team during the course of the project took place in the Antelope House, and Cebul remembers the interior as a source of inspiration. "Having the tree in a certain spot, or the honeycomb, was prompted by the building," she explains. "We were looking for ways to get people up into these wonderful spaces."

The building was restored with an eye toward function rather than historical accuracy. The exterior (which had been multicolored) was painted complementary shades of green and its stonework repointed. A new cupola, located where an original removed in the 1930s had been, makes room for the 24-foot-high, 16-foot-wide ficus tree inside. The interior, says Izenour, was always green, and the columns bow out approximately five degrees, distorted by the heavy slate roof, which has been replaced with a lighter material. "It's stable," comments Izenour of the skewed structure, braced with tie rods, "and it adds a little charm."

As eccentric a project as the Treehouse could not be designed on paper. Izenour likens the process more to the way buildings were created a century ago, when artisans and craftsmen worked in unison with the architect. "We'd have squats," he says, "morning sessions with our core group of people, and we'd work for maybe two months on one area, hashing out what we were trying to teach here, what was the goal, the best environment to teach those ideas, what it would look like." The ideas were transferred to a model (which changed continually), materials were experimented with to create the effects sought, mockups were made, and more ideas were thrown back and forth. This hands-on involvement with the project, Izenour points out, was similar to the goal of the Treehouse—to engage imagination and creativity through physical activity.

The collaborative talents of the team are revealed in the use of new materials and techniques to bring the Treehouse to life. Fred Kreitchet, whose Sculpture Workshop did all of the environments, usually works with molds. That process was prohibitive in cost for the Treehouse, so Kreitchet and a team of 15

Above left, Treehouse's restored exterior; left, stages in life of a monarch butterfly in the milkweed meadow. Above right, reaching for a frog's lunch; right, inside a tunnel of frogs' eggs.

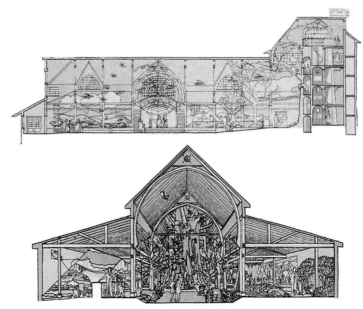

Above left, Treehouse nave with ficus tree in apse, punctuated by George Izenour's lighting design. Above and right, visitors explore a honeycomb and view the world through the head of a bee.

sculpted most of the pieces with urethane foam. "It's terrific to work with because it sets up fast, and within 10 minutes you can carve it," Kreitchet says. For many of the pieces foam was applied to a wire mesh armature, sculpted, and then coated with glass fiber. For the tree, fabric sheets were hung to enclose a staircase and then sprayed with foam, which replicated the creases and folds. After coating with glass fiber, holes were cut and then color-impregnated resin was applied. When sculpting prehistoric creatures such as the hadrosaur or dragonfly, Kreitchet used information supplied by the zoo or a model. "The Philadelphia Academy of Natural Sciences loaned us a dragonfly and we just enlarged it," he says.

To create the sound effects that pervade the Treehouse, film maker and audio technician Christopher Speeth says that he relied heavily on sounds collected by naturalists all over the country. He combined their contributions and some sounds that he recorded to create a special sound track for each environment. Speeth, who studied classical violin, says he "took the best recordings based on my musically trained ear—they were clear, clean and crisp—and then mixed them to make musical tunes out of them. I call them animal songs." Where he couldn't obtain a sound directly from nature—in the case of the prehistoric hadrosaur—he collaborated with paleontologist David Weishampel, an expert on the animal. "The hadrosaur had a bone cavity in its head," says Speeth, "and that hollow bone chamber was actually a horn." To duplicate the sound, Speeth recorded a tuba and the breathing of zoo tigers, both slowed down an octave, and combined the two sounds.

For the overall environmental sounds, comprised of from three to six tracks, Speeth used loop tapes that repeat every dozen minutes or so. For the short sounds like the dinosaur or the frog (which croaks when somebody sits inside), the sounds were transferred to solid state computer chips—the first time chips have been used in such a way, Speeth believes. "The sound is digitalized into a binary system," he explains, which is burned onto the chips and then can be "read back" by a computer to produce the sound. "There are no moving parts, except for the electrons that are running through these microchips," says Speeth. This means that the sound system should last indefinitely, because there is nothing to wear out.

The animal sounds and a host of other special effects are triggered by "magic rings," given to every visitor over the age of 3. Mounted on the rings are small magnets that when held against pinholes of light found throughout the Treehouse cause a small piece of metal to move into a fiber optic light path. When the light is blocked an electric impulse is transmitted, activating a "gizmo" (the collective term used by the design team to refer to the mechanical special effects). The magnetic switch, the rings, and a host of gizmos are the creation of architect Lou Rodolico. Rodolico likes to fiddle with machines, and either designed his own or combined pieces of off-the-shelf mechanisms to make crickets sing, plants grow, bunnies pop from their war-

187

Below, lenses fitted on PVC pipe allow visitors to see live fish in the beaver dam. Right and across page, views from and of the ficus tree, which visitors can climb inside to its peak.

rens, bees perform their waggle dance. Some gizmos, such as the growing plants, are operated by reconditioned power steering transmissions picked up in a junkyard and guaranteed by Rodolico "for 50,000 miles or five million kids, whichever comes first."

Joyce Nathan, manager of the Treehouse, says that the gizmos have been "every bit as durable and as consistent in performance as Lou promised." Nathan is responsible for day-to-day operations and after six months' observation of the Treehouse in use says that it prompts many different reactions. For those under 3, who cannot readily distinguish fantasy from reality, the Treehouse can be frightening. "With the noises and the size of the creatures, it's more than they can separate in their own minds," she says. Visitors between 4 and 10 can spend hours pretending to be animals and role playing. "Other kids have a good time finding the magic ring lights," says Nathan, "like an Easter egg hunt." The best visits occur when kids and their parents discover the secrets of the Treehouse together. There are no signs in the building, which puts young and older visitors on an equal footing. "The kids can be as expert as the parents if what you're doing is discerning information from the clues that are given," Nathan explains. This leads to some surprising oneupsmanship, as in the exchange I heard between a woman and her 5-year-old daughter, who was sitting beneath the monarch butterfly in a chrysalis: "Are you a pea in a pod?" asked Mom. "No! I'm a caterpillar in a cocoon!" There are usually five Treehouse volunteers on the floor to help kids and their parents with the discovery process. They also police the place, wary of visitors who climb too high on the beehive or grab hold of a rafter from the top of the frog egg mass. There have been only a few skinned knees, however, and only one magic ring swallowed.

Treehouse exhibits are to change yearly. Most importantly, the Treehouse appears to be encouraging its visitors to use their imaginations to explore the natural world. "It's really an education of the senses we're after," says Cebul.

Alice, no doubt, would feel right at home. □

© Jane Lidz

Purposeful Chaos on Cannery Row

Monterey Bay Aquarium.
Esherick, Homsey,
Dodge & Davis.
By Carleton Knight III

Right top, front facade of old cannery was reconstructed while bulk of aquarium is all new construction. Right middle and bottom, exhibit area and cafe wrap around deck and tidal pool. Old foundations serve as base for deck. Below, aerial view and plan show rambling nature of facility. Left, portion of deck, which overlooks Pacific Ocean and enables visitors to see exhibits and natural habitats of aquatic mammals and fish.

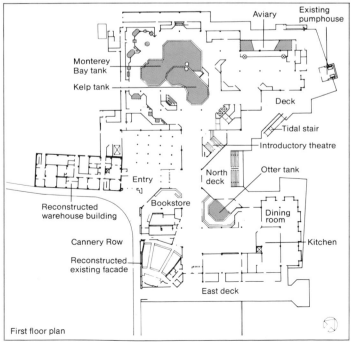

Aviary

Existing pumphouse

Monterey Bay tank

Kelp tank

Deck

Tidal stair

Introductory theatre

Otter tank

North deck

Entry

Bookstore

Dining room

Reconstructed warehouse building

Cannery Row

Reconstructed existing facade

Kitchen

East deck

First floor plan

A poem, a stink, a grating noise, a quality of light, a tone, a habit, a nostalgia, a dream. . . . The gathered and scattered, tin and iron and rust and splintered wood, chipped pavement and weedy lots and junk heaps. . . ." With those words, John Steinbeck described Cannery Row in Monterey, Calif., in his 1945 novel. Not long after the book appeared, however, the sardines—the lifeblood of the area—disappeared. Why they left or where they went remains a mystery, but with the demise of those little fish, the colorful life as Steinbeck had portrayed it slowly went too. The canneries ceased operation, and eventually the buildings were gentrified, becoming restaurants and boutiques for the myriad visitors drawn to the area. The last and largest of those facilities shut down in 1972, but today it has sprung back to life in a variation of its earlier role, one inspired in part by Steinbeck's description.

The old Hovden Cannery is now the new Monterey Bay Aquarium. Although portions of the old were saved, the public areas are nearly all new construction. What is most surprising is that it looks and feels like the old canneries that Steinbeck haunted, no mean accomplishment by architects Esherick, Homsey, Dodge & Davis of San Francisco.

Before we get into a detailed look at the aquarium and its design, a bit of history. In 1967 Stanford University purchased the Hovden Cannery as a buffer between the increasingly tourist-dominated waterfront and the university's neighboring Hopkins Marine Station, a research facility. The idea of an aquarium, to be located in the old Hovden Cannery, was born at a 1977 cocktail party attended by several local marine biologists. Two of them were sisters, Nancy Burnett and Julie Packard, who wrote their parents seeking support for such an idea. Their father is computer mogul David Packard of Hewlett-Packard. He agreed to fund the entire $40 million cost, on the condition that the facility become self-supporting.

A foundation to operate the aquarium was established, and the old cannery was purchased for $900,000. The Packards took a strong interest in the facility—Julie is director—and its design. Charles M. Davis, AIA, principal in charge, describes Packard's approach simply, saying, "He told us, 'I'm going to build the best aquarium in the world.'" Davis indicates his firm was selected because it had designed a marine laboratory in Santa Cruz and had experience with recycling old buildings.

The original idea had been to install a modest aquarium inside the existing cannery, but that approach did not work. Instead, by utilizing some older parts such as the warehouse and boiler house as "anchors" and fitting new construction in and around them, the architects were able to create a complex that is contemporary in nature yet respectful of the past. The aquarium is a massive structure—177,000 square feet—but this bulk is reduced by dividing the complex into what appears to be a number of small buildings. Davis says the result is "almost chaotic with lots of little roofs," but the resulting design looks like the old cannery. Viewed from the sea or the shore, the complex fits into its context, something the California Coastal Commission insisted upon. (Design review by that panel and 13 others took an entire year.) The old boiler house chimneys, for example, had to stay; remade in glass fiber, these triple stacks act as a signpost.

It was no easy task to recreate that historic legacy, according to Davis, who spent five months in Monterey to soak up the atmosphere. "There was no written program," he notes. "The building just evolved. We worked with the staff continually to massage the building." Davis says it helped to have the old cannery, whose character they wanted to preserve, next door to his temporary offices. "Every day we walked over and through the building. It was a kind of Piranesian fantasy with two by fours all painted white and sloping roofs. We regarded it as a special place. It's an area filled with history and metaphor that had to be imbedded in the building."

© Jane Lidz

© Jane Lidz

Nicolas Sapieha/Art Resource Inc.

He recalls especially the tremendous range of light—foggy, filtered through clouds, and bright sun reflected off the water—that he was able to see over several seasons. One result of viewing this varied light, he notes, was "to make the building more transparent." While the street facade is much as it was originally with few openings, the ocean side is heavily glazed and offers 20,000 square feet of decks, all of which reinforce the connection between the exhibits and the real world of the sea, as well as taking advantage of California's unique climate.

In his introduction to *Cannery Row,* Steinbeck wonders, "How can the poem and the stink and the grating noise—the quality of light, the tone, the habit, and the dream—be set down alive?" In other words, what is the best way to tell his tale? Answering his own question, Steinbeck says, "open the page and let the stories crawl in by themselves." And that is just the approach taken by the aquarium's planners with the exhibits. Unlike most similar facilities, visitors to the Monterey Bay Aquarium are not programmed or confined to a predetermined path. Rather, they are left to wander about, seeking out whatever interests them, much as one would when skin-diving on a coral reef or rocky shore.

There are some 83 exhibit tanks in two dozen galleries, all of which are devoted solely to the study of Monterey Bay, whose unusual geology (its bottom is deeper than the Grand Canyon) and habitats (protecting everything from tiny birds to mammoth whales) make it one of the richest aquatic treasure troves in the world. The centerpiece of the aquarium is a pair of huge tanks, including the largest in the country at 355,000 gallons. That one, 28 feet tall by 66 feet long, features a growing kelp forest, while the other is a figure-eight-shaped, 90-foot-long section of Monterey Bay, designed to allow sharks to swim freely, along with other fish and creatures of the deep.

In addition, there are petting tanks, where children may touch starfish and other creatures, a sandy beach with birds, and a tank for an entertaining group of sea otters. Overhead, there are life-size replicas of whales and other fish as well as small boats. The exhibits were all created in-house with the aid of consultants Frederick A. Usher of Santa Barbara, Calif., Ace Design of Sausalito, Calif., and Bios, Inc., of Seattle.

Views across tidal pool to main exhibit building, which makes extensive use of natural light. 'Conning tower' at far right is top of pump house used to bring in fresh seawater for tanks.

Right, exposed ceiling with ducts creates factory-like image and permits easy hanging of mammoth glass fiber models of whales and other nautical memorabilia. Below, postmodern bookshop is visible through boat rigging. Below right, kelp in tank.

"For all the exhibits, you don't see the architecture," notes Davis. But the architecture is there, purposely tough and industrial to stand up to the corrosive action of the environment, but softened by the addition of wooden railings and benches, which also provide a nautical flavor. Overhead, the ceiling ducts, piping, and framing are exposed, just as in the original warehouse, which was saved and with a new foundation and roof made into the administrative offices. At the boiler house, the walls were removed exposing the structural frame and boilers, now displayed as artifacts. New construction, half of which is over constantly moving water, features concrete walls with corrugated mineral-fiber siding. All materials had to be impervious to the corrosive sea air; the rebar in the specially mixed concrete is epoxy coated, the gutters are copper, and the downspouts are plastic. The industrial steel sash is PVC coated and painted a deep sea green. Inside, the floors are covered with a thick golden-green Rhodesian quartzite tile that has a give when stepped on. Cast acrylic bubble windows, seven-and-one-half inches thick, permit visitors an unusually close look inside the tanks.

The rambling facility has all the exhibits facing the ocean. Two sections, divided by the entry, wrap around a tidal pool at the center. To one side is a three-level exhibit area whose prow sticks into the sea like a ship. Above, there is a conning tower/pump house for the twin pipes that bring in fresh seawater from 1,000 feet out in the ocean. On the other side, a lower structure contains classrooms and an auditorium and is accessible after hours for community use. This wing also holds the delightful Portola Cafe whose interior was done by Marie Fisher and Marnie Wright. Their concept from the start was to differentiate the cafe from the mostly gray interior of the aquarium. They used a green and maroon palette, picked up from a WPA mural discovered in Monterey and given to the aquarium. These designers also planned the bookstore/giftshop, which offers a distinctly postmodern flair, again to give it contrast.

The space seems to work as intended; children especially are enchanted by the variety of experiences. The only problem, if there is one, is in the numbers. Studies indicated the aquarium could expect annual attendance of one million visitors; in its first seven months of operation since the October opening, it registered 1.3 million visitors. That is 10,000-plus daily on weekends and does create overcrowding. Other museums should be so lucky.

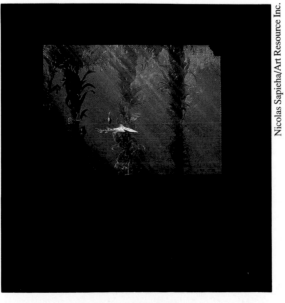

Above, old cannery's trademark smokestacks were recreated in glass fiber. Right, walls of boiler house were removed to expose furnaces, piping, and other mechanical equipment. Treated as a historic artifact, this industrial composition serves as the frontispiece to the facility. Main entry to aquarium is through glass doors at right. □

1986

H.E.B. Headquarters

U.S. Chancery, Malaysia

World Financial Center

Wenglowski House

Seeley G. Mudd Chemistry Building, Vassar College

Hood Museum, Dartmouth College

Complex of Solid Regional Character

H.E.B. headquarters, San Antonio, Hartman-Cox. By Allen Freeman

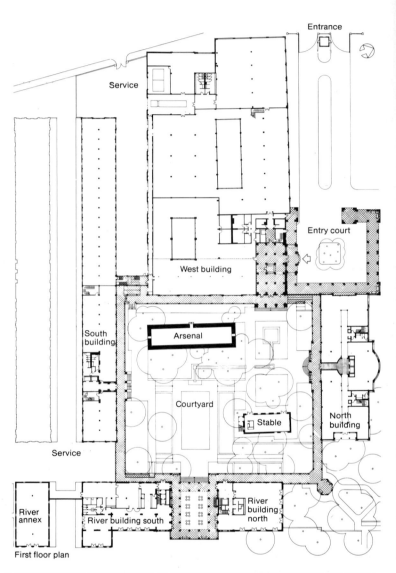

Service

Entrance

Entry court

West building

South building

Arsenal

Courtyard

Stable

North building

Service

River annex

River building south

River building north

First floor plan

Recognizing potential in a derelict, overbuilt Army ammunition depot required an impressive leap of imagination by Warren Cox, FAIA. The result is an even more impressive achievement. Blessed with a sophisticated client, Hartman-Cox with Chumney/Urrutia have made over San Antonio's old arsenal complex into a corporate office complex of extraordinary Southwestern character.

During the Civil War, the Confederate Army manufactured bullets and leather saddles here; during the First and Second world wars, the U.S. Army stockpiled munitions. Today the complex comprises six dissimilar buildings—two of them faithfully restored, two extensively altered and adapted, one renovated, and one entirely new—on 12 acres south of and adjacent to downtown. One of the pleasures of visiting the H.E. Butt Grocery Co. headquarters is trying to discern the old from the new.

Another is the transition from the street entrance (photo above) to the interior courtyard. You enter the grounds on the west side—away from the San Antonio River that flows in a concrete channel on the east—through gates protected by a little military-style guardhouse. Hard on your right is a long, mostly one-story building; directly ahead and a little to the left is an echo of the

guardhouse, a drop-off pavilion attached to a covered arcade. Together, the pavilion and arcade define an entry court from which you penetrate the building on your right at its double-height end piece, an entrance marked by a portico with heroic but friendly looking eared pediments. Now you are in a 35x65-foot entrance hall, distinguished by 20 oversized columns, that seems neither grand nor small.

From a central reception desk you turn 45 degrees and proceed through oversized glass doors into the courtyard. Roughly 200x225 feet, its four sides are enclosed by an arcade, and behind it buildings of one to four stories, all in cream stucco.

Previous spread, H.E.B. from across the river in photo © Peter Aaron/ESTO. Above, complex through the entrance gate. The form of the guardhouse in left foreground is repeated farther down at the entry court. Straight ahead is the north building; the west building is to the right. Aerial photo at left is oriented like the plan, with the San Antonio River at the bottom and gazebo at the lower right. On the plan, north building is all-new, west and river buildings are largely adapted, south building is renovated. Twin of the south building is expansion space.

At opposite corners of the courtyard, as if protected and afforded places of honor, stand two simple, limestone buildings—a long, uninterrupted arsenal (with thick walls, only two little slits for windows on the ends, and a vaulted ceiling under a gable roof, again with eared pediments)—and a stable. The arsenal is to become a museum; the stable a conference facility.

The courtyard, punctuated with rectilinear gravel pathways and limestone watercourses, is serene. It is not a place that you enter for the first time and want to say "Wow!" The subtleties of the courtyard and the play of buildings that surround it are best absorbed slowly. Had these buildings been sited, designed, and built from scratch, for example, the walls of the arsenal and stable probably would have aligned perfectly with the enclosing buildings (which they do not), and the long, west elevation of the arsenal, which contains that building's only entrance, would not have fit so snugly against the courtyard's west building. And the ensemble would have been duller for being more neatly configured. As in urban streetscapes built over time, imperfections have created tensions borne of necessity. What might have been turned into a movie set seems instead solid, permanent.

Interiors are also untrendy. Interior finishes are mostly plain

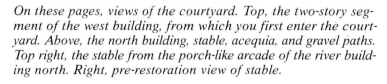

On these pages, views of the courtyard. Top, the two-story segment of the west building, from which you first enter the courtyard. Above, the north building, stable, acequia, and gravel paths. Top right, the stable from the porch-like arcade of the river building north. Right, pre-restoration view of stable.

vanilla—no rich marbles, no exotic woods. In public spaces, the floors are gray-green slate, and panel reveals are gyp board trimmed in painted wood. There are many different colors in the executive suites of the all-new north building, for instance, but none is saturated. New windows have been detailed to match the simple, old metal frames retained in the recycled buildings.

Selling groceries is an unglamorous, low-margin operation in which most of a company's workers toil in stores removed from headquarters. This was a prime consideration for the officers of H.E.B. Charles C. Butt, president and chairman of the family-owned chain, says that the last thing he wanted was an ivory tower for 500 of his 21,000 employees. (All 21,000 are called "partners . . . to reflect their participation in the management and growth of the company," according to a handout.) Opposed to corporate or personal ostentation, Butt told Cox that he wanted

the headquarters to be comfortable like a sturdy San Antonio leather belt rather than flashy like a Houston alligator belt.

Butt had selected Cox's Washington, D.C., firm from a list drawn up by Jonathan Barnett, FAIA, of New York City. Barnett, who rarely consults for corporations, made an exception for H.E.B. "because they wanted to do something of high quality," he says. Of his final selection, Butt says simply, "I wanted an individual—not just a firm—who could lead us through the process, beginning with site selection." (Chumney/Urrutia later associated with Hartman-Cox and, under a separate contract, designed some of the office interiors. James E. Keeter was landscape architect.)

Before selecting the arsenal, the first choice of Cox, H.E.B. had three additional sites under option, all green fields or wooded, on the developing north end of town. Butt's initial reaction to the arsenal was that it was too much work. It seemed a hopeless hodgepodge of nine crammed-together buildings, with only the arsenal and stable having any architectural interest and the stable particularly ramshackled. The former dates from the Civil War; the latter from Reconstruction days. The rest were routine, built during the First and Second world wars and, though

structurally sound, in general disrepair. Cox's proposal of selective removal and rebuilding around a courtyard was the clincher for Butt, who already appreciated the river setting, the practicality and symbolism of a central San Antonio site accessible to "partners" from all parts of town, and the potential for public good will generated by restoration of a local landmark. (H.E.B. conducts tours of the complex.)

Reportedly, Butt's contribution to the design was his tendency toward simplification. Flagpoles substituted for a tower at the entry court ("Charles said he didn't want a Blenheim," remarks Cox), and a swath of English grass for a courtyard pool. And simplicity is carried through in the choice of materials—common but durable, in the spirit of the stable and arsenal—and in execution of details. The details reference new to old, and they are integrated so well that you are hard pressed to know which are old and which are new.

The seamless look of H.E.B. hides five years of hard work. When I visited the complex, some droll "partner" had floated a rubber duck in one of the watercourses. It seemed a good analogy for H.E.B. Stay calm on the surface while you paddle like hell.

Below, the hypostyle entrance hall, with centered reception desk, in view toward the courtyard. Column capitals in this new room were borrowed and adapted from a cornice detail of the 1917 south building, seen through sapling branches at left edge of photo at right. Bottom, lobby of all-new north building. □

The U.S. Chancery in Malaysia: Neither Fortress nor Hut

Hartman-Cox makes it both secure and successful as architecture. By Carleton Knight III

"Don't bring in an American building and leave it among the palm trees. On the other hand, don't put the chancery in a grass hut." Those were the words of a diplomat, Ambassador Robert H. Miller, speaking to an architect, George E. Hartman Jr., FAIA, about a difficult job, designing a U.S. chancery in Kuala Lumpur, Malaysia. Hartman, of the firm Hartman-Cox, resolved this seeming conflict between "waving the flag and going native," as he puts it, with a stylish, contemporary building that evinces demonstrable concern for the local vernacular architecture. It makes a spirited addition to this nation's designer collection of embassies overseas and may indeed be the best yet. Importantly for the U.S. Department of State, it also goes a long way toward meeting growing security requirements.

Kuala Lumpur was the site of one of the first acts of modern-day terrorism a decade ago when soldiers of the Japanese Red Army invaded the American embassy and took several diplomats there hostage (after negotiations, the diplomats were released and the terrorists allowed to depart, flying to Tripoli). The embassy offices, atop Kuala Lumpur's first highrise office building, were deemed unsafe for both security and fire hazard reasons, and plans were begun for a new facility. Eventually, after some land trading, the present site, at the edge of a residential area built by British colonials during the 1920s and 1930s two miles from downtown, was obtained. The three-acre lot fronts on the city's major ring road, a six-lane divided highway.

From the start, security considerations, even stronger today than in 1979 when planning started, were primary and drove

organization of the internal space. Programatically, the architects saw the building as having three major divisions. The support function—service, shops, warehouse, parking—acts as a base for the bulk of the embassy offices on one side and the U.S. Information Service cultural center including an auditorium, library, exhibits area, and offices on the other of the H-shaped plan.

This meshed with security requirements because it enabled the creation of a multilayered plan that places the most sensitive areas—communications and the ambassador's office, for example—high and to the rear while the more accessible areas are low and to the front. This vertical stratification in which public functions are limited to the main floor is enhanced by the placement of the lobby in the center. There, visitors come under initial screening: Those seeking visas from the consular section turn to the left, those with business at the cultural center turn right, while those visiting embassy officials go straight ahead.

As security considerations were driving the plan, Hartman sought context to shape the overall look. Until the mid-1970s, Kuala Lumpur was still a rather sleepy town that had been founded by Chinese miners 100 years ago, but during the past

Varied roof planes break up massing of chancery so that it fits into residential neighborhood. Perimeter fence/wall reduces impact of the building's large, windowless base. Below, a fast-moving afternoon storm approaches.

© Peter Aaron/ESTO

few years graceless skyscrapers have become the norm. Initially Hartman was concerned about what he perceived as the city's lack of an identifiable stylistic character, not hard to understand considering the wholesale destruction of Kuala Lumpur's architectural patrimony for a frenzy of new development.

Although the architects maintained their programatically layered approach, their first design was a modernist exercise inspired in part by Le Corbusier's Chandigarh complex in India. The architectural panel that the State Department's Office of Foreign Buildings Operations uses to help it commission and review buildings liked the concept, but the architects kept fiddling with it. A second scheme derived from the initial one, but the exterior was pulled back to form a screen wall. Hartman, however, was still not satisfied.

Eventually he found a combination of contextual elements—shaded verandahs, wide eave overhangs, balustrades, exterior stairways, tiled roofs, lattice-covered openings—in buildings such as the railroad station and a girl's school and in houses, and this third design worked. As William L. Slayton, Hon. AIA, former deputy assistant secretary of state for foreign buildings, recalls, "They kept improving the design." Ambassador Miller, now assigned to the Ivory Coast, attributes much of the success to the use of traditional elements.

(A sidelight: Early on, some Malaysian architects thought the design looked too derivative of their nation's British and Dutch-ruled colonial past, apparently preferring instead a Houston-styled glass box. Many in the third world believe that such modern buildings, including skyscrapers, are a sign that a city or nation has "arrived," at considerable expense to fragile cultures. As Lee Becker of Hartman-Cox notes, he and his associates—foreigners in Kuala Lumpur—were striving to create a traditional, vernacular look to the building, while the natives were seeking the styleless image of modernism. "No one is advocating they stay in grass huts," says Becker, but he believes important regional styles ought to be preserved.)

The resulting building combines a range of requirements, from security to esthetics and from climate to function. Take the deep verandahs, for example. They cut the glare and provide shade from the sun (Kuala Lumpur is only 3.5 degrees above the equator), but they also offer protection from the frequent, but short-lived, heavy rains (six to ten inches a month). In addition, they allow use of a glass curtain wall to maximize views. The solid balustrade provides protection against projectiles. The building consists of a poured-in-place concrete frame with brick infill walls covered with Shanghai plaster, a material common in the region. Similarly, an indigenous red clay tile unifies the varied roof forms.

The chancery demonstrates successfully how to introduce a necessarily large building—approximately 100,000 square feet—into a neighborhood of 6,000-square-foot homes. By placing the largest portion, the embassy offices, on the northern or com-

Transparency of building becomes evident at twilight. Below, site plan with chancery, U.S. Marine security guard quarters, and extensive recreational facilities.

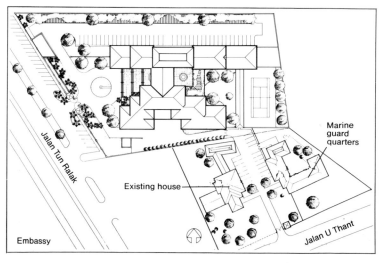

mercial side of the site, the architects were able to take advantage of the prevailing breezes and views. Then they stepped the mass down to the more residential scale of the southern exposure. Thus the overall design, which allows the communications equipment and elevator penthouse to be integrated into the scheme at the top, is broken up to resemble residential buildings, reducing its apparent bulk.

Since the narrow ends of the long buildings are perpendicular to the street, and the roofs step up and away, passersby get little sense of its massiveness. This effect is accentuated at the entry, which features a pair of 40-foot-wide wings—a dimension common in residence design there—that reach out to shelter the grand staircase while funneling visitors into the open-air lobby.

Despite the fact that the building by necessity must be closed, it has a welcome transparency. One can look from the front gate through the lobby into a courtyard. The verandahs also give depth, and therefore a degree of what seems transparency, to the facade. On the other hand, the architects disguised the fact that no windows were permitted within 16 feet of the ground. A nine-foot-high perimeter wall surrounds the building, effectively cropping off visually the windowless base of the structure, which holds the parking garage. The architects also raised the entrance some seven feet above grade, with a series of cascading steps. All these elements add to the sense of protection, but, as Slayton notes, "Hartman made the security not seem ominous and ubiquitous."

Hartman describes the building as "a reinforced concrete pillbox, broken down in scale to resemble a house. It looks friendly, but it is built like a fortress." Ambassador Ronald D. Palmer, who oversaw construction and left Kuala Lumpur in 1983 just after the building was completed, says that in contrast to what one might expect in such a heavily safeguarded building, the chancery has an unusual sense of light, space, and freedom. That may come as a surprise until one discovers that behind the balustrade most of the exterior is a glass curtain wall. Appropriately enough, it was fabricated by a California manufacturer of jail windows from a design based by the architects on an old British-constructed window wall in Kuala Lumpur. It was assembled with heavier-than-standard steel and wired glass, but the primary difference between old and new, says Hartman, was the addition of more muntins for security. They are hardly noticeable, however, as views from the offices have an especially open look, with the extensive, nearby foliage creating an almost jungle-like atmosphere. Visual interest is added to the curtain wall by a number of grids, from the wire in the glass to the steel framing to the columns on the verandah, all of which work to soften the overall appearance.

Top and above, rear of building, which overlooks lower-level courtyard and tennis court with covered colonnade. Right, view from interior shows gridded, glass curtain wall with doors to verandah. Across page, mesh security doors lead to fountain courtyard at rear of lobby.

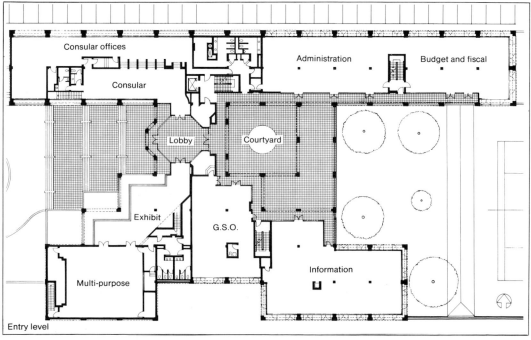

Consular offices

Administration   Budget and fiscal

Consular

Lobby   Courtyard

Exhibit

G.S.O.

Multi-purpose   Information

Entry level

Although the program precluded dramatic interior spaces, the architects designed a series of courtyards on several levels. Palmer, who is now a visiting scholar at the Center for Strategic & International Studies of Georgetown University pending another ambassadorial assignment, compares the main courtyard at the rear of the lobby to a "Renaissance piazza with a fountain. It has an intimate character and allows you to observe others without intruding." This space, enclosed by a latticed pergola, stands on the roof of the dining room, which overlooks another courtyard opening on the tennis court. A colonnaded walkway serves as a divider and provides a welcome spot of shade for late afternoon parties. The colonnade roof is a multilayered series of beams, trusses, purlins, rafters, and battens covered with tile, another gridded design that creates its own special interest.

There is more to this $8 million (including furnishings) facility than the chancery. A somewhat dilapidated house has been renovated as a community recreation center for the American families stationed there. And there is a tennis court, a swimming pool, and a squash court in the chancery's basement. The U.S. Marine security guards have separate quarters in a build-

Below and across page, main courtyard with fountain is surrounded by lattice-roofed pergola.

ing on the grounds designed by the architects to echo the chancery design.

According to M. Lyall Breckon, deputy chief of mission during construction, it is unusual to have such facilities all in one place, but, he notes, it helps morale by allowing families to get together during the day. The current ambassador, Thomas P. Shoesmith, who describes the complex as "the nicest I've seen in Asia," says it is "absolutely first class as a workplace. I've never heard a single complaint, functionally or esthetically." The chancery has also met with public acclaim, and Breckon says the design has had a positive effect, inspiring a renaissance of sorts for older style buildings in Kuala Lumpur. At the chancery's dedication, Palmer, who says the building reminds him of "Tara after the ball was over," reports that one Malaysian, a leader in the preservation movement there, told him the building ought to be designated an instant historical monument. That's not bad for a brand new American embassy. □

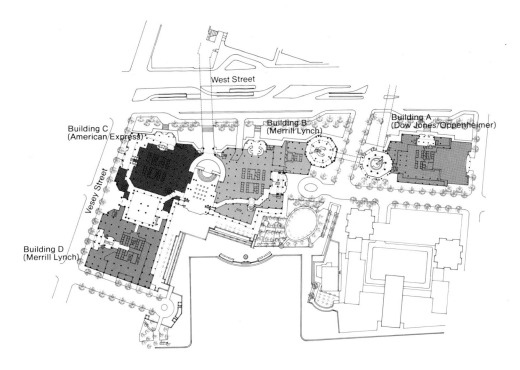

The Rockefeller Center of the '80s?

Battery Park City's core. By Andrea Oppenheimer Dean and Allen Freeman

Three of the World Financial Center's four towers at Battery Park City and its two "gateway" buildings are nearing completion, and its vast, enclosed winter garden is glazed. How does the complex look? What does it feel like to be there? Is it "a new Rockefeller Center," as some observers have claimed? Is it perhaps an embodiment of peculiarly 1980s ideas and attitudes toward urban design and architecture?

Approaching from the south, along West Street, the lower Manhattan towers look refined, wellspoken—downright eloquent next to the Le Frak housing to the south (an early phase of Battery Park City's housing program that will in time yield 14,000 luxury units).

The four new skyscrapers also do wonders for their neighbor to the east, the World Trade Center. Rising from 33 to 50 stories, the World Financial Center's towers, each with a different silhouette and geometric top, mediate between Yamasaki's flat topped shafts and those of the neighboring Wall Street area and mercifully transform the Trade Center into background.

Viewed individually the new complex's towers are neither breathtaking nor meant to be, though they put the new midtown Manhattan buildings to shame. The emphasis was on their grouping against the skyline and on their identical and extraordinary skins.

The skin show should come as no surprise with master architectural clothier Cesar Pelli, FAIA, as designer. In an effort to reduce the massive towers' bulk, he peeled the granite and glass cladding back a notch at each of four setbacks and made the buildings look increasingly immaterial as they rise—as though painted against the sky—by changing the relationship of glazing to stone from base to crown. He enlarged and elongated the windows at each setback, finally overlaying them with finely drawn mullions and tautly stretching them against a granite grid of similar color value. As Pelli says, "At the base these are skins of stone with windows in them; at the top they are skins of glass with a tracery of stone marking the modular system."

He adds, "I tried to design the buildings to be as intelligent

Left, in a helicopter view from over the Hudson River, the new towers cluster around a rectilinear cove. Behind are the World Trade Center twin towers and, beyond, Wall Street skyscrapers.

and clear as a modern building but to also be responsible to the silhouette of the city, to the sidewalk, and the traditional buildings of downtown New York. The whole issue to me was to do a building that is of our time, responding to our sensitivities, our ideology, the history that exists behind us, but without historic borrowings."

This characteristically 1980s attitude of accommodation marks one of several differences between the basically conservative World Financial Center and Rockefeller Center, a revolutionary urban design concept. For the latter, Raymond Hood's team of architects turned their backs on the lowrise tenements dominating the midtown neighborhood. Even Le Corbusier, while quarreling with its detailing, regarded Rockefeller Center as the harbinger of "a new age."

Pelli's subordination of his scheme to the existing city coincided with the guidelines spelled out by Battery Park City's master plan of 1979, which broke with canonic modernist thinking and succeeded a series of unbuildable schemes, two of them by Harrison & Abramovitz. The first, kindred in spirit to Albany Mall, dated back to 1966, the beginning of Battery Park City's rocky history.

The project's life as a combined effort of state and city management fueled by private investment began in 1979 when it was bailed out financially by the New York Urban Development Corporation. Before inviting developer bids, the UDC hired the firm of Cooper, Eckstut Associates to draft a master plan. Their work, based on rezoning that extends the grid of lower Manhattan and preserves view corridors to the water, is "a celebration of New York that recognized the city's strength, diversity, and existing architecture," in the words of Meyer Frucher, current president of the Battery Park City Authority.

Cooper, Eckstut's plan and guidelines defined, among other things, exact street patterns, the general location and massing of buildings, waterfront treatment, connections and circulation, and physical and visual relationships to the surrounding neighborhood, and set superior design standards. Shortly after accepting it, the UDC named Olympia & York as developer and gave the Toronto-based firm a 10-year tax deferral. The first $400 million in taxes will be used to finance low- and moderate-income housing elsewhere in Manhattan. Frucher says this will be the

219

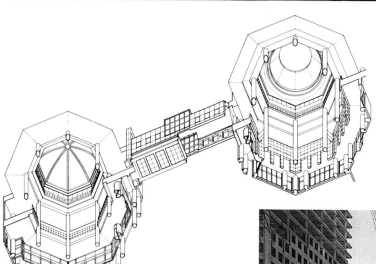

Top, the complex along West Street from the platform of the World Trade Center. The tower in the distance, occupied by Dow Jones and Oppenheimer, was first to be completed. Between it and the unfinished Merrill Lynch building (right in photo) are the 'gate house' extensions, whose interior rotundas are shown above in axonometric. Right, another view across West Street, with the same Merrill Lynch tower above the north bridge, the vault of the winter garden, and the heroic entrance and shifting facade of the American Express tower. Opposite, the 40-foot-wide north bridge.

nation's largest housing trust "and its most significant linkage between market rate and low-cost housing." The UDC's deal with Olympia & York was in exchange for the developer's offer to build the project in half the expected time and to single-handedly develop the entire $1.5 billion, 14-acre site. It was to include six million square feet of commercial space, 100,000 square feet of retail, 150,000 square feet of recreation and exhibit space, and 3.5 acres of public parks and plazas.

It is the vast scope of its intentions that makes Battery Park City most unequivocably analogous to Rockefeller Center. A closer look, however, underscores the differences, the first having to do with location and site plan. While Rockefeller Center is in the middle of Manhattan and resembles a doughnut in plan, Battery Park City is at its edge, on landfill. It is configured as an L embracing a plaza facing the Hudson and away from the city from which it is separated by West Street, a 10-lane thoroughfare.

Absent also is the drama one feels approaching Rockefeller Center's vertically ribbed towers. The World Financial Center's buildings are not only fewer and stockier but somewhat bulky and anchored to the ground by a two-story, wall-like masonry base containing retail whose horizontality is underscored by carefully crafted banding and a continuous row of recessed square windows at the third level. What drama there is comes from the cladding, the tops (which are packed with mechanical equipment), and from Pelli's having rotated the axes of the two northernmost buildings above the ninth level. This twist makes their lower portions follow the proximate street grid while their upper sections align with Wall Street to the east.

Also different from Rockefeller Center is the lack of street activity at the World Financial Center. Shops, in the manner of the 1980s mall, will face inward, while the towers' West Street elevations are edged with grass—to a peculiarly non-urban effect—and each has only a single, albeit monumental, front door created of layers of marble cladding, colored glass, and a bronzed metal. The basic design elements are the same for each portal but variously sized, shaped, and colored.

They follow a principle applied throughout the complex: use of an overall language of elements with different "accents," as Pelli calls them, to give each building its own identity.

In image and detailing these entrances—and, for that matter, shapes and detailing throughout the project—bear resemblance to work of other architects (Graves, Kohn Pedersen Fox, Rossi). Pelli acknowledges this, explaining, "We are all affected by our times and many of our concerns are the same." Among these he stresses an attempt to find expression for current technologies, such as the ubiquitously used, many-layered, thin envelope.

The monumental street level entrances are largely symbolic. The estimate is that eventually they will be employed by up to 30 percent of the building's users. But now about 90 percent of the approximately 9,000 office workers already installed at the World Financial Center enter the complex in a singularly pedestrian manner, via two second-story enclosed bridges crossing West Street that resemble airport corridors. The north bridge, the larger of the two at 40 feet wide, connects buildings B, C, and D (respectively occupied by Merrill Lynch, American Express, and Merrill Lynch again) to the World Trade Center and its underground transportation hub. The towers are interconnected at the first two levels.

The south bridge leads directly to the octagonal domed atrium of the "gateway" building attached to building A (occupied by Oppenheimer & Co. and Dow Jones). This atrium is an airy, beautifully modulated space ringed by two balconies, capped by a stenciled ceiling, and terminated at ground level by two semi-circular, almost baroque stairs flanking an escalator. An as yet unfinished bridge leads to a similar atrium in "gateway" B.

The lobbies of the office buildings are, again, all variations on a theme. In each, the elevator core is covered in a differently patterned damask "to avoid the typically unfriendly marble or granite elevator box and serve as an orientation point," in Pelli's words. A constant in all public interior spaces is painted black structural columns, which seem somewhat obtrusive at first. Pelli wanted them to be read as "serious things holding

Left, the lower, West Street lobby of the Dow Jones-Oppenheimer building. Right, the three-story rotunda of the adjoining nine-story 'gate house' contains a broken curving stair with escalators up the center. Doors at second level connect to one of two bridges across West Street.

up the building," analogous to set changers in Kabuki plays who become almost invisible once you're accustomed to them.

Each lobby has a dominant flecked gray marble with different accent colors: red in one, green in another, purplish in the third. Walls are white, ceilings a cool bluish white to give depth. Pelli explains, "We started with one color and chose others that would go well with it, sometimes complimentary, sometimes similar, to avoid a simplified or simplistic design decision." Most of the second story lobbies are ringed with retail space (still unoccupied) that is separated from the commercial space by freestanding marble screens—punctured walls, Pelli calls them.

In the lobbies generally, nothing is over-designed, overscaled, or less than gracefully proportioned. Most appealing are the Dow Jones-Oppenheimer building lobbies with their combinations of curved and rectilinear, symmetrical and irregular shapes. Least pleasing is the lower level of American Express's lobby whose retail spaces were removed to give it an open look from outside, leaving great expanses of arbitrary-looking glazing and a lot of vacant, leaky-looking space. Pelli has recommended plans for exhibits and demonstrations in these lobbies, but awaits American Express's decision.

The winter garden, the World Financial Center's pièce de resistance, and the waterfront plaza are intended as the principal destinations for the public at Battery Park City. Pelli, who designed the future plaza in collaboration with artists Scott Burton and Siah Armajani and landscape architect Paul Friedberg, says he hated the idea of the collaboration at first, fearing that "the artists would use the plaza as a canvas for personal expression."

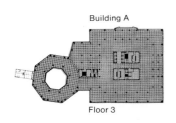

Building A
Floor 3

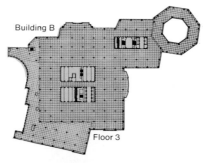

Building B
Floor 3

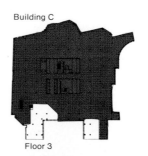

Building C
Floor 3

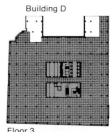

Building D
Floor 3

Floors 26-37

Floors 26-40

Floors 26-47

Floors 26-31

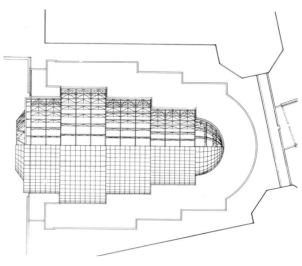

Above, winter garden roof plan, showing ribs and glazing pattern. Photos left indicate the room's grand scale. Right, a twilight view above the winter garden's glazed roof, with Merrill Lynch's building D beyond, now undergoing completion.

As it turned out, he says, both artists and architects agreed to discard anything that "smacked of an art statement and wasn't responsive to public use, and our different attitudes added vitality to the design." When we visited in late October the plaza was still mud-filled and covered with construction trailers.

The winter garden, a huge space the size of Grand Central Station's concourse, is framed by 120-foot-high arched steel vaults clad with clear glazing. These telescope from the east in increasing diameter, then bump back down "to contain the space," as Pelli says, before ending in a sheer wall at plaza's edge. In section, as he notes, the humped shape resembles an elephant.

This fall, the winter garden's interior characteristics were just beginning to become apparent—the marble flooring was still covered, the huge columns mostly unpainted, the retail and dining spaces undefined. It was far from ready for the 40-foot palm trees that will inhabit the space. But one could see how it might soon resemble an enclosed, small city square with the sun filtering in through its overarching filigree of steel trusses, and people dining, browsing, strolling. It is already the project's most dramatic space.

The winter garden's grand half-circle stair, with an hourglass-like tuck at its middle, will lead in from the north bridge and be a processional entryway—the only one in the complex. Planned by Pelli as a "hangout" as well as for circulation, he saw the stair as functioning like that outside New York's Metropolitan Museum of Art. At floor level will be two white tablecloth restaurants, according to Michael James, Olympia & York's vice president for retail development and leasing. The balcony ringing the second story will be mostly for circulation, and surrounding the space at grade will be upscale stores containing "antiques, collectibles, and things that appeal to the intellect," says James.

One expects to see a door or two leading from the winter garden out to the plaza. The reason for omitting openings here is obvious, once Pelli explains that "putting in doors would have made the whole space into circulation." In concept, however, one is reminded again of the 1980s shopping mall with its inward-looking, no-easy-exit orientation.

The World Financial Center is, as Pelli hoped it would be, "a complex of our time." In fact, it is almost a compendium of 1980s urban design ideas in accommodating existing city patterns, adjusting its scale, proportions, and shapes to people—rather than the other way around as in the International Style—in being the source of redemption for a neglected waterfront, focusing inward, and appealing to the affluent.

In 1969, AIA gave its 25-year award to Rockefeller Center, the jury calling it "a project so vital to the city and alive with its people that it remains as viable today as when it was built." Can we expect such a future for Battery Park City's World Financial Center? We think it likely. □

Photographs by Allen Freeman

Triad of 'Temples' in the Woods

Wenglowski house, Deer Isle, Maine; Peter Forbes & Associates.
By Robert Campbell

The Wenglowski house, silent and monumental, stands like a cluster of temples on a rocky little acropolis overlooking the incredibly beautiful, island-studded Penobscot Bay off the coast of Maine. Two of the temples are anchored by overscaled, nearly freestanding granite fireplaces at one end, as if the fireplaces were the surviving ruins of an earlier civilization and the architect, Peter Forbes & Associates of Boston, had discovered them already here on the site and had merely attached his new temples to them.

There are three temples in the main complex, two of them glass pavilions, one a wood cottage. The pavilions are a living/dining room and a master bedroom; the cottage is a children's house. All three have similar shapes and gray lead-coated copper hip roofs. Together they triangulate a family courtyard, paved in granite and grass and furnished with slim firs and birches.

This courtyard and the whole complex are hushed and austere. Neither the trees nor the buildings have fussy shapes or ornamental features. There are no other houses within a half-mile on the coast, and the only sounds are the wind in the trees and the slow roll of the ocean against the dark rock and shingle of the beach.

Peter Forbes, FAIA, has designed a number of vacation houses on the New England coast, all in the same uncompromisingly austere design vocabulary. In each house, he has explored some variant of a single continuing theme, that of a long, tall, barn-like or basilica-like volume. His architecture arises out of the disciplined exploration of this formal idea, not merely out of the circumstantial chances of the site or the client. Like the writer of a sonnet or a fugue, he chooses to work within a given formal envelope.

At the Wenglowski house, the basilica shape isn't obvious at first because it's been broken into two parts. It includes both of the living pavilions and is bookended by their two fireplaces. A granite flagged path, emerging like an arrow from the children's house, splits the two pavilions and opens a slot of space and a view to the ocean beyond. At the slot, a great deal of energy collects; it is the place at which you find yourself pausing again and again as you explore the house.

Of the three components that make up the house, the children's cottage is the most ordinary. Made of conventional wood framing and siding, it contains two bedrooms and a loft for music, television, and the like. It presents a windowless blank wall to the rest of the complex, preserving the privacy of both generations of the family. The blankness of this facade, together with its symmetry and its placement at the end of the axis that splits the pavilions, give it a surprisingly monumental character.

Much more surprising, however, are the two glass living and bedroom pavilions. Here Forbes has indulged a love of explicitly dramatized structure and of massive piles of masonry, as well as a taste for a monkish gray severity that is the antithesis of the conventional seaside vacation house with its clutter of cheerful porches, awnings, dormers, and flagpoles.

Structurally, each pavilion is a kind of tent. A light, rigid, welded framework of white steel tubes rests, at its corners, on four massive round concrete columns, as if the Wright brothers had landed on Stonehenge. The steel frame in turn supports,

Across page, Wenglowski house as it sits amid trees atop its rocky, Maine coast 'acropolis.' Below, view west between living and bedroom pavilions, toward wood-sided children's cottage.

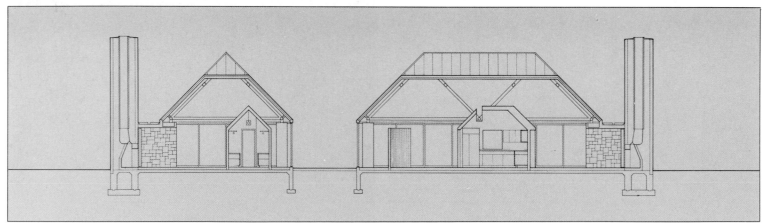

Photographs © Paul Ferrino, 1986

Across page, living pavilion from northeast with view through the building toward the ocean. Bedroom pavilion is at left in photo. Above, bedroom (at left) and living pavilions from chil-den's cottage, framing view across site with water beyond.

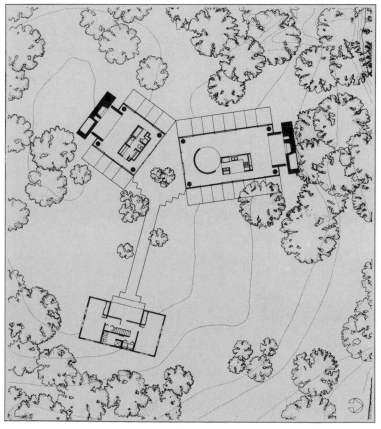

by means of elegant little steel clips, the rafters and decking of the roof. Every joint in this elaborate system is crisply celebrated, with the kind of joy in exposed construction that has largely passed out of contemporary architecture. The spans are, of course, enormous for a house, and they give the living pavilion something of the sense of a public hall or meeting room.

Aside from the structure, there is little else to the pavilions except the immense fireplaces, each of which fills an entire end of its pavilion. The walls are sliding glass, opening onto con-tinuous wood decks that hinge up ingeniously to cover the glass when the owners are away. The floors are granite, without car-pets. In the living pavilion a small wood house, reminiscent of the children's cottage, encloses the kitchen, and a half-circle, freestanding wall, reminiscent of the Tugendhat house by Mies, shelters the dining room table.

The pavilions are as exceptional for what they do not con-tain as for what they do. There are no bookshelves, no places to hang paintings or family photographs, no obvious place for shell collections or stacks of forgotten board games or trunks full of old *Life* magazines to leaf through on rainy days. The house, instead, demands to be understood as a retreat, a retreat almost in the religious sense, from all such pleasant fripperies of every-day life. It is a place where you come to draw closer to your-self, to your family, and to nature. Its tentlike forms suggest an

Left top and bottom, interior of living pavilion is populated with simple, white structures that enclose kitchen space and form backdrop for dining room, all beneath a hefty frame. Above, at night enclosure dissolves to render interior dominated by fireplace.

impermanence, a sense of camping out in the great natural setting.

One of the owners is a painter, and for her a studio, a fourth temple, filled with evenly glowing north light, has been built in the woods at a distance from the others. A fifth, not yet built, will be a garage, blocking the driveway's vista toward the ocean and deflecting visitors into the courtyard, so that their first view of Penobscot Bay will be through the glass pavilions themselves. A sixth will be a guest house, two stories high and sited at the

edge of the little acropolis, between the children's cottage and the living pavilion. The guest house will disrupt the axial symmetry and uniformity of rooflines that now exist, and will make the family courtyard feel both more enclosed and less formal.

Of all the places in this somewhat stern house, the most impressive is the master bedroom pavilion. Here two heavily symbolic icons of domestic life, the bed and the fireplace, confront each other at surprisingly close quarters. The fireplace is as big as a cave—you can walk into it—and it makes the bed, on its granite floor under its tentlike roof, feel half outdoors, as if it were camped on a granite ledge in front of the cave/fireplace. To either side the walls are all glass, giving a view toward the far horizon of the wilderness bay on one side and toward the enclosed

domesticity of the courtyard on the other. There is a primitive power in the elemental simplicity of this space.

In the living pavilion, by contrast, things aren't quite so clear and strong. The kitchen-shed and dining-wall seem unrelated to the larger volume in which they stand, confusing it a little. But the great granite-block fireplace, almost identical with the one in the bedroom and quarried, like all the granite in the house, from a nearby island, has tremendous presence inside the room, as does the view of the bay.

Remarkably original in both concept and execution, the Wenglowski house is austere but not unpleasingly so. It joins a bold, formal concept with a striking natural site and makes, out of the two, one place. □

'Indeterminate But Handsome'

Seeley G. Mudd Chemistry Building, Vassar College; Perry, Dean, Rogers. By Michael J. Crosbie

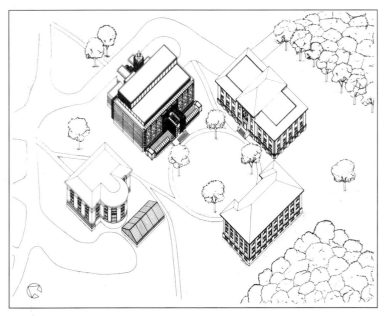

The Seeley G. Mudd Chemistry Building at Vassar College in Poughkeepsie, N.Y., responds on a variety of levels to its context, but it does so without sacrificing its own unique and powerful identity. Designed by Perry, Dean, Rogers & Partners of Boston, it assumes a posture on the campus that is respectful but not timid.

The 42,000-square-foot building is composed mostly of laboratory spaces for undergraduate chemistry instruction, with support spaces that include offices, classrooms, and lounges. It is sited just southeast of Vassar's imposing Main Hall and next to the facility whose function it replaces, the Sanders Chemistry Building of 1909. The old chemistry building and the Sanders Physics Building of 1926 sit at right angles to each other, forming two sides of a rectangle. Diagonally across this quad is New England Hall of 1901, which, although small, defines a western edge.

The new Mudd building's program dictated energy efficiency, so a clear southern exposure was required. Sited northwest of the old chemistry building, Mudd neatly completes the quad, with its south wall facing the open space. Charles F. Rogers, principal in charge of the design, explains that after construction began on the

Above and across page, Mudd building's all glass solar wall as it faces quad that it completes. Twilight view reveals square windows behind solar wall that align with wall's patterned design.

new building a photograph of the site was discovered in Vassar's archives that showed the college's first science building, constructed in 1881, sitting precisely where Mudd is today. Although it recalls none of the Victorian/Romanesque architecture of the original building (which was demolished in the 1930s) Mudd reestablishes a presence that the architects of the Sanders buildings no doubt responded to in creating the quad in the first place. So sited in the company of symmetrical buildings, Mudd in kind is symmetrical, the same width as the physics building, and placed on axis with it.

Mudd's exterior is indeterminate but handsome at the same time. Walls of solid brick seem pushed apart (or glued together?) by a rectilinear web of translucent glass block. On the north, the block is a veiled housing for the wealth of mechanical equipment necessary for the labs, culminating in a central tower crowned with vent pipes. Mudd's brick and limestone trimmed wall establish the cornice line of its neighbors and are scored to recall the

decorative brickwork of the older structures. Above Mudd's cornice line the building extends another story and a half, devoted entirely to mechanical equipment space, whose sheet-metal enclosure is rendered in verdigris green, alluding to the physics building's copper roof (the old chemistry building's roof, like Mudd's, is green painted sheet metal).

Sheltered by brick to the north, east, and west, Mudd demonstrates its energy features as it faces south with a long, solar wall. Patterned to recall the bay and panel composition of the Sanders buildings, the solar wall is all glass and creates a two-foot slot of air space against the building's brown, concrete block wall. Open at the bottom, air rises through the cavity and is heated. Fans at the cornice line pump the heated air into the mechanical system, which distributes it through the building. This surplus air is essential in the efficient operation of the 46 exhaust hoods in the labs, under which students work with chemicals. At this time, the hoods do not operate as effectively as they should, Rogers explains, because of the insufficient dampening, requiring all the hoods to exhaust when only one is being used. Modifications to the system should solve this problem. The building also has active solar collectors on the roof.

As a link between the science quad and the larger collection of public spaces north, the Mudd building's "front" is necessarily ambiguous. Buildings on quads usually front on quads, as the older Sanders buildings do, and Mudd's south side is distinguished by a glass-block entrance that appears to grow out and down toward the quad like a crystal. But that's not Mudd's front. The north side is the main entrance to the building, and it is much more symmetrical and formal than the south side. You pass through a heavy, brick portal, which sandwiches a glass-block in-

terstice, and on into a tall lobby. The lobby is midlevel between the partially sunken first floor and the second floor. It's vaguely shrinelike too, displaying a portrait of the building's donor, which recalls the elaborate concrete plaque outside. These talismans were program requirements, and the architect has displayed them with relish.

Entering the building on axis, one then moves west to a staircase and up. The second floor, like the first, is devoted to lab spaces, dense with pipes, tubes, and other mechanical hardware, and not entirely welcoming to the visitor because of its no-nonsense quality. It's proper for these labs to be uninviting to the outsider, maybe a little intimidating, because this is where most of the instruction and learning takes place, and a visitor should feel no more comfortable waltzing through than into a classroom. A row of work tables is strategically placed across the axis, in effect barring casual passage through the labs.

The vaulted and light-filled third floor, in contrast, is very hospitable, made so by the immediate visual connection through a public lounge and a large, square window to the physics building across the quad, whose limestone plaque is perfectly framed. It beckons you on. To the east are two classrooms that are pinned together with a glance of the eye through a series of superimposed windows (shades can be drawn for privacy), offices, and a wavy, glass-block-walled faculty lounge. To the west are lavatories, a seminar room, and a library. Having reached the central lounge, you are midway through your journey, and again move

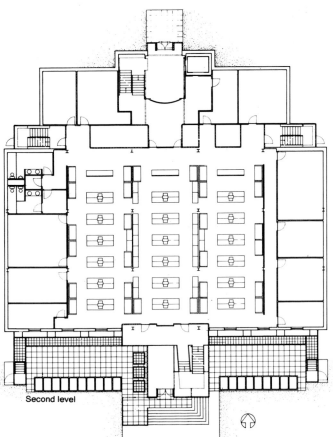

Second level

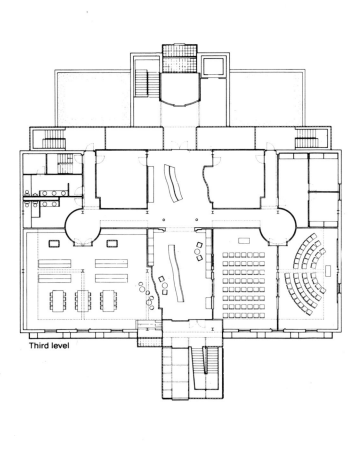

Third level

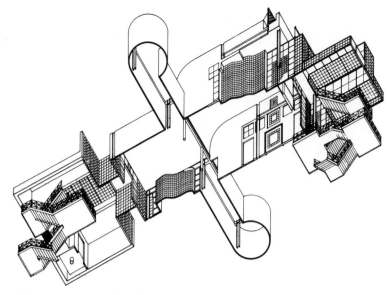

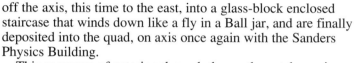

Above, axonometric of processional path through building; left, third floor lounge midway through procession; below, typical lab spaces on lower levels; right, shrine-like north lobby.

off the axis, this time to the east, into a glass-block enclosed staircase that winds down like a fly in a Ball jar, and are finally deposited into the quad, on axis once again with the Sanders Physics Building.

This sequence of entering through the north portal, passing through the building, and then arriving at the open quad replicates in miniature the experience of entering Vassar's campus through the main gate (which is actually a building), passing through it, and then arriving in a grand, open space on axis with Main Hall. Apparently the students have caught onto this shortcut through Mudd, Rogers reports, because they regularly go through it rather than around it.

The only problem with the Mudd procession is that upon close inspection one discovers that the building is actually off axis with the physics building by about three feet to the east. It's such a small error, of course, that you're not even aware of it while moving through the building, and it probably wouldn't make much difference to anyone but an architect. But in a quirky way it's appropriate, being detectable only by viewing the building from across the quad, because that's the view of Mudd from the quarters of the college's resident physicists, who know that even the seemingly ordered and rational universe has its own unsettling indeterminacy.

Mudd's interior is all nuts and bolts, taking its cue from the building's most important spaces, the labs, which occupy the center and are ringed by offices and service spaces. The two levels of labs, which were planned in collaboration with the chemistry faculty, appear to be models of efficiency, with all structure and mechanical equipment exposed. Each floor of labs is divided into three areas, defined by movable cabinets, shelves, and exhaust hoods. The work tables are rendered in Vassar's own collegiate color of rose, and can be disconnected from the overhead mechanical equipment and moved around. Fluorescent task lighting, which can also be relocated, cuts energy consumption.

Spaces outside the labs are likewise bare-bones. In the north lobby the steel frame is mauve with staircase and railings (sporting the same ornamental cross-bracing as found in New England Hall) in green. In the lounges and classrooms partitions are always exposed as infill between the steel members. As Rogers points out, this kind of interior demands that the building trades pay close attention to the quality of their work, which is usually concealed. Except for some instances of shoddy drywall work and sloppy painting, the trades shine through. Revealing the building in this way, such as how the brick curtain wall ties into the steel frame, is pedagogically akin to the work conducted in the labs: an investigation into the nature and structure of things. As such, the Mudd building wouldn't make a bad architecture school either. □

An Architecture of Verve and Invention

The Hood Museum at Dartmouth, Charles W. Moore and Centerbrook. By Robert Campbell

College students love to explore the new university world they find themselves in. They yearn to achieve a sense of belonging by becoming the inside-dopesters of their environments, the initiates who know where all the secret places are.

The new Hood Museum at Dartmouth seems made for the purpose of catering to this collegiate and youthful impulse. It's a building so ungraspable you could spend your whole four years trying to figure it out and not succeed. You can discern clearly enough the Hood's center—it's the top-floor Churchill P. Lathrop Gallery, dominated by a huge bright Frank Stella collage—but you can't tell at all where its perimeter is. The Hood's edges interdigitate, as the scientists like to say, with everything around it and especially with two older buildings on either side. No matter how many times you wander through the Hood and its neighbors, in and out and up and down among its numberless entrances and staircases, you never succeed in forming a clear mental image of this essentially indeterminate building. Instead, you begin to think of yourself as the inhabitant of a graphic by Escher, doomed to climb forever the staircases of a universe of shifting perspectives.

The Hood's architects are Charles W. Moore, FAIA, and Chad Floyd, AIA, of Centerbrook Architects with Glenn Arbonies,

AIA, as managing partner. Moore and his colleagues have long been known, of course, for whimsical buildings that often seem to be mocking their own pretensions. The Hood is sober for Moore & Co., with a sense of solidly built fabric and institutional permanence that is rare in their work, yet it retains all their usual invention and quirkiness.

A simple but inadequate description of the Hood might go like this. It is a two story (plus basement) building made of red and gray brick, dark bush-hammered concrete, and copper. It plugs a gap between two older buildings at a corner of the Dartmouth Green, the grassy common that is the heart of both the village of Hanover, N.H., and the college. It contains 10 gallery rooms, one auditorium, and various support spaces in 60,000 square feet. It also contains very good collections in both art and archeology.

Unfortunately, that description fails to convey anything significant about the Hood. It fails to note, for instance, that the Hood wanders around its site as aimlessly as a lost cow, ignoring the orthagonal grid with which other buildings in Hanover

Across page, the Hood Museum's entry vestibule, where circulation paths converge; below, entrance from south courtyard.

239

Top, the Hood's concrete and copper entry gate from the north, between Hopkins Center and Wilson Hall; above, view of the courtyard framed by the gate, with far portal leading to second courtyard. Across page, reception area near entry vestibule.

are aligned. The Hood has many entrances, but no main entrance. It shapes three courtyards so irregular that they cannot be experienced as outdoor rooms but seem, rather, to be clearings in an architectural forest. All the Hood's parts look different from one another, they tend to be incomplete in themselves, and they collide at random angles and levels. If there is a single governing metaphor, it is that of the Victorian New England mill village. But the Hood is a mill village romanticized into something more like an Italian hill town, picturesquely punctuated at the skyline by theatrical gables and cupolas.

Often charming, this exterior occasionally lapses into confusion or self-indulgence. The problem is most serious at the most important place, which is the facade facing Dartmouth Green.

Since the Hood itself is set well back from the Green, Floyd and Moore have tried to give it a presence there by means of a false front. This is a ceremonial gateway made of darkened, bush-hammered concrete, lacking detail or ornament and facing north. It is simultaneously timid and grim. The architects had wanted granite here, real blocks of solid granite from the Granite State. But the budget would have allowed only thin granite veneer; the architects chose concrete instead. From any distance out on the green, you hardly notice the gate; the Hood instead presents itself as a shapeless heap of copper roofs in the middle distance between and behind its two neighbor buildings. When the roofs turn green the museum will read as a bosque. As you approach the Hood from the green and notice the gate, you also perceive the museum's name boldly carved into it. This named gateway is an architectural promise that if you pass through, you will arrive at the Hood. Alas, you find yourself only in a mysterious courtyard, facing a lady-or-tiger choice of two ramps, one curving up, one going straight down. I watched while one unfortunate elderly couple started down, then backtracked and started up, then gave up and departed. Had they persevered, they would have found that both ramps lead to entrances at different levels, but they had no way of knowing that. Moore and Floyd here play a little too aggressively the game of setting up expectations only to undercut them. Failing to provide a legible entrance is coy. And the split-level courtyard that results, intended for future sculpture, is an awkward and unpleasant space.

Other parts of the Hood's exterior are more prepossessing. The copper roofs, to be sure, are a little unsettled, sloping and intersecting in too many ways, like a flight of copper-colored paper airplanes. But the Hood nevertheless achieves a kind of precarious wholeness through the use of a consistent palette of materials. The red brick walls with punched, mullioned windows are enjoyably like-but-unlike traditional New England vernacular. The gray brick, stack-bonded in friezes, helps belt together the diverse shapes. And the three colors of green—plain green, blue-green, and olive green—brighten the eaves and windows, echoing the future color of the copper while perhaps gently parodying the ubiquity of green (in another shade) at Dartmouth.

The Hood's interior, not its exterior, is where the big architectural successes are scored. Almost everything inside works well, and the whole sprawling complex comes together with a satisfying crescendo at the Lathrop Gallery, one of the remarkable recent rooms in American architecture. It is this room—just as Floyd and Moore predicted before the building was finished—that is the memorable experience at the Hood. The approach is dramatic: You climb a stair that hugs a glass wall, a wall double-glazed in such a way that each layer has its own separate grid of mullions, so that the grids slide past one another as you move. Light fixtures in the shape of flaming torches line this stair, as if a medieval banquet awaited you at the top. What does await you is a gallery crossed at its gabled ceiling by a catwalk, above which a skylight spills indirect daylight down onto the gallery walls. The room is dominated by the 15x17-foot Stella metallic collage, on loan from the artist, a work which radiates energy from the far wall with a verve equal to that of the architecture.

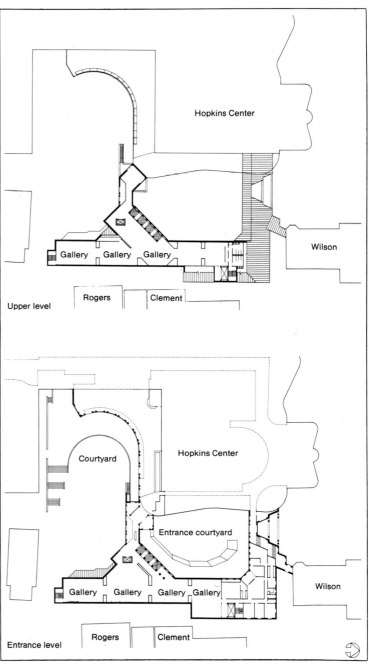

Top, cupola-crowned Harrington Gallery at west end of museum's upper level; above, grand stair leading from reception area to Lathrop Gallery; across page, 'focal point of two axial vistas.'

Standing in the center of the Lathrop Gallery, you realize you are at the focal point of two separate axial vistas, each of which penetrates a series of galleries arranged enfilade. The vistas extend outward from the Lathrop at angles, like two trains departing from a station in different directions. You feel yourself to be at the center of something, in a space that commands and magnetizes everything around it.

The Hood interior offers many further delights. All the rooms and passageways are treated differently. As Moore has noted in a published statement:

"Among my favorite museums are the little ones with lots of special places—like the Phillips in Washington; I wanted this museum to be a series of rooms of very different proportions, grandeurs, and characters, where the art would not just appear in some anonymous matrix but have the opportunity to enjoy its own environment."

The Hood interior succeeds in the way Moore intended, as a linked grouping of individual places. If a building is a family of rooms, as Louis Kahn suggested, then the Hood is a sort of reunion of the members of a very idiosyncratic family, some of whom have chosen to arrive for the festivities in costume.

The auditorium, for instance, is a game of hide and seek played with columns. A row of three real, freestanding columns runs down one side. The middle column lacks its base and most of its shaft, which would have impinged on the seats: Its capital hangs like a severed head, suspended from the ceiling. On the opposite side, three corresponding column shapes are painted in silhouette on the wall, as if they were shadows of the first three but with the middle one now complete. All six "columns" serve as light fixtures.

The entry vestibule is another pleasing anomaly. Here several circulation paths come to resolution at a little octagonal circus with a ceiling of criss-crossing blue beams, an arbor-like place that opens out into the nearest thing the Hood has to a main lobby. Everywhere you go in the Hood, details like stair rails and lights are freshly invented. The architects toy with the risks of staginess or gaucherie, but never lose control. And the installations of the art and artifacts, too, are exceptionally well done, kept carefully in scale with the architecture. Rooms seem made for their contents, contents for their rooms.

P. Lathrop Gallery

To save confusion, I've left discussion of the two neighboring buildings until last. On the Hood's west is the Hopkins Center, a pretentious, disorganized, barrel-vaulted building of the 1950s by Harrison & Abromovitz, which contains a theater, a cafeteria, and a mishmash of student activities. The Hopkins shares with the Hood one quality, which is explorability. On the Hood's east is Wilson Hall, a good Richardsonian ex-library.

One of the best things Moore and Floyd have done is reach deeply into the Hopkins Center and renovate some of it into a new cafeteria, relocated next to the entrance to the Hood. As you now approach the Hood through the Hopkins, the cafeteria tables lead you seductively, step by fatal step, toward one of the Hood's numberless entrances, much as bait scattered on the ground might lead game into a trap. Student life and the world of art here interpenetrate so indiscernibly that you aren't really aware when you've left one and entered the other. And the cafeteria extends outdoors, too, under a long awning (green, of course), with tables facing the Hood across one of those clearing-like courtyards—another way of linking the Hood to its surroundings. At its other end, the Hood connects with, but doesn't really interact with, Wilson Hall, much of which has been renovated by Floyd and Moore as art and music facilities.

An unusual design process produced the Hood, greatly influencing its final form. Centerbrook began work by setting up an office in the Hopkins Center, next to the college snack bar. Here the architects could soak up college life while simultaneously being heavily kibbitzed by a 30-person building committee. Even so basic a decision as where to site the museum came out of this collaborative client-architect process. Centerbrook simply designed six buildings for six different sites, and the committee picked a winner.

The Hood is a building of wonderful parts that seems to wish to convey—but doesn't always succeed in conveying—the sense of an order won momentarily from chaos. Like a college student's room, the museum is filled with shrines and sacred places while remaining, as a whole, not fully formed. In its indeterminancy it perhaps resembles the personality of its senior architect, Charles W. Moore, who in the days prior to the Hood's opening was, as usual, dodging around the world on airplanes (Brazil, Berlin), while simultaneously building in Texas the eighth of the houses he has designed for himself. The Hood possesses Moore's own trait of a nervously amused inventiveness that never quite risks coming to closure. It is a measure of the high quality of this building that one intensely wishes for it the very greatness it seems perversely resolved to fall just short of.

Despite such paradoxes or because of them, the Hood Museum is a building which, once seen, lodges forever in the memory, growing in interest the longer you think about it. □

Top, smaller, more intimate gallery spaces north of Lathrop Gallery; above, larger gallery space on entrance level, with illuminated display alcoves on angled wall; right, auditorium on south end of lower level. Across page, light fixtures along the grand stair.

1987

Fuller House

Menil Collection of Art and Historic Artifacts

Conrad Sulzer Regional Library

O'Hare International Airport Rapid Transit Extension

Forms as Rugged as Their Desert Setting

Fuller House, Antoine Predock, FAIA.
By Allen Freeman

The Fuller house by Antoine Predock, FAIA, in suburban Scotts-dale, Ariz., is original and introverted yet in sync with its natural setting. It composes into a series of low forms that seem to have settled softly on the floor of the high Sonoran desert in angular imitation of the rugged peaks and eroded ridges beyond.

The first indication that the house is different comes when you ask directions at the Desert Highlands subdivision gatehouse and are told to look for the pyramid on the right. Indeed, a four-sided, partly freestanding, stepped pyramid of pinkish gray adoquin stone is the signature form of the 5,500-square-foot house. (A skylight at the peak reminds you of the eyeball atop the pyramid on the dollar bill.) The rest of the building, clad in stucco painted two complementary grayed-down colors, hunkers low behind, except for open-air, second-story lookout pavilions at the extreme ends. The corner lot is a mere 35,000 square feet, but its apparent size is more than doubled by an adjacent open space that is to remain undeveloped. This, combined with an inward-focusing plan, makes the house seem solitary.

Timothy Hursley/The Arkansas Office

Desert Highlands is dotted with saguaro, cholla, ocotillo, and prickly pear cacti, palo verde and ironwood trees, and jojoba and creosote bushes. Predock let the indigenous vegetation grow next to the house, thereby heightening the sense of wedding the building to the site. The long axis lies east-west, and the building is slightly recessed into the sand at the east end, where the entrance is tucked into the back of the building next to exterior stairs leading up to a pavilion.

Predock says he conceived the house as an east-west procession of space ordered by daily routine. The plan starts with a line-up of four orthogonal rooms—breakfast, kitchen, dining room, and study—against which lies a hall that widens in a shallow arc and ends at a window wall. From there you jog to the right and then continue to the bedrooms at the west end under a curving loggia that edges the courtyard. Or, you can cut through the living room along the curved wall that forms the inner boundary of the loggia. A guest bedroom and bath anchor the northwest corner of the house; a dog-legged master suite defines the west end

In view from the southwest, tumbled ridge profile forms a backdrop for the house, with lacy palo verde trees and ocotillo sprays in the foreground. Plan shows house's organization around pool and patio, with A.M. and P.M. pavilions at either end.

of the courtyard. The west pavilion, intended as an evening sitting space, is reached by stairs that wind up from the master bedroom.

The character of the house shifts from room to room, yet the building seems all of one piece. The main hall, called the gallery, is sheathed in white wallboard on the flat side and, on the curved wall, in horizontally applied deerheart redwood. The floor is square adoquin pavers laid on the diagonal. A two-inch-wide water channel, straight as a laser beam, cuts a course down the length of the hall floor, its implied source being an exterior fountain just outside a window slit into the east end of the house. Just inside that window, water bubbles up over a precision-cut black stone and flows down the hall and then under the window wall at

the far end (from which it empties into a round pool that is the centerpiece of the courtyard). The gallery is full of tension, and it is a little eerie. You are drawn down the widening space toward the daylight (mitigated by deep aluminum grilles) at the end, but the slit in the floor and the echoing splash of water make you feel uneasy.

Plugging into this amorphous space like modules are the breakfast room, the kitchen, and the dining room, all rectilinear but each slightly different in size, shape, and window placement. The two eating spaces flank the kitchen and are linked to it through doors that form a second corridor parallel with and adjacent to the main hall. These rooms (and the pyramid that is the fourth room in this line) have vertical slits for windows placed in punched-in nooks that bring the desert floor close to eye level since the house is slightly depressed at this end. This makes for good viewing of desert critters that scurry or slither around the house.

For the dining room, Predock designed a semicircular table and bench, something like a nightclub booth, that all but fill the square room. Custom cabinets in the corners behind the bench display a spoon collection. The architect calls the room a cockpit.

A suitable nickname for the pyramidal study used as an office might be the throne room. Outfitted in dark woodwork against white walls and rising to the four-sided peaked skylight, it is a room like no other in the house (or in my experience). Intimate yet formidable, the room has a geometry that makes you think there just may be something to Pyramid Power, whatever that is or was. Although the glass area is minimal—vertical slits in two sides, plus the skylight—the room is bright with Arizona sun, of

Series of photos swings around the house from the east end fountain (above) to the south elevation from the southeast (above right) to patio from southwest (right) with 'invading' rocks.

which you stay at least subliminally aware as shafts of light swing around the space.

Across the gallery is the media room, which is the pyramid's spatial antithesis, as open and undefined as the study is closed in and constricted by geometry. It is almost a nonroom, a space to cut through on your way to the living room. The latter spreads from a fireplace toward the patio; glue-lam ceiling beams are arranged like ribs in a fan.

The most remarkable feature of the two bedrooms is the built-in bed designed by Predock for the master suite. Its canopy is a cascade of drywall with concealed lights that emphasize the angular lines. In all, the total bedroom space allotment seems tight compared with the generous spaces elsewhere. Predock has designed a third-bedroom addition if and when it is needed.

Perhaps the most thoughtfully orchestrated space in a house full of them is the unenclosed patio around which the house is arranged. Here, perfectly regular man-made forms—the pyramid, the water channels, the round pool—meet the softer shapes of the stucco walls, which are in turn set off by the rugged landscape beyond this tiny realm. To clue you in, Predock piled up indigenous rocks and spilled them down a terrace inside the low, south patio wall. Their irregular stony forms contrast with the smooth patio floor, and they seem to be advancing toward the house. Several have invaded the pool, where they protrude from the glasslike surface of the water. It is a subtle version of SITE's decomposing walls, but with a more timeless message.

Photographs © Timothy Hursley/The Arkansas Office

At top left, the pyramid's stepped profile is seen through grille-covered windows, its glass peak in line with peaked portal. Grilles, four inches deep, cast pyramidal shadows on gallery floor. Top right, inside the pyramid. Above, water channel bisects the gallery and spills down toward the patio. Above right, the curved wall of the living room. Facing page, view from one pavilion to the other. □

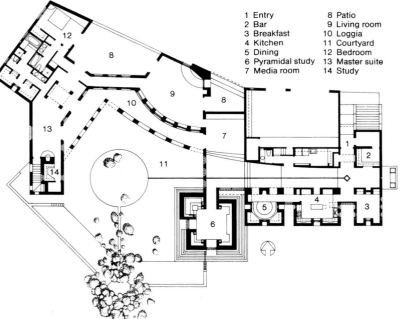

1 Entry	8 Patio
2 Bar	9 Living room
3 Breakfast	10 Loggia
4 Kitchen	11 Courtyard
5 Dining	12 Bedroom
6 Pyramidal study	13 Master suite
7 Media room	14 Study

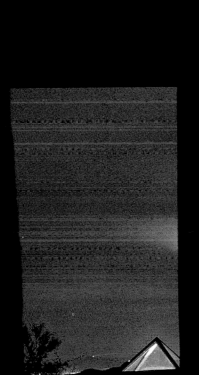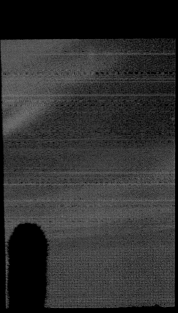

Simplicity of Form, Ingenuity in the Use of Daylight

Menil Collection of Art and Historic Artifacts, Piano & Fitzgerald.
By John Pastier

There can be no doubt that we live in a golden age of
museum building. Throughout the developed world, public
and private bodies have been erecting and expanding
museums lavishly and in such numbers that one wonders if there
can possibly be enough good art to fill them. Beyond sheer
quantity and generous budgets, it is a time of unprecedented
diversity of expression; there is no conventional wisdom or
reigning style among today's museum designers.

In the American sunbelt alone, one can see this diversity.
Richard Meier's High Museum in Atlanta pays homage to early
Le Corbusier. Edward Larrabee Barnes's Dallas Museum of Fine
Arts blends abstract modernism and equally abstracted Roman
revival. Frank Gehry's Temporary Contemporary, a now permanent part of Los Angeles Museum of Contemporary Art
(MOCA), is a converted warehouse that evokes the loft spaces
where so much art is made. Arata Isozaki's main MOCA building is a witty postmodern stew of new wave and antiquarian
ingredients. Hardy Holzman Pfeiffer's sizable addition to the
Los Angeles County Museum of Art flies off in many directions, but is at bottom a reprise of authoritarian monumentality
of the 1930s. And the most recent sunbelt museum, Piano &
Fitzgerald's $25-million Menil Collection of Art and Historic
Artifacts in Houston, is a singular exercise in domesticated
high-tech.

If postmodernism is nostalgia for the premodern past, the
Menil may be seen as nostalgia for more recent times. Renzo
Piano's quite evident influences are those of a mere generation
ago: the metal space frames of Buckminster Fuller and Konrad
Wachsmann, the thin, curving ferrocement shells of Pier Luigi
Nervi and Felix Candela, and the domestic-grade industrialism
and Miesianism of the California Case Study Houses fostered
by *Arts & Architecture* magazine. In the spirit of the '80s, these
'50s elements are collaged and hybridized rather than smoothly
integrated, but the collage is polite and refined rather than
confrontational or dramatic.

Piano's previous museum, the Centre Pompidou (done in partnership with Richard Rogers, Hon. FAIA), proclaimed a
dynamic future of brightly painted exposed ducts and structure,
but this newer one looks back to a tranquil recent past when
technology was as much concealed as revealed and when architectural magazines published their photographs in black and
white. And where the Pompidou brashly ignored the adjoining
urban fabric of one of the world's most cherished cities, the
Menil modestly defers to a seemingly ordinary neighborhood
of a sunbelt boomtown that is not on very many people's lists
of favorite destinations.

But while the Menil's Montrose district environs may seem
ordinary, they are far from it. Thanks to a 30-year involvement
on the part of the de Menil family, this enclave, situated about
midway between Rice University and downtown, is well stocked

*Left, the east end. Ferrocement light diffusers form colonnade
around entire building. Below, west end of south elevation.*

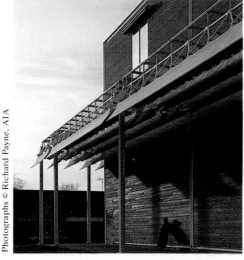

255

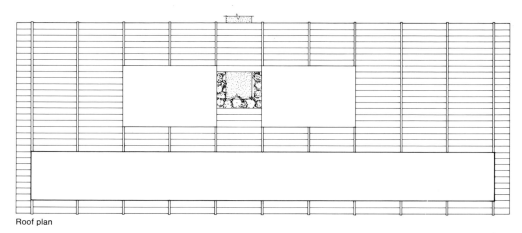

Roof plan

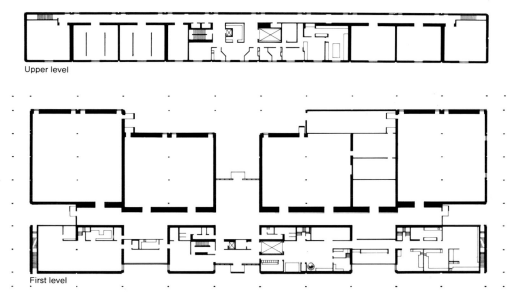

Upper level

First level

Opposite, the context of the museum is modest, residential—one-story brick and frame houses painted gray. Plans, left, reflect client's desire to show only a small number of works at one time, with the remainder available to scholars in top-floor study rooms.

with architecture and even richer in art. The family first patronized the University of Saint Thomas, establishing its art department and the core campus buildings that constituted Philip Johnson's first important commission. This grouping was an unusual combination of Thomas Jefferson's organizational scheme for the University of Virginia campus and Miesian building forms and details. The nearby Rothko Chapel was another family project, both the building and the paintings within. Major modern sculptures are found informally distributed throughout the district, all outdoors and all the product of de Menil largesse. Not far away, Rice University also has been given arts facilities and program support by the family. And finally, the Menil Foundation has steadily bought up bungalows in the district, repaired them when necessary, and painted them all gray. This property acquisition has progressed to the point that several blockfronts are entirely or almost entirely under the foundation's ownership. Some of these house foundation offices; others are rented out to a wide variety of tenants.

A major objective of that program was to assemble a land bank for the museum while keeping the neighborhood character stable. The idea of a permanent museum was explored as early as 1972, when Louis Kahn was retained to make preliminary designs for a site adjoining the Rothko Chapel, a block east of the present museum. After Kahn's death, Houston architect Howard Barnstone, FAIA, prepared another design that wasn't carried forward. In 1980, as the project moved off the back burner, Dominique de Menil asked Pontus Hulten, director of the Centre Pompidou, about architects who might be able to design a very different sort of museum from his own. Somewhat unexpectedly, Hulten suggested Renzo Piano, Hon. FAIA, and perhaps surprisingly, Mme. de Menil gave Piano the commission in 1981. In retrospect, the advice and decision to take

it were both sound; it is hard to think of a case where any other designer has been able to make such a dramatic about-face on two successive commissions involving the same building type.

It was the gray bungalows on the site and on the adjoining blocks that led in great part to the museum's exterior appearance. Dominique de Menil wanted the new building to respect the prevailing scale of one-story, single-family houses, and therefore asked for a building that would be "small outside and big inside," a museum that was residential in feeling although generous in size. The result is a 140x400-foot structure occupying a large block, capped by an elaborate system of skylights, ferrocement light diffusers, and ductile iron trusses that shows up on the exterior in the form of a colonnade roof. In contrast to this tour-de-force of applied technology, the museum is clad in simple, gray-painted cedar siding. Contrary to what one might assume, that latter decision was made not by the client but by Piano himself.

The museum is one story high over most of its extent, with a narrow second floor and mezzanine running along its south side. Generous setbacks on the north and east are analogous to the enlarged front and side yards of a corner-lot house. Given the 10,000-piece collection that it houses, the building is relatively small. From the beginning this was a matter of intent, facilitated by a decision to show only a small part of the collection at any one time, while also making the balance available to art historians and students by appointment. That was achieved through the device of a "treasure house," i.e., a series of secure, climate- and light-controlled rooms that are more restricted than normal museum spaces but more gallery-like than normal storage facilities. Under this arrangement of "concentrated installation," paintings cover the walls several rows high and in some ways have even greater impact than they would if displayed

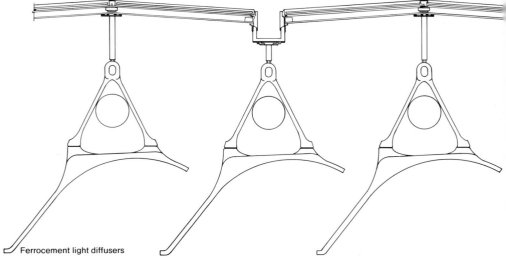

Ferrocement light diffusers

Below right, Piano's early conceptional draw-ing of the light diffusers. Below, section through external wall. Right, the concrete diffusers and support system. Opposite, main entrance court on north side.

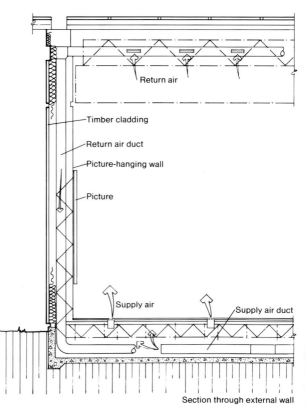

Return air

Timber cladding

Return air duct

Picture-hanging wall

Picture

Supply air

Supply air duct

Section through external wall

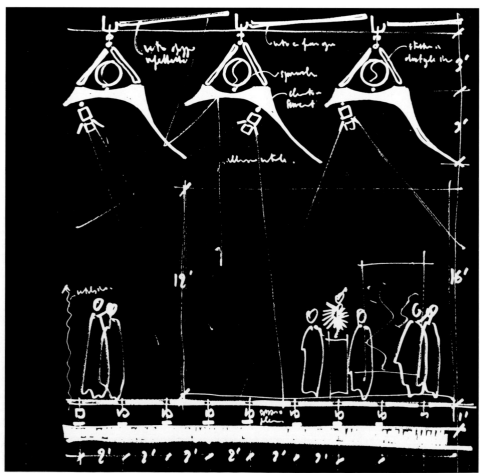

conventionally. Because Houston is prone to flooding, the treasure house is on the second floor rather than in the basement. The Contemporary Arts Museum, less than a mile away, had many works damaged when water poured into its basement some years ago.

The Menil Collection is as much a system as it is a building. A cross section along its short dimension reveals strict zoning by function: the treasure house occupies the narrow second floor, a mezzanine for staff offices lies just below, and other nonpublic working spaces fill a corresponding zone on the first floor. Laterally adjoining this last zone is the 320-foot-long public circulation spine, or promenade, and, beyond that, the exhibition galleries. Utilities occupy the basement, and the larger and noisier mechanical equipment is located in a satellite plant nearly a block away. This arrangement also safeguards the artworks from any possibility of explosion.

Given such rational placement of functions, it goes without saying that the building is also modular. The planning and structural modules are each five feet but are offset slightly from one another. Structural bays are 20x40 feet, and all galleries are either 40 or 80 feet wide. The module is experienced most directly in the form of the ferrocement light diffusers that form the ceilings in the promenade and most of the gallery spaces. Piano refers to these 7,000-pound, nearly 40-foot-long objects as "leaves," but that word, conjuring up such light and frail things as fluttering appendages of plants or pages in a book, does not do justice to the massiveness of what is being named. These cyclopean vanes are analagous in form and function to the blades of a Venetian blind, except that they are not adjustable. (In light of Piano's home base, perhaps this invention should be called a Genovese blind.)

These baffles are part of a complicated symbiosis of elements

that Piano worked out in close conjunction with Peter Rice of Arup Associates, the engineering consultant. The vanes are structurally integral with their three-dimensional matrix of supporting trusses, and their trailing edges terminate in lighting tracks running their full length. The galleries' return air ducts run within the triangular space formed by the trusses, and the trusses also support the continuous glass skylights and drainage gutters that make up the roof. Thus, structure, natural and artificial light, spatial definition, ventilation, weatherproofing, and drainage all are addressed in a single system that Piano calls a light platform. Outside the museum, it extends beyond the building walls (minus its glass and ductwork) to form a *brise-soliel* roof for the perimeter colonnade.

The light platform is the heart of the museum's design and represents a remarkable feat of logical and physical integration. In an era when so many designers have directed so much of their energies to surface esthetics or visual complication, it is heartening to see such an elegant and rigorous intellectual exercise brought to reality. In this building, Piano is keeping alive an important tradition of architecture as an evolving building art, as problem solving, and as comprehensive thinking, and he is doing so with humanistic clarity rather than technocratic dogma.

Having said all this, I must also point out that the light platform presented problems of execution and, in some degree, of logical and visual consistency. Both main structural elements, the vanes and the hand-cast ductile iron trusses, were harder to produce than originally thought, and both were installed in a form that diverged from the intended design.

The vanes were handmade in a boat-building factory in Norfolk, England. The process was one of forming the armature of reinforcing rod and mesh, and then troweling a dense mixture

of cement and marble powder into the interstices and shaping the surface to the desired profile. The goal was a smooth finished surface that would not need painting, but some of the vanes show permanent streaks of discoloration caused by uneven proportions of marble and cement. Also, it wasn't possible to make the vanes as thin as designed, so they became significantly heavier than anticipated. To carry that extra weight, the trusses were reinforced by collars bolted onto alternating chords, thereby diminishing their original elegance. The British foundry originally selected was unable to produce enough castings sufficiently free of cracks, and, after some delay, the work was turned over to a foundry in Arkansas.

There is also some paradox involved in the concept. Mme. de Menil wanted the gallery light to vary with the seasons and the weather, but it still seems odd to invest so much energy in a system that does not adjust to those changing conditions in the slightest. The fixed vanes exclude 99 percent of the light on a bright summer noon, and an equal proportion on an overcast winter afternoon. Even though the Texas sun can be strong, Houston's skies are often cloudy, and much of the time the galleries will seem dim, with artificial light dominating. Alas, current museum wisdom values natural light highly, yet limits it severely. One wonders why a system of movable louvers, made of lightweight materials and supported by readily available structural members, wasn't used instead to provide less extreme variations in lighting level, a lighter structural system, and greater economy and speed of construction. (Building delays caused the museum's opening to be rescheduled twice.)

The vanes also cause some esthetic problems. In a large gallery, their scale is congruent with that of the space, but in the promenade they seem rather large and unrefined. Further, their wavelike shape is somewhat incongruous juxtaposed against the strict orthogonal geometry of the museum as a whole. Piano's original idea of a circular arc would have been more visually compatible, but that shape provided insufficient light control and a compound curvature was found necessary. On the exterior colonnade, where the vanes can be seen end-on and where their function is largely symbolic, the wavelike forms look ba-

roque and even fussy. Attached to the simple gray cubic forms of the building, they represent at best a semicompatible esthetic system and design philosophy. Fortunately, the disagreement is gentle rather than violent.

To many museum-goers, the disparity will not be very noticeable. While the light platform carries the intellectual and performance burden of the design, the museum's character is primarily a product of the other enclosing surfaces. Except for its size, the low-slung wood and exposed steel exterior is very much in the tradition of the Case Study Houses built in California during the first two decades following World War II. (Of these, the most famous was the Eames house, while the most typical were products of Craig Ellwood and Pierre Koenig.) Notwithstanding its domesticity, the stained cedar siding is part of a sophisticated wall system whose precision and complexity are left unexpressed save for one small detail: each board is attached to its backing studs by five precisely placed pairs of Phillips-head screws.

Inside, the ceilings are high, the walls simple, and the spaces calm. Floor-to-ceiling glass illuminates parts of the circulation space, and some of the galleries have windows overlooking garden courts. (Indeed, on gray days, these windows admit perceptibly more light than the baffled ceilings.) The floors are a departure from standard museum practice: not light-colored hardwood, but black-stained pine. The effect is rich and dramatic but also diminishes the light levels perceptibly.

The Menil's Miesianism is one of rectilinearity and expression of structural detail. Fortunately, it is not one of vast universal space; while two of the galleries are an impressive 80x80 feet, they can still be seen as rooms, and their largeness is acknowledged by unobtrusive internal columns rather than denied by immense roof spans. The other galleries are 60x80 feet but will be subdivided by internal partitions that will change with the exhibits. My having seen the building completed but before any art had been installed makes any statement about its final quality speculative, but its comfortable size, spatial generosity, good proportions, and unobtrusive detailing all point to a civilized and satisfying experience for its users.

And beyond the museum-going experience in itself, there is the issue of the design in its own temporal context. The Menil Collection will offer visitors a unique environment among today's plethora of new museum spaces. The galleries might seem slightly old-fashioned, if that term can apply to a design smack in the middle of the modernist tradition, but the attitude behind that design is refreshing and probably more advanced than most of its contemporaries. Where they seek to reflect art by being art objects in themselves, the Menil Collection reflects art by embodying a process of informed creation. Where they seek to reflect cultural continuity by reworking images of the past, the Menil does so by reviving a now dormant tradition of pragmatic experimentation and research. This is not confined to the previous generation's influences cited near the beginning of this article but extends in spirit to the great Victorian engineering feats that transcended the limitations of cast-iron construction: the Crystal Palace and countless train sheds and bridges. In this building, Piano is tipping his hat not only to Fuller and Nervi but also to Paxton, Eads, and Eiffel.

In another context, Piano once said, "My buildings? Well, they are my children, yes—but they are not all perfect. . . ." The Menil Collection likewise is not perfect, and while it may in places frustrate a critic, that imperfection also gives a strongly technological building much of its humanity. Piano's rationalism is sufficiently evolved to allow itself occasional inconsistencies, and his careful methods are not so cautious as to preclude all possibility of failure. In these respects, his painstakingly thought-out piece of architecture has much in common with the art that it shelters. □

Dignified Presence in a Neighborhood

Conrad Sulzer Regional Library, Hammond Beeby & Babka. By Nora Richter Greer

Above, the formal symmetry of the library's front facade as seen from across Lincoln Avenue. Right, its rounded south facade.

Inserting a large public library into a well-established urban neighborhood without creating discord is no easy task. Such a problem was successfully solved in Chicago's Ravenswood area by architects Thomas Beeby, AIA, and Tannys Langdon of the Chicago firm Hammond Beeby & Babka (with Joseph W. Casserly, city architect). Through an eclectic mixture of styles, Beeby and Langdon created a 65,000-square-foot regional library that is monumental yet not overbearing, inspirational, welcoming, and already well loved by Ravenswood residents.

The shape of the Conrad Sulzer Regional Library was determined by its irregular site: a long, triangular plot, the hypotenuse of which is a major artery (Lincoln Avenue). Instead of creating a triangle to perfectly fit that site, the architects made the south end of the plot a small park and the south facade a round "park pavilion." On the front facade (the Lincoln Avenue side) the fenestration takes on a formal symmetry; the rear facade, which faces a residential neighborhood, is of deliberately different massing with a bustle containing offices and service spaces and a stair and cooling tower.

The building's exterior is a reinterpretation of an older language—that of German neoclassical, in part to reflect the heritage of the Germans who were the predominant settlers in Ravens-

wood. Particularly influential was the Arsenal in Berlin, designed by Nering, Grunberg, Schluter & de Bodt in 1695-1706: the articulated masonry base; deep, arched openings; stone sill; a more recessed, smoother, and taller upper story with pilasters between the bays; and the projecting, gabled, central entrance bay. For the Sulzer library, a majestic purple, iron spot brick and matching granite base were chosen. The main entrance is marked by a thickened brick base. As in the Arsenal, the brick is pushed back slightly at the second level. Also on the second level, semicircular steel coverplates set over steel columns separate the bays; on the first level the division is a thin line of steel set into the brick. Windows are outlined in steel, and the standing seam roof creates a textured border.

Immediately inside the building, the historical allusions shift. The main lobby—an oval-shaped rotunda—is clearly classical in origin, but with its somewhat abstracted columns and light sconces takes on a postmodern flavor. Its glazed ceiling allows glimpses into the second story, a space radically different in design. The columns and sconces are repeated in the first-floor

Left, the oval-shaped, classically inspired lobby, with the entrance to the community auditorium beyond. Above, the main circulation 'house' with stairs behind leading to second floor.

spaces, which include the children's library and some of the adult services. Repeating the classical motif is the main circulation desk, which is actually enclosed in a little "house." Behind it are two stairways up to the second-story reading room.

It is in the second story that the industrial nature of the building manifests itself. Here the historical reference is Henri Labrouste's Bibliothèque Ste. Geneviève of 1845–50, expressed through the exposed, prefabricated metal structure and roof. In the case of the Sulzer library, a skylight runs the entire length, flooding the second floor with an abundance of natural light. Eight giant columns (colored purple to match the exterior) march down the center of the expansive, 20-foot-tall space. In an attempt to bring some classical order to the space, a symmetrical horizontal zone is created at the center: the top of the glazed, elliptical rotunda (around which is placed the index table) is balanced by the two stairways. A mezzanine is placed in the rear bustle overlooking this horizontal zone. Located here is the historical room and the director's office.

Altogether different in nature is the furniture that project architect Langdon designed for the library. Made of plywood slabs painted with surface ornament, the chairs and tables introduce lighthearted whimsy into this stylized environment. As motifs, Langdon used Midwestern plant and animal forms, as well as mythological themes. Also playful is the children's storytelling room, where, under the city's "percentage for art" program, Sandra Jorgensen created surreal landscapes that are said to delight children of all ages.

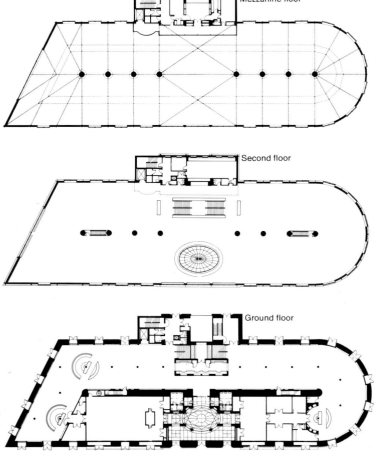

Mezzanine floor

Second floor

Ground floor

Left above, the second floor viewed from the mezzanine. Left, the oval ceiling of the lobby is the index table. Right, the children's storytelling room, with murals by Sandra Jorgensen. Architect Tannys Langdon's imaginative furniture, as seen in storytelling room, right and below. □

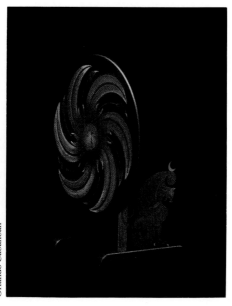

Movement and Color as Themes

*O'Hare International Airport Rapid
Transit Extension, Murphy/Jahn.
By Nora Richter Greer*

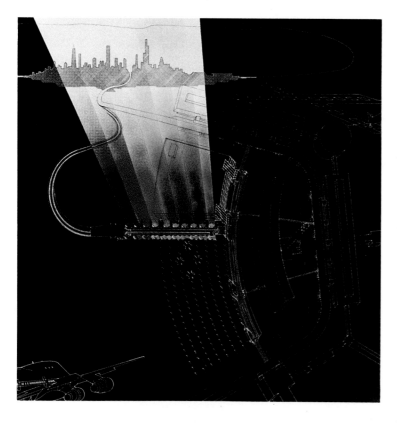

Chicago's subway stations generally fall in the same class with
New York City's: they are dark, dingy, dank, noisy—an altogether unpleasant, sometimes unsettling, environment. One
exception in Chicago is the new underground station at O'Hare
International Airport, where color, light, texture, and form are
manipulated to produce a dynamic, inviting setting.

Designed by Helmut Jahn, AIA, of the Chicago firm Murphy/
Jahn, in association with Joseph Casserly, AIA, the city's architect, the 105,000-square-foot station first opened its doors in Sep-
tember 1984. It is located beneath the airport's multistory parking
garage and is the final stop on a subway line running between
O'Hare and the Loop. (It's also one of five stations designed by
various local architects as that line was extended to O'Hare;

Above, red columns and a 'classically inspired' tiled entablature mark the transit station's entrance. Left, drawing suggests colorful station's role as 'gateway to Chicago.'

the other four are above ground.) The O'Hare station is connected to the three terminals and the airport hotel via underground pedestrian tunnels containing moving sidewalks. Eventually, a people mover will greatly diminish what now can be a very long walk from the subway station to the terminals.

Only a hint of the station's richness is found in the pedestrian concourse and station entrance. Located one story above the trainroom, the area is high-tech in appearance, with chrome ticket booths and entrance carousels. The entrance is marked

by four red columns, which support a tiled entablature, the whole of which is meant to be abstractly classical. The predominant color is gray, ranging from light to dark, to provide a smooth transition to the rest of the airport spaces, which also are mainly gray toned. Beyond the entablature, the entrance ceiling is dropped to nine feet from 15 feet in the concourse. As one progresses through the station's entrance, more and more of the trainroom is revealed through windows of a shape that emulates those found covering an airplane. From the front of the "plane," escalators extend to the trainroom below.

In the trainroom, the hard edge of chrome, metal, and grayness gives way to a soft light show of water, earth, and sky tones in a column-free, 30-foot-high, 70x600-foot room. Post-tensioned

269

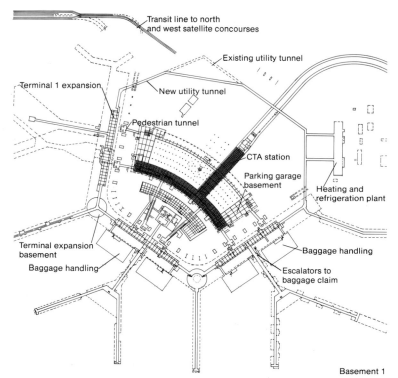

Basement 1

Right. the large trainroom is distinguished by its undulating. colorful glass block walls. An open room for the three tracks is achieved by the use of post-tensioned concrete girders.

concrete girders transfer the weight of the parking structure columns above the trainroom. Open-cut excavation produced sloping berms that became the trainroom's walls. which now are totally covered by undulating glass block screens. The luminous colors are created by bouncing light off the painted bermed walls and through the glass blocks. A patterned effect is achieved in the glass block walls through the device of varying the mixture of transparent and frosted glass.

The overriding image is of movement: on the three tracks. trains zip in and out; the escalators constantly carry passengers into and out of the station; the undulating glass block walls create the illusion of waves rolling from one end of the station to the other in a forceful. syncopated rhythm. Sometimes, though. when the frenetic movement slows down, the trainroom seems to take on an entirely different quality—that of a Seurat painting in which all movement is frozen in time yet is not static. Overall. the O'Hare subway station achieves what Jahn set out to create—a "powerful statement that is deserving of its stature as the gateway to the City of Chicago." □

Use other platform

STAIRS

1988

Tegel Harbor Housing, West Berlin

Guest House, Wayzata, Minnesota

Science Discovery Museum

Becton, Dickinson Headquarters

Cooper Chapel

274 Photographs © Richard Bryant

Waterfront Housing
At Once Exuberant and Classical

Tegel Harbor Housing, Moore Ruble Yudell.
By Andrea Oppenheimer Dean

The village of Tegel is perched near a harbor of the same name and is surrounded by forested open space laced with canals. It's a bucolic spot, one of the few in West Berlin that was spared in the air raids of World War II. Tegel is also about as far from downtown as you can go before coming up against the East German border. As a result the village and its harbor are a favorite destination for Sunday outings, and Tegel Harbor was chosen by the International Building Exhibition as the site for a miniature new town, including housing and cultural, educational, and recreational facilities.

The ensemble was master planned by Charles Moore, FAIA, and Moore Ruble Yudell, which also designed housing, a library, and a recreational center. Stanley Tigerman, FAIA, Robert A.M. Stern, FAIA, and John Hejduk, FAIA, are among American architects whose "villas" are taking shape on the site. Tegel Harbor is becoming an exhibition of late-1980s design.

Moore Ruble Yudell's recently completed 170-unit, subsidized housing complex at Tegel Harbor is probably the most satisfying example of postmodern architecture yet. It has none of postmodernism's usual thinness, conveys a sense of substance, and eschews the cute, the ironic, the cartoon. It has the stage set quality common to postmodernism, the sense of being a get-away from the grit of everyday reality. But that's appropriate in this instance. For Tegel is the closest thing this cordoned-off city has to a suburb or countryside.

Most fundamental to the project's appeal is its site plan. The architects decided to use the water—partly for its calming presence—as a major organizing element and therefore widened the harbor to pull it right up to the edge of their buildings. They linked all built elements to the water via a sinuous promenade, as well as bridges, walkways, and paths, and the site has been splendidly landscaped by a German firm. The curved complex is layered, with shapes becoming larger, their details more colorful and

Left, the building edges the water, curves landward, and ends in an octagonal court, defined by more subdued buildings.

their colors stronger as they approach the water. The idea, explains principal-in-charge John Ruble, AIA, was "to create big, interesting shapes near the water that can be seen from afar."

The complex slips along the promenade, then circles clockwise and landward to create a grassy common in the shape of a backward C, and ends in an octagonal courtyard edged by five-story buildings. It is a case of buildings shaping usable space rather than usurping it.

One of the complex's most appealing qualities is its combination of opposites: the informal and formal, the picturesque and classical, animation and composure. The buildings lining the octagonal courtyard are symmetrical, classical, quiet, and self-contained, while those shaping the common and winding along the promenade are asymmetrical, more colorful, quirky, and exuberant.

From the fifth floor up, the main building is full of dormers and gables and penthouses, over which spills a prominent standing-seam tin roof. Toward the center of the building, it climbs abruptly to form a towerlike element topped by twin chimneys. You can't help but think of Hansel and Gretel—slicked up, grown-up, and graduated to high rise. Ruble explains that the intention was to make the complex "look villagey, spontaneous, very picturesque where it got high, like architecture that is built up over the years rather than being carefully composed."

If the upper portions of the building allude to the spontaneous and vernacular, its lower parts become more formal and classical. Apart from the tripartite organization and rusticated base, which grounds this sometimes frolicsome object, there is the detailing. And this is somewhat puzzling. For the complex's shapes and colors are variations on the village architecture—which is untouched by classicism. Moore's bric-a-brac-like pilasters, cornices, capitals, and the like seem a misfire in this city, since serious classical detailing in Berlin is confined mostly to overblown, authoritarian-looking public edifices, built first by 19th-century imperialists, then by National Socialists (Nazis), and more recently by East German Socialists (Communists). Also, the surface

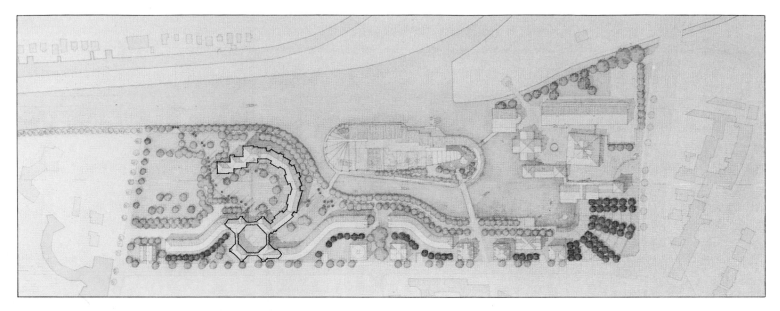

Photographs © Richard Bryant

appliqué makes these very large volumes look even bulkier than they are from some angles—but still thankfully on the benign side of Bofill.

The complex has, predictably, been criticized as overly picturesque, too nostalgic. Even the colors—ocher, peach, yellow, oranges—seem awfully sweet. But they are a welcome lift under Berlin's usually leaden sky. Ruble explains, "We took a risk, because the project is very 19th-century, and some people think it's just quaint and bourgeois and can't bear it. But people have been living for decades in urban houses with flowerpots, and we've designed a building where people can have that. I see a lot of Berlin composed of that." In the end, when we say something is too picturesque or too nostalgic, we mean it's kitsch, or pretty close to it, and Moore Ruble Yudell's complex is too dignified and esthetically inventive to be kitsch.

Still another criticism of the complex is that the exterior often belies what lies within, with floor slabs, for instance, nonchalantly crossing large, vertical panes of glazing. Ruble explains that more important than what the modernists called structural honesty was "the requirement of creating an order for the exterior of this large building that you can read from the distance and that feels comfortable up close."

Incredible as it may seem to Americans accustomed to a generally shoddy level of subsidized housing projects that segregate the poor, the units in Moore Ruble Yudell's building receive government subsidy. The amount depends on the resident's income; thus laborers live beside professionals. There are, however, no apartments designed specifically for the elderly or handicapped, as is usual in German public housing, and you see few dark faces here. Still, the project has a public component despite the fact that it is comparable in quality to prestige condominiums in the United States.

Working within Berlin's strict housing codes, the architect used a variety of devices to stretch and open up spaces, such as combining dining and living areas and appending loggias, nooks, and breakfast areas. And because the building is narrow, apartments typically extend through its width, giving views in two directions, cross ventilation, and lots of light.

The building was fully rented a year before completion, and there is now a lengthy waiting list. Is it any wonder? □

Facing page, the taller building seen from the horseshoe-shaped green it forms. Above, the roofline drops abruptly from a high point, marked by twin chimneys, and the building is terminated by a quiet, anchoring element. Left, dormer apartments.

Assemblage of Disparate Objects

Guest house, Frank O. Gehry & Associates. By John Pastier

© Michael Moran

This witty and genial guest house in Wayzata, a distant suburb of Minneapolis, forms half of a distinguished residential compound occupied by prominent patrons of contemporary art. Taken together, the original house and its guest quarters provide graphic evidence of how dramatically architecture has changed over the last 35 years.

Both were designed by prominent architects working in their trademark style of the time. Philip Johnson's large main house of 1952 is, exactly as one would expect, a quintessentially rational and modular Miesian essay. This simple, expansive, one-story brick and glass pavilion commands a pastoral view of gently rolling, tree-framed lawns and Lake Minnetonka.

Frank Gehry's small guest house of 1987, sited about 120 feet from the main quarters, is a picturesque and highly subjective conglomeration of sculptural forms. In line with one of Gehry's current preoccupations, it is a village where each room is a little building unto itself. But unlike its articulated predecessors, it joins its discrete elements into an irregular pinwheel.

When the clients, who are the second owners of the house, decided to add guest quarters, they went to Philip Johnson. Occupied with much larger projects, he declined the assignment. They next approached Gehry after reading a profile of the architect in a newspaper magazine. He accepted, but was concerned about the relationship between Johnson's Apollonian pavilion and his

own Dionysian assemblage. Accordingly, he sited it behind a hedge, so that it would not be visible from the main dwelling. The clients, however, are happy with the combination and so have removed the hedge.

From the beginning, the guest house design concept was one of a different form and material for each room. The early schemes were purely orthogonal, except for a simple pitched roof or two, and the forms huddled tightly together. Eventually, the room elements began to separate from one another, twist off the grid, and assume more varied and less conventional shapes. Paradoxically, the final version is simpler and clearer than its compact and purely rectilinear predecessors.

The living room forms the geometric and functional center of the house. The 35-foot-high, truncated pyramid, clad in dark gray painted sheet metal and terminating in a flat skylight, anchors four other elements that project, pinwheel-fashion, from its corners. The largest in plan is a long garage and kitchen wing clad in Finnply, a rich reddish-brown, phenolic-coated plywood normally used for concrete formwork. A skylighted, cube-shaped, galvanized metal sleeping loft is perched precariously atop this form, its overhanging corner supported by a thick metal cylinder.

Diagonally opposite this wing is the house's smallest component, an inglenook that has become a miniature room in its own right. Built of brown brick, it too is roughly cubical, with a skewed

Gehry's guest house is composed of irregular geometric forms clustered around a truncated pyramid that functions as the living room. Each room, 'a little building unto itself,' is expressed by form and material, drawing from a conglomeration of materials—painted sheet metal, phenolic-coated plywood, galvanized metal, brick, and Kasota stone veneer.

fireplace chimney extending above its roof. A pair of bedrooms engage the other two living room corners. One is shed-roofed and rectangular and sheathed in the same gray metal as the main element. The other forms a circular segment in plan and section and is covered with a creamy Kasota stone veneer.

Some of the interior spaces are relatively simple, but most are not. Both bedroom wings contain articulated bathroom elements, clad in Finnply, that form solid volumes within the sleeping quarters. The stone-clad bedroom is also spatially complex due to its curved wall and vaulted ceiling. The kitchen is punctuated by a steep twisting staircase that leads to the sleeping loft. The stair originally was designed to be enclosed, but during the framing stage Gehry liked the way it looked exposed, so he revised its detailing to allow the underside of one short run to be visible in the kitchen.

The inglenook is relatively simple in itself, but, considered as part of the living room, it represents a dramatic change of scale and compression of space. And the living room itself is dramatic and unusual, being much taller than any of its plan dimensions and having most of its wall surfaces out of plumb. The outdoor spaces also are interesting in that some of them are shaped and sized similarly to adjoining rooms. Diversely sized and placed skylights and windows allow natural light to differentiate the spaces even further.

The effect of the entire composition is at once artful and child-like. The simplicity and improbability of some of its forms are analogous to a youngster's drawing of a house, and so is the extreme differentiation of elements through color and shape. At the same time, the ensemble's sculptural aspects and object quality exhibit a well calculated mastery. A generous budget allowed better materials and workmanship than is usual for Gehry, and he deployed those resources with telling restraint. This is clearly one of his finest works.

The evocation of childhood is appropriate, since the clients' five grown children are beginning to produce families of their own, and those grandchildren will be frequent visitors. It is also a thread that runs through many of Gehry's best designs, such as the interior of his own remodeled Santa Monica house, and the unfortunately never built Camp Good Times, in which he collaborated with Claes Oldenberg.

The youthful brio of Gehry's guest house is a nice foil to the calm and self-effacing manner of Johnson's older design. And, taken together, these two efforts form a parallel to Johnson's own house in New Canaan, Conn. His world-famous main structure, being all glass and having no blinds or drapes, totally lacked visual privacy, while his guest suite, built at some physical remove, amply provided that quality by being a nearly solid mass of brick. Just as Johnson made his New England home a study in complementary opposites, so did Gehry provide a quality missing in Johnson's house in Minnesota.

Although this was not a conscious parallel in Gehry's mind, the New Canaan house was part of his design thinking in a different, more intuitive fashion. At first he "didn't want to mess around with Uncle Philip's baby," he said, because he was sure that Johnson was "horrified" when he heard Gehry was doing an addition to one of his works. It was in deference to those assumed feelings that he kept his building on the far side of the hedge. But after completing the design, Gehry realized his living room bore a strong conceptual resemblance to Johnson's conical-roofed and skylighted library in New Canaan, and he called to tell him so. In an ending straight out of O. Henry, Johnson replied that he had just built a chain-link fence pavilion on his own grounds as an homage to Gehry. □

A series of complex and discomposed spaces defines the interior of the guest house. The kitchen area, linking the garage with the living quarters, incorporates an exposed staircase that winds up to a sleeping loft. A brick inglenook, located off the central living area, provides an intimate and simple space in contrast to the larger area and its 35-foot-high ceiling punctuated with irregularly sized skylights, its wall surfaces out of plumb (photos at right).

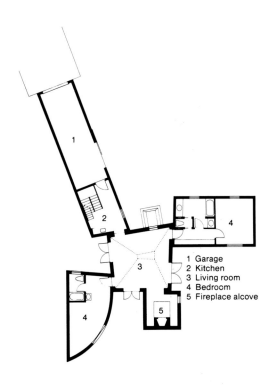

1 Garage
2 Kitchen
3 Living room
4 Bedroom
5 Fireplace alcove

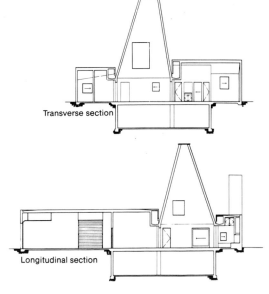

Transverse section

Longitudinal section

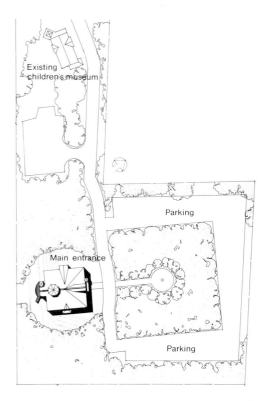

'Nutty, Delightful' Children's Museum

Science Discovery Museum, Acton, Mass.,
E. Verner Johnson & Associates.
By Robert Campbell, AIA

An ideal marriage of architectural style and programmatic substance is what we find in this little museum in a bedroom suburb of Boston. All the gripes about postmodernism's antic ways vanish, at least for the moment, as we contemplate this gem.

Postmodernism is just a game you play with colored cutouts from architectural history books? You just paste them together and call it a building? It's childlike? It isn't really serious? It's full of puzzlement and ambiguity? It will melt in the rain?

Oops. That last one just may turn out to be a problem when a few New England winters have had their way with the Science Discovery Museum in Acton, Mass. But even if the carpenters and painters have to come back now and then, it will have been worth it.

Looking at the nutty, delightful, multicolored entrance facade, architectural buffs will immediately recognize motifs cribbed from such high postmodern icons as Robert Venturi (his mother's house) and Michael Graves (numerous works of the late 1970s). Inside, there's a lot of Charles Moore, especially in the cutout holes in the walls and in the big stair that rises toward a skylight. Since all those sources are now a decade or more old, I suppose we must call the Acton museum postmodern revival.

As for those benighted persons who couldn't care less about architectural history (a group that presumably includes the kids visiting the museum), they will see in this architecture something else: a wondrous array of faces, robots, clocks, triumphal arches, fanlights, towers, arches, keystones, crow's nests, bowers, and trellises. This is storybook architecture. It's architecture made out of pictures of architecture.

None of those pictures is quite literal. All are slightly abstract. The round "clock," for instance, in the gable high above the entry, is really only a window with a green wedge in it. It takes imagination to see the window as a clock. Imagination is what

the Science Discovery Museum is all about. And of course the clock isn't just a clock. Its abstraction allows us to imagine it in many ways. Like all clocks it's also a face, and the blue gable above it becomes its hat. Or it's an eye, with the gable its brow.

There is another and more general metaphor at work, too, one deeply rooted in Western children's culture. The museum is a magic house, a house discovered in a clearing in a forest like the houses of Hansel and Gretel and Little Red Riding Hood. Surrounded by a dark woods that gives it no social context, it is like the dream of a house, placeless and surreal, more vivid than life.

The architect of this remarkable museum is E. Verner Johnson & Associates of Boston, a firm that specializes in museums. The client was the museum's founder and director, Donald Verger. Both were influenced by another museum that already existed on the same piece of land, the Children's Discovery Museum, which Verger also founded and which he still runs for younger children. The earlier museum occupies a Queen Anne house that, like all Queen Annes, exhibits an amazing variety of shapes and of shingled and clapboarded exterior surfaces. Verger liked the old house's shaggy, exuberant exterior with its oddly Victorian quality of being a sort of sampler of architectural surface treatments. He insisted that new Science Discovery Museum also be an enthusiastic exploration of all the things you can do with wood.

Verger also liked the "houseness" of the earlier museum because it doesn't intimidate children. Its mazelike floor provides nooks and crannies where kids can be by themselves in small places. In the new Science Museum, Verger wanted to replicate that sense of a complicated house in which every room comes as a new and private discovery. But he also wanted bigger spaces for bigger kids.

Facing page: below, main entrance with abstract round 'clock' in the gable; above, the secondary entrance and balcony on the building's opposite side. This page, clockwise from bottom: the second floor looking toward the 'clock,' across the atrium, and up into the atrium.

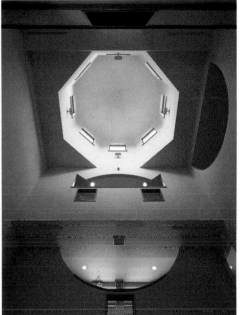

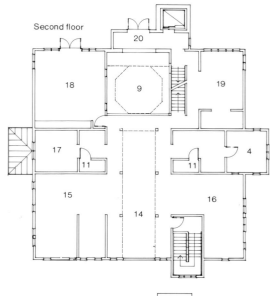

Second floor

The interior celebrates architecture as well as science. Below, smaller spaces for study give way to larger communal areas (bottom and facing page). Wall cutouts create views into and across the atrium.

First floor

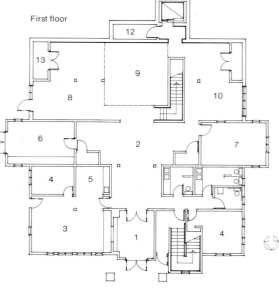

The architect responded by creating a 60x60-foot, three-story building ordered by a 12-foot grid, with small spaces around the perimeter and an atrium near the middle. Outside, clapboard and trellises and pitched roofs recall the local farmhouses, but there is a curious quality in the architecture that locates it, even to a child, firmly in the contemporary world. This quality is its resemblance to toys like Lego sets or Transformers. You get the sense of a kit of parts that could be rearranged in some other way. But since the clapboard is there too, it's as if in some preservationist horror film a familiar family farmhouse has been invaded by aliens from Lego-land who are gradually transforming the house into one of their own.

Indoors, the atrium rises the whole three stories to an octagonal tower. Things grow brighter the higher you climb. Exhibits can be tucked into the nooks around the edges or placed in the more open spaces that overlook the atrium. Cutouts in the walls, in geometric shapes that often suggest architecture (e.g., a Palladian window), establish vistas through layered space. Staff offices are scattered and visible through glass.

The exhibits, not done by the architect, are as delightful as the architecture. None is operated by push button. They are exhibits to be played with, not canned and pretentious "learning experiences." All involve things you can pick up and mess around with. It is doubtful whether the museum has ever had a visitor, child or adult, who resisted the urge to play with them. Scientific principles are always involved, often ingeniously so, but the principles are for you to discover to your own delight—although there are helpful staff wandering around who make unobtrusive suggestions.

The Science Discovery Museum is part of a master plan that eventually is to include other small museum buildings and a nature walk on the three-acre site. □

Arts and Crafts Spirit Pervades Corporate Offices

Becton, Dickinson Headquarters, Kallmann, McKinnell & Wood. By Robert Campbell, AIA

Most of the famous American suburban corporate headquarters—Weyerhaeuser, John Deere, Connecticut General, General Foods—seek to communicate an overwhelming sense of organization. The corporation wants you to think of it as well organized, and it wants its headquarters to express that quality. The resulting buildings are like palaces set in deer parks—stately, centered, aristocratic, hierarchical.

The new Becton, Dickinson headquarters by Kallmann, McKinnell & Wood is something very different. (Becton, Dickinson is the little BD you probably never noticed on virtually every medical thermometer you've ever used.) The headquarters stands in 114 acres of rolling scrub woodland in the posh New Jersey suburb of Franklin Lakes. The architecture is rich and graceful but it isn't grand. It seems to have emerged from a more relaxed sensibility, one self-assured enough not to need to assert its importance.

Corporations, after all, aren't monarchies, and their leaders aren't czars or dukes. CEOs don't arrive at their rural headquarters with processions, and they don't go hunting, at least not on the premises. There's an absurdity in the aristocratic deer-park image that has dominated our architects. Why should a headquarters be a stately mansion? Why should its surrounding landscape be a mere setting, applauding and glorifying the building?

At Becton, Dickinson, all is more modest. The landscape is primary, on a par with the architecture. The company was keenly aware of the desire of wealthy neighbors that the new building shouldn't destroy the rural, residential character of Franklin Lakes. "The neighbors knew what they didn't want," recalls BD vice president Wilson Nolen, "which was anything that would remind them of the Route 1 corridor in Princeton."

There was another motive for modesty. "We make medical products," says Nolen, "that is to say, things for people who are sick. We didn't think the building should transmit a message of corporate grandeur. It shouldn't suggest that we've become overly affluent at the expense of sick people."

The master planner and landscape architect, Morgan Whee-

lock, chose to leave the woodland in its natural state and in places to let it creep up close to the building. "Our original concept," says Nolen, "was that the building should appear to have been dropped in the woods, with planting native to New Jersey coming right up to it. We thought of it as a home in the woods. I think of the woods here as a Neil Welliver environment."

Wheelock added to this concept a recontoured, saddle-shaped expanse of grass known as the "Great Lawn." Across this lawn, employees will walk from Phase I of the headquarters, the part that's been built, to Phase II, now under construction.

Walking across landscape is basic to the experience of Becton, Dickinson. When you arrive at the building (crossing one of the two elegant highway overpasses designed by Kallmann, McKinnell & Wood), you immediately stash your car in an ingeniously engineered garage (Zaldastani Associates, consultants) and, emerging from it, walk in snow, sleet, rain, hail, or sunshine across a broad courtyard toward the building.

The client admits to wishing, often, for a tunnel, but luckily

Above, glassy executive wing. Left, main entrance.

the solid rock ledge below grade makes one too costly. Thus
the landscape becomes, as in a good college campus, something
more challenging and bracing than a mere picture seen through
the frame of a window.

Like all the recent work of Kallmann, McKinnell & Wood,
BD is eclectic. The materials are traditional—pale brick, limestone, copper roofs. Their warm-toned pallor suggests the palette of the architecture of the Tuscan hills. The craftsmanship
is outstanding. Nearly 40 brick shapes were needed to achieve
the angled corners and bull-nose trim work. Stone, copper, wood,
and brick are fitted together with care rarely seen.

In style BD resembles the same architect's American Academy of Arts and Sciences in Cambridge, Mass. Oddly enough,
the program for each building contained, in nearly the same language, a proviso that the building should not reflect the architectural tastes of any one moment in time. Sketches of the

academy, on KMW's office wall, influenced the client's choice
of this architect.

"I knew right away when I saw the sketches that that was
exactly what we wanted," Nolen remembers. "The academy was
a working environment for knowledge workers. It was expressive of values that are attractive to people who work with their
minds. It had a university rather than an industrial atmosphere."

Both buildings are strongly influenced by the arts and crafts
movement, with its message of human scale and hand workmanship as well as its vague, comfortable air of Edwardian clubbi-
ness. Especially evident at BD are the influence of Mackintosh
and Wright, with hints perhaps of Aalto, Asplund, Scarpa. "Early
on," recalls Nolen, "I bought the architects a Greene and Greene
T-shirt."

But there's also that Tuscan look, emphasized by arches,
arcades, and hip roofs. Even the parking garage has an applied
false front of Tuscan towers and arcades. Why a Tuscan villa is
the right embodiment for the headquarters of a manufacturer

of medical equipment, on a site in the Jersey woods, is a reasonable question. Aside from their simple love of Tuscany, both the architect and the enormously sophisticated client seem to have been searching for an image that would retain some of the aristocratic dignity of the corporate deer-park tradition but that would suggest a much looser organization and a much closer working relationship to the land. Michael McKinnell, AIA, compares the parking garage, for instance, to the farm outbuildings of Palladio—prosaic, in both cases, and incorporated without fuss into a total building-land composition. If BD has a flaw, however, it is that the architect perhaps veered a little too close to the picturesque and the scenographic in the use of this kind of imagery. The arch at the entrance jars a little, and the garage's false front seems slightly overdone—"the slipcover," as Nolen irreverently calls it.

As you approach BD across the courtyard, the front door is easily found but doesn't leap out at you. That fact is the first indication of the building's lack of conventional hierarchy or authority. Says McKinnell, "The client told us, 'we're not on a power trip.' So we tried to achieve something more episodic than the usual headquarters, something that would pose choices and would be more interesting for the daily user."

Thus the building tends to reveal itself slowly, unrolling or unraveling gradually to your perceptions. This is true on the exterior, where BD is not a unity but presents itself in separate chunks. It's also true inside, where there is no impressive lobby or grand spine or any other obvious organizing principle. This is a building you have to explore over time. The exploration offers joys and surprises—for example, in the sudden long views that open up through skylighted atria or out into the landscape.

The typical exterior facade is among the triumphs of BD. There are three stories, and usually all are devoted to essentially the same office uses. But the exterior in no way expresses this plain fact. Instead of looking like a package of uniform cubage, it is a careful fiction that humanizes the building and relates it to the site. The ground-floor windows look like French doors, as if

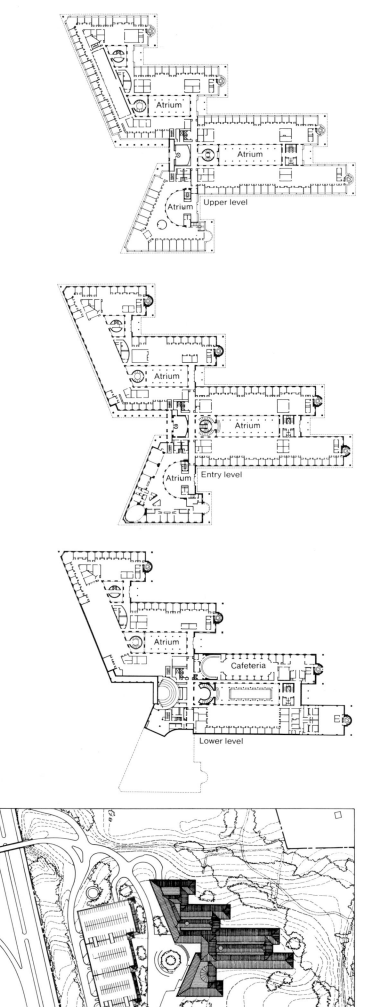

At dusk, the warm-toned hues of the Tuscanlike building.

they could be thrown open to the outside from spacious interior reception rooms (most really don't open at all and have ordinary offices behind them). The middle floor has square windows. The top floor, deeply shaded by an overhanging eave, is continuously glazed, as if it were a single gallery or studio space. All the windows have green mullions that relate them to the scale of a human face. The result is a very handsome facade that offers the executives inside a variety of window conditions.

If the message of the windows is that office workers are not interchangeable digits but human beings and that their workplace is not a human filing cabinet but a house, the same message is proclaimed in the space layouts inside. As far as possible, BD's interiors do not consist of large, subdivided space, where people must work within a labyrinth of little partitions. Instead, the interior is divided into rooms—rooms with high coffered ceilings and, because of the building's 56-foot typical span, a generous,

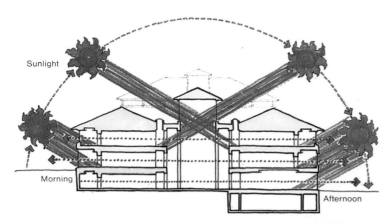

Sunlight

Morning

Afternoon

Below, the large atrium's centerpiece is a flower-water garden shaped like an excavated quarry. Above, the executive wing lobby with its mushroom column and sunburst wood skylight.

open feeling. Few places in the building lack a view of daylight either through windows or bouncing off the walls of the atria.

The high point of BD is surely the two interior atria, both designed in collaboration with sculptor Michael Singer. In the larger atrium, the floor is a water garden that Singer has shaped into an excavated quarry from which the materials for the building are perhaps being extracted—but with a strong suggestion, too, of an archaeological dig, as if we were uncovering the ruins of the building. Photographs don't begin to do justice to this atrium and its floor-garden sculpture. It is a magically silent and serene place that poignantly relates the building to the means of its making and its eventual unmaking.

All of Kallmann, McKinnell & Wood's work has explored the theme of the tragic side of architecture, the conflict between the proud built artifact and the slow eroding processes of time. Nature chews into one corner of the American Academy of Arts and Sciences, and Boston City Hall resembles the surviving ruin of itself. The large atrium at Becton, Dickinson is another mov-

Arcade encourages an interchange with the natural surroundings.

ing expression of the same theme. A smaller atrium, almost equally eloquent, contains another Singer sculpture with a quarry cart and piles of cut stone and wood.

Art is present elsewhere, indeed everywhere, at BD. Environmental artist Richard Fleischner was given the cafeteria terrace to design. Fleischner planted a long, straight row of birches, visible through the cafeteria windows. The birches begin on the terrace and penetrate several hundred feet into the woods, where they gradually peter out. They state Fleischner's theme, which is an exploration of the difference between the formed and the natural and all the stages in between—a theme that becomes a device for relating the architecture to the landscape. Fleischner also paved the terrace, placed benches in it, and planted yarrow and sumac. A "green room," an 80x80-foot, geometric clearing in the woods, was planned as a sort of negative image of the interior atria, but it was cut because of budget limits.

Much of the pleasure of BD lies not in its big ideas but in the simple delight of its detail. Kallmann, McKinnell & Wood has never before done a building so fully realized.

Among its joys are the eloquent freestanding corner columns at the exterior; the crisp red trusses that span the atria; the spatially rich, cylindrical stair towers of the atria, which frame views and incidentally serve as the building's shear walls; the forestlike eaves with their wood brackets; the granite base with its trim of bull-nose brick; the braced metal railings around the atria, hinting, perhaps, at Mackintosh's windows for the Glasgow Art School; the sunburst wood skylight, atop a mushroom column, in the lobby of the executive wing; the handsomely tiled servery in the cafeteria, a room rather than a production line; the very turn-of-the-century, arts-and-crafts cafeteria.

Becton, Dickinson is a design that repays your attention at every scale, from the landscape down to the brick. It proposes a healthy and modest attitude toward the design of the rural corporate headquarters as a building type. □

Encore Delivered with Strength and Delicacy

Cooper Chapel, Arkansas, Fay Jones & Maurice Jennings.
By Karen Cordes

In a variation on his Thorncrown theme, E. Fay Jones, FAIA, has touched the Ozarks once again, this time in the small retirement community of Bella Vista, Ark. Conceived by Bella Vista developer John Cooper Sr. in memory of his wife, the Mildred B. Cooper Memorial Chapel is a gift from her children to the 7,000 townspeople.

Cooper Chapel quietly commands a dignity and presence uncommon among buildings of our era. It is a harmonious celebration of strength and delicacy, owing much to its predecessor, Jones's celebrated Thorncrown Chapel in Eureka Springs, Ark. Both chapels have a power that stems from an expression of the nature of the materials, and their grace is found in a translation of Gothic architecture capturing the emotions of that age of faith. Like Thorncrown, Cooper Chapel employs what Jones and his partner, Maurice Jennings, AIA, refer to as Gothic's "operative opposite," which reverses the structural system to use members in tension rather than members in compression. This reversal is derived from the materials themselves, exchanging the medieval masses of stone for today's lighter materials. And it is here that Cooper Chapel departs from its predecessor.

Left, front elevation. Right, lighting is from floor fixtures along perimeter.

In Cooper Chapel wood and glass are combined with a third material—steel—allowing Jones to design with an expression natural to it: the curve. This simple form relays a gentle flow quite unlike the crispness in Thorncrown's straight wood members, strengthening the allusion to the Gothic. Says John G. Williams, FAIA, founder of the school of architecture at the University of Arkansas and a close friend of Jones: "People ask me which I like better, Thorncrown or Cooper. I ask them, 'Which is more beautiful, a straight line or a curved line?' Both are beautiful."

Protected by a wooded hill, Cooper Chapel is undetectable from the Interstate highway and shopping center only a few hundred yards away. The path to the chapel lies along the slope of the hill; the walk is dotted with intricate foot lamps that hint the building's presence. As you round a curve and the cars and noise fade, the chapel appears.

Its delicacy is striking. The wood frame is pierced by a large entry arch and a circular opening reminiscent of a rose window. Through these openings the curves of the steel structure appear against the wooded backdrop. The curves intersect one another high overhead, forming a lacework of members into a series of pointed arches. As each member extends toward the ground, only the outermost pieces reach the flagstone floor. The remaining are suspended in the air, ending with a curved slice. The entire structure supports a roof with a long central skylight and

Left, lights border the approach path. Above right, front door is recessed two bays. Below right, view toward pulpit.

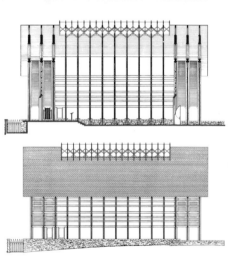

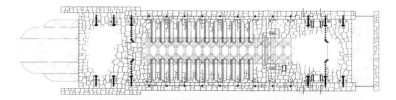

large overhangs, giving the steel network light and shadow to play in and against. The wood frame joins with the outermost steel members, resting on the low stone walls that border the flagstone floor. Wood members give form to the building; the steel structure supports it.

The chapel speaks simultaneously of enclosure and openness, bringing the outside in while at the same time making a place within the woods. Jones spaced the columns six feet apart, combining the wood and steel pieces to minimize their presence. This maximizes the meeting of the interior and exterior, making one an essential part of the other. The close relationship of chapel and nature becomes most apparent through time and season, as daylight continually changes the patterns made by the steel structure and the seasons create a range of enclosures.

The mechanical system consists of outside units with the ductwork enclosed in each of the two low walls running the length of the building. Vent openings are actually holes within the mortar, surrounded by the moss and lichen that still grow on the rocks. Pews, doors, and other wood trim are oak; structure is redwood. Oak and redwood are stained to blend with the bronze finish of the steel. The red pew cushions and the colors in the flagstone harmonize with the bronze, creating a warm tone for the chapel.

Set like a dark jewel in a deep setting, Cooper Chapel is a place of splendid solitude. □

Above, note patterns in skylight; apparent second skylight is reflection in side wall glazing. Left, cross motif in perimeter lighting. Right, the effect of stained glass.

1989

IBM Regional Headquarters

Hynes Convention Center

The Walker Art Center Sculpture Garden

Australian Parliament House

IBM's Colorful 'Place in the Sun'

In Westlake, Tex., Legorreta Arquitectos. Mitchell/Giurgola. By David Dillon

W estlake doesn't show up on many Texas maps, and its neighbor Southlake appears only as a speck on the fringe of Dallas/Fort Worth Airport. Together they have a population of 3,500, enough to support a Dairy Queen, a Circle E convenience store, and the Flying Burrito restaurant.

But this pastoral tranquility is disappearing as IBM relocates its regional headquarters to the area. Two thousand employees already have made the move, with another 2,000 to follow in the next few months. Nearly 2 million square feet of space have been completed. Within 10 years this 900-acre swatch of rolling north Texas prairie is expected to contain a dozen corporate headquarters, mainly electronics and communications firms that are considered the salvation of Texas's depressed and chemically dependent economy. As many as 20,000 people eventually may work and live in Westlake and Southlake, making a city where only farms and pastures existed before.

IBM Westlake—now rhapsodically renamed Solana or "place in the sun"—is the latest satellite city to go into orbit around Dallas and Fort Worth, taking its place in the regional galaxy next to Las Colinas, the Galleria, and the Dallas Parkway corridor. Although not the largest of these new urban centers, it is arguably the most thoughtful and instructive.

Above, overview shows integration of roads and buildings. Left, the Marketing Center, a multi-jointed building.

From a distance, Solana is only a magenta pylon and a cadmium-yellow column poking above the tree line on either side of State Highway 114. Southlake residents once threatened to sue IBM over these colors, claiming that they were loud and un-Texas. And they were right. The colors are loud and Mexican and were introduced by architect Ricardo Legorreta, Hon. FAIA, to give Solana a distinctive psychedelic presence on the rural horizon.

"I wanted to make color part of the entire design, not something added on," Legorreta explained. "Instead of saying I will make a wall and paint it red, I said I will make something red and it will be a wall."

But bold color is only one of the things that sets Solana apart from other corporate campuses in the region. The Texas Highway Department, in a rare burst of inspiration, permitted Legorreta to design the bridges and underpasses leading to and from the project. So, instead of taking another nondescript off-ramp, with a traffic island and a stop sign, visitors exit Highway 114 into a dramatic outdoor room, complete with plazas, foun-

tains, and tall, slender obelisks. The adjacent berms and slopes, planted with fruit trees, are like miniature orchards that mediate between the raw prairie and the artful parterres around the individual office buildings. Legorreta also placed two red stucco walls parallel to the overpass, further evidence that this is a gateway rather than simply a freeway interchange.

Those who drive to the Westlake side of the project find another surprise: two long, low parking garages, with arcades and double rows of trees, that create a baroque forecourt for the office complex. Seventy-five percent of the parking at Solana is covered; this is an unusually high ratio for a suburban development. Equally impressive is that the parking garages have been used to make public spaces instead of being appended crudely to the backs of buildings. Here the UPS driver feels he has arrived at Vaux le Vicomte.

Freeway interchanges and parking garages, though not the main attractions at Solana, demonstrate how meticulously the entire project has been planned. It is not a typical suburban scattering of discrete buildings on individual sites but rather a series of precincts or rooms in which the automobile has been accommodated and also tamed. There are edges, boundaries, and hierarchies. Roads keep to the high ground, with the buildings set

Photographs © Richard Payne, AIA

in low areas against a background of trees and rolling hills.

Solana is a joint venture of IBM and Maguire Thomas Partners. Maguire Thomas hired Legorreta Arquitectos to design the IBM complex in Southlake, as well as the hotel, shops, and office buildings that make up the Village Center across Highway 114. Mitchell/Giurgola designed the Westlake campus, which consists of six five-story office buildings, two parking garages, a cafeteria building, and a computer center. Landscaping for the entire 900-acre site was done by Peter Walker/Martha Schwartz, while the master plan was the responsibility of Barton Meyers, AIA, in consort with all the other key participants.

Assembling so many stars on one team could have been a disaster, like George Steinbrenner's grand designs for the New York Yankees. Yet one of the pleasures of Solana is how well the individual pieces work together. Whatever the stylistic differences, they reflect common objectives and a shared point of view.

Everyone agreed at the outset that the site was the most important element, not simply because it had a history and an identity that were worth preserving. The challenge was to put buildings in the place yet to allow the place to shine through. Consequently the architects agreed to build only on 10 percent of the land, leaving the remainder as fields, meadows, and woods. One hun-

Facing page above, the Village Center, patterned after a plaza in a small Mexican town; below, entrance axis of the IBM office complex. Above, cross axis of the same complex, showing interior courtyard with pools and pergola.

dred fifty acres have been replanted with the wildflowers and prairie grasses that once flourished there. Buildings have been kept below the tree line—roughly five stories—so that they always are seen across a landscape. In form and materials they are South-western, though without the usual postcard clichés. Connecting these far-flung pieces is a network of lakes, streams, ponds, and pathways that represents an architectural stylization of the natural features of the site. Within these general guidelines the architects were free to do as they wished.

The most distinctive single building at Solana is Legorreta's Marketing and Technical Support Center, a low, multijointed structure with large stucco walls, small mullionless windows, and five interior courtyards. CEOs from around the world gather here to inspect IBM's most sophisticated new products. The center was intended to be a compound, a place apart, and Legorreta responded by turning the building in on itself.

Visitors enter the Marketing Center through a tall vaulted room,

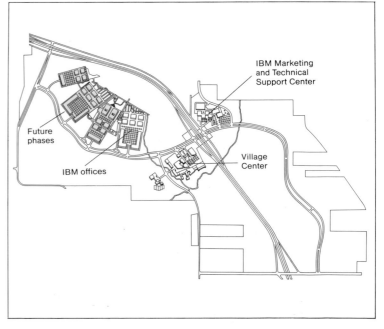

painted blue, with a slatted arched window at one end and a spartan reception desk at the other. It is Giotto's chapel updated for the computer age, ideal for putting customers in a receptive frame of mind.

Beyond are the numerous offices and conference rooms where IBM's latest modems and mainframes are given their whizz-bang presentations. Here the interiors—by PHH Neville Lewis—are nearly as spare as in the vestibule chapel: white walls, Mexican tile floors, oak trim, and a few latia ceilings, like those in Legoretta's resort hotels.

But the real interior decoration is the gardens, designed by Legorreta and Walker/Schwartz. They give the building a clarity and openness belied by its stolid stucco exterior. The main entry courtyard, with its cedar trees, misting fountain, and magenta sunscreen, is an intense contrast to the cool, dark, barrel-vaulted lobby. Another courtyard, clearly inspired by Luis Barragán, consists of willow trees and a series of narrow, rectangular reflecting pools. A third is a spare gravel space with benches around the edges and a few small trees. Here is an interior world of crisp geometry and carefully framed views that manages to be restful rather than manipulative. After an hour in these green spaces, any sales pitch becomes bearable.

Above, Legorreta's long entrance to the Marketing Center. Facing page, above and below right, vaulted Marketing Center lobby, moodily lit from small windows; below left, grand stairway leads from this vaulted room up to offices on second floor.

The Village Center is intended to be an intimate and informal counterpart to the corporate preserve, the small town at the edge of the army base. Instead of Cancun and Barragán, Legorreta borrowed from the markets and plazas of small Mexican towns. So far, the Village Center consists of restaurants and retail spaces opening onto a paved courtyard with fountains, trees in large clay pots, and a soaring (and enigmatic) fuscia pylon that could be a commercial version of a Mayan stela. Opposite the plaza are two spec office buildings by Legorreta—architecturally the weakest parts of the development—and the beginnings of a 300-room hotel. If Solana is to have a civic realm, the Village Center is it.

Compared with Legorreta's underplayed vernacular designs, Mitchell/Giurgola's Westlake complex appears formal, rigid, almost classical, with buildings arranged foursquare on a neat rectangular grid. Romaldo Giurgola, FAIA, has continued the Southwestern theme by cladding most of the buildings in red

or tan stucco, yet the general feeling is of another place, suggesting at times the firm's Volvo headquarters in Sweden. In keeping with the master plan, Giurgola distributed the 900,000 square feet of office space among six identical buildings, each five stories tall and tucked into a natural hollow on the site. And, whereas the Marketing Center turns inward toward gardens and courtyards, Mitchell/Giurgola's buildings turn outward toward the landscape. Arcades run along the base of the buildings, while on the upper floors the perimeter is a wide corridor that gives everyone a view of the surrounding woods and prairies. The space between the buildings is a long symmetrical courtyard with trellises and reflecting pools, like a formal garden in a country estate. The one splash of traditional corporate high design occurs in the cafeteria building, one end of which is clad in polished gray granite and features a grand stairway that comes straight from the Volvo headquarters. The idea here seems to be that, because in a remote place like Solana lunch becomes a major social event, employees should have an elegant place in which to eat it. Nice thought, but somewhat schizophrenic as a design. The other cafeteria interiors—by CRS Sirrine—carry on the low-key Southwestern motif to more pleasing effect.

Weaving around and through the entire project are the paths,

Above, purple pylon and fountains at Village Center. Right, one of the entry fountains at the Marketing Center.

ponds, streams, and parterres shaped by Walker/Schwartz. It will be years before this work can be fully appreciated, yet already it has set the tone for Solana by showing how large buildings can be set in a landscape without obliterating it. The obvious development pitfalls—ubiquitous parking lots, overscaled buildings, gratuitous diversity—have been avoided. There is order at Solana but also diversity in the form of hills, lakes, boulevards, hiking trails, public spaces, and private retreats.

The real test for Solana will come a few years from now, when the second generation of corporate tenants arrives and decides it wants to tweak the original master plan. Build a little taller, perhaps, or creep a bit closer to the highway for better exposure. Many good plans have crumbled under this kind of assault. Maguire Thomas says it won't cave in. "We are under no pressure to start a helter-skelter development," says managing partner Robert Maguire, "and we won't do it. We won't lose control."

Phase I of Solana is so good, so filled with lessons for other developers of the new American landscape, that one can only hope that Maguire is a man of his word. □

Boston's 'Best New Piece of Public Architecture'

Hynes Convention Center,
Kallmann, McKinnell & Wood.
By Robert Campbell, AIA

A convention center that is neither a huge cube of black mirror glass, nor a vast block of concrete, nor yet a gift box wrapped in bright high-tech frippery, nor an underground concourse with a park on top—can such a building be conceived?

Conceived it has been, and not only conceived, but built. The new John B. Hynes Veterans Memorial Convention Center—to give it its full, ludicrous, all-things-to-all-constituencies name—differs from other major American convention centers in that it appears to be a place intended for human habitation rather than a fish warehouse or bird sanctuary or bus garage or high-security bomb factory. The Hynes is clearly a real building, with a roof and a base and floors and windows, with recognizable parts and materials and an attitude to the street and even a front door.

But it's far more than that, although that alone would have been a unique achievement for this forlorn building type. The Hynes is the the best new piece of public architecture in Boston, one of the few buildings of our own time that can be at least mentioned in the same breath with the masterpieces of a century ago, with the Boston Public Library or Trinity Church.

The architect, Kallmann, McKinnell & Wood, faced a daunting problem. Most convention centers, everywhere in the United States, are nothing but walled containers. The convention center is not a building type that suggests rich possibilities for architectural expression. All the life takes place deep inside, in deliberately windowless showrooms and lecture halls.

How can such a building be made *public?* How can it open itself, with sociable trust, to the life of the street and the city? How can we, standing across the street and looking at it, be encouraged to fantasize ourselves inside and thus begin the crucial act of interacting imaginatively with the architecture?

The architects have solved this essential problem by bringing the human part of their building—the lobbies and corridors where

Right, Hynes Center seen through a Back Bay street. Below, the remodeled box is at left and part of the addition at right.

conventioneers walk, meet, and party—out to the street front of the building. Luckily this is a north-facing facade that can accept generous windows. Some of the windows even have curtains. So far from being a blank wall, the entire major street frontage of the Hynes, on all three floors, is a row of windows, windows that connect the life inside the building to the life outside in the street.

Somehow, KMW persuaded the client, the Massachusetts Convention Center Authority, to fund another essential of good public architecture: wasteful, inefficient interior space. All those lobbies and corridors are big enough to function as great public living rooms. This is especially true at the top level, the third, where the lobby along Boylston Street is a stunning public gallery, two stories high and a city block long, vaulted at the ceiling, flooded with light, and opening to a view over the roofs of the Back Bay with the Charles River and Cambridge beyond. This gallery is one of the great rooms of Boston of any period. Part of its impact derives from the fact that it has been carefully prepared for. As you rise through the Hynes on its various stairs and escalators—rising toward this gallery—you are always moving up from darker and smaller spaces into brighter and larger ones, until you reach the top and emerge, as a climax, into the explosion of space and light that is this superb gallery.

There are many more things to praise about the new Hynes. Not the least is its success in completely hiding the old Hynes. For the Hynes of today is not an entirely new building, although you can't tell that either inside or out. A hideous old blockhouse, the former Hynes still exists, completely renovated, inside the new. What the architects have done is to wrap the old building on two sides with the new one, which contains a great variety of meeting rooms and auditoriums that cater to the newer kind of convention crowd, more interested in holding a symposium than in staring at boats or tractors. The old contains, as it always did, big loft spaces for product displays.

The Hynes is unique in one other way as well. Instead of being sited out on the Interstate or in a downtown neighborhood of wholesalers, it stands on a street in one of Boston's best residential and shopping neighborhoods, the Back Bay. The Back Bay has its public monuments—the library, hotels, churches, clubs—but it has no other public building of the size of the Hynes. KMW has succeeded, or at least has come amazingly close to succeeding, in giving its building the rhythm and texture of the traditional Back Bay block without at all compromising its proper grandeur as a major civic institution. The Hynes is a very big thing in a neighborhood—or on the edge of one, at least—that is made up generally of much smaller things. Yet the Hynes is respectful in every way that it could be without abandoning its public character. The granite of its exterior matches the granite of the Boston Public Library a few blocks down Boylston. The spacing of its columns and windows matches the rhythm of housefronts. Its height matches closely the heights of older buildings across the street, including the Tennis and Racquet Club, which KMW renovated and in which the firm now has its own offices.

Things would be better if the ground floor along the Boylston sidewalk could have been lined with commerce instead of, as it is, by a relatively useless arcade. But the owner didn't want shops. In their absence, the arcade is a device for giving the building an articulated base and a sense of transparency along the sidewalk. It also is an extraordinary urban space in its own right.

Much has been written in recent years about the importance of the "street wall" in traditional cities. KMW has interpreted that concept in an amazingly literal way. The architects have conceived of the Boylston Street facade as one long wall, pierced but never violated by rhythmic windows and by the openings of the ground-floor arcade. Even at the main entrance, the continuity of the street wall isn't ruptured. Instead, the entire facade,

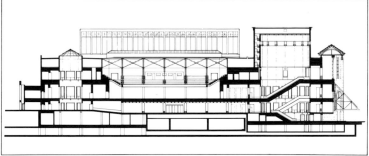

Top, the Boylston Street gallery that fronts the 'hideous old blockhouse' of the original convention center, now refaced. Far left, the consecration of Episcopal Bishop Barbara Harris in the convention center last February. Left, a corridor etched in red.

© Peter Vanderwarker Photographs

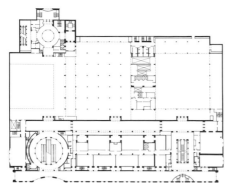

Second level

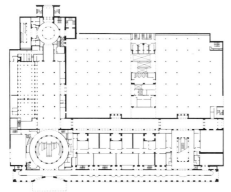

Plaza level

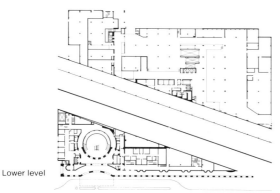

Lower level

unbroken, cups back in a welcoming curve, while an enormously bold glass canopy juts forward to signal the entrance. The balance here, between continuous wall and invading entrance, is exquisitely kept. In the larger cityscape, the Hynes's entrance terminates an important vista up Gloucester Street from the residential Back Bay. That vista is made absolutely wonderful by the delicacy with which KMW has placed its bold entrance just enough off the axis of the street to emphasize the primacy of the street grid over the monumentality of any single building.

The wallishness of the Hynes reminds you that the houses on nearby Commonwealth Avenue also line up to make block-long walls—walls that shape the space of the street into a great outdoor corridor. The Hynes has restored a similar feeling of streetspace to this long-fragmented end of Boylston Street.

On the facade itself, the architects have played a conscious and rather sophisticated game of trying to relate the new Boston to the old. At the sidewalk, the Hynes begins with a traditional material—granite—cut into shapes that recall, in a diagrammatic way, the details of the buildings of Boston past. But, as your eye moves up the facade, strange things happen. The warm-toned granite gives way more and more to steel and glass, materials more expressive of our own time. At the top, simple blue-black steel plate girders, like those of a bridge, span the window tops and support the roof. It's as if the Hynes's granite skin were being progressively peeled back to expose the steel skeleton of which the building is actually made. This pseudonarrative gives the facade a lot of interest and gives the architects the chance to play with more than one material. And it helps create the clear bottom, middle, and top. The effect is truly elegant.

Viewed from the street, the facade dramatically expresses what's going on inside. The tall third-floor windows tell us there must be a grand piano nobile inside, like the ballroom floor of a palace or the upper-floor reading room of the Boston Public Library. The windows don't lie: behind them is the great public gallery.

One thing you don't notice about the Hynes is the fact that much of its ground floor is mere headroom for the Massachusetts Turnpike, an Interstate highway that barrels at an angle through the entire length of the building. You don't notice that because, as soon as you enter, you are whisked up a rapid escalator while your attention is distracted by extraordinary interior space.

This, the center of circulation, is a mighty drum, a great vertical cylindrical room that rises the full height of the building and pokes up through the roof. Escalators rise in its middle, and stairs climb its curved walls. Architects will quickly recognize, as one source, the classic Stockholm Public Library by Gunnar Asplund, where the drum houses the lending room as well as stairs. At the Hynes, the cylinder form does many things. On the exterior it makes a round foil for the long, flat street wall. Inside it makes the circulation memorable and thus organizes your perception of the whole interior. You are always emerging from and returning to the drum as you move about the building. From it, you can see straight through the building to the rear door where the Hynes opens onto the plazas of the Prudential Center complex—plazas that connect, over bridges, with two convention hotels and a shopping mall. From the drum, too, you can look down the long Boylston Street galleries at all three levels. You can see out to the streets of the city at each landing. Unlike so many convention centers, the Hynes is never a maze, never disorienting. You always know where you are in the building and where the building is in the city.

The next thing you probably notice after the drum is the quality of materials. Where else can you find a convention center whose floors are surfaced not in bland terrazzo but in patterned inlaid granite of different colors? Where else do ordinary meeting rooms have coved or vaulted ceilings, so that they will feel like complete, self-contained rooms instead of like mere segments of some endless space that has been arbitrarily partitioned off?

Left, inside the circulation drum. Right, vaulted ballrooms that can be used separately or as one great luminous space.

315

A few questionable things also should be noted. Some of the circulation areas, especially on the lower levels, are perhaps a little too dark. Wide wooden benches in the great galleries are elegant but seem overwrought in shape and uncomfortable in use. There's a lot of hidden pochet area in the plan, which serves well to create a sense of depth at room entrances but which might also perhaps have been put to some practical use.

Besides the top-floor gallery, several other interior spaces are remarkable. A trio of vaulted ballrooms can be used separately or thrown together as one big room. Either way, they feel complete and beautiful. The transverse hall on the third floor, which serves these ballrooms as circulation and reception area, is astonishing. Its walls are bright red, and down both of its sides huge blank dark doors (many of them false panels) seem to march. The effect recalls some of the grim Valhalla interiors by the German painter Anselm Kiefer.

This red room reminds us of a certain angst that has persisted in the work of this remarkable team of architects ever since its extraordinary debut in 1962 with the competition-winning design for Boston City Hall. Kallmann-McKinnell buildings are always far more than accommodations of the client's program. Like good poems, they offer a dense compaction of possible readings and metaphors. They also derive from an amazing range of sources. They are eclectic in inspiration but never in expression, because the sources are always digested, abstracted, and transformed.

Despite the eclecticism, one theme does continue throughout the firm's career. This is the tension between survival and decay, between the temporal assertions of humanity and the timeless processes of nature. At KMW's American Academy of Arts and Sciences, the landscape chews into the architecture at one corner, presaging an eventual reversion to nature. At the firm's fine Becton-Dickinson headquarters in New Jersey, an atrium floorpiece—a collaboration between the architects and artist Michael Singer—takes the form of an excavation that seems to contain building materials but also mysterious artifacts. It is at once the fresh breaking of earth for the new and an archeological digging up of the old, and it relates the building to the process of its making and its eventual unmaking.

The Hynes has that metaphoric richness. The red third-floor hall, suggesting the set for a dramatization of the Masque of the Red Death, is part of it, but so is the more hopeful movement of rising up through the building from darkness into light. The great drum reminds us of Asplund, but also of Stirling in Stuttgart. Though KMW's work always seems tectonic and fully built, as opposed to pictorial or narrative, it is amazingly rich in ghostly messages, references, metaphors, and demarcations.

With the completion of the Hynes, KMW has created more significant public architecture in Boston than any other architect or firm since Charles Follen McKim. KMW has emerged as a sort of designated civic architect. It seems likely, too, that the firm, long saddled with its reputation as designer of the now hopelessly unfashionable (though still powerful) Boston City Hall of 1968, is about to re-emerge into the consciousness of the profession and of architectural schools and historians in the United States. Hynes is in many ways the best and most interesting of recent Boston works of architecture and deserves that kind of attention.

Perhaps the Hynes presages something else: an era in which Americans again will be ready to spend as much money on the public realm as on our private worlds. Perhaps Bostonians are once again realizing that a wonderful private world—a great car, house, stereo, art collection, whatever—means little unless there's a great public realm to walk out into. It was just such thinking that created, a century ago, the public streets and squares of the original Back Bay. The Hynes is a fitting addition to that great piece of urbanism. □

This page, from top: skylight entices visitors up to light-filled gallery; view into meeting room from Boylston Gallery looking across the granite-tiled floor anteroom; the stark and sleek 'mighty drum' of the full-building-height rotunda. Facing page, top floor of stairway that wraps around the rotunda.

Design Clarity and Urban Synthesis

The Walker Art Center sculpture garden, Minneapolis. By Barbara Koerble

If clarity has become a byword for the design approach of Edward Larrabee Barnes, FAIA, his plan for the new Minneapolis Sculpture Garden also represents a notable synthesis. Barnes's design draws the envelopes of space within the Walker Art Center outside, where modern sculpture can play against the strong classical foil of his garden plan.

The 7.5-acre sculpture garden is one of the largest urban sculpture centers in the nation. A joint project of the Walker Art Center and the Minneapolis Park and Recreation Board, it will also feature year-round horticultural displays in the new Sage and John Cowles Conservatory, located on the grounds and designed by Barnes's partner, Alistair Bevington. The sculpture garden was designed by the Barnes firm in association with landscape architect Peter Rothschild of Quennell Rothschild Associates; the conservatory's Regis Gardens are by Barbara Stauffacher Solomon and Michael Van Valkenburgh.

In many ways, the Walker Art Center finds itself at the vanguard. Programmatically, under the leadership of Martin Friedman, it has established a national reputation as a leading center for the study of the most avant-garde developments in contemporary art. Physically, the museum nestles comfortably against a residential backdrop to the west, sharing its site and a central lobby with the Guthrie Theater. Yet to the east it confronts 16

lanes of high-speed freeway traffic that sever it from downtown Minneapolis and the city's Loring Park.

But the Walker seems to have a knack for turning liabilities into assets. Barnes's memorable 1971 design, with its vertical progression of boxlike galleries, was necessitated by the many physical constraints of a difficult site. His plan also reflected Friedman's strong interest in contemporary sculpture. To provide more space for large works, Barnes designed the rooftops as sculpture terraces, continuing the helical procession from indoors to outdoors. His 1984 addition to the Walker extended its central helix by burrowing underground, creating more sculpture terraces around the base of the building.

Despite the Walker's special accommodation of sculpture, the underutilized park across the street irresistibly beckoned to Friedman. He and David Fisher, superintendent of the park board, saw creation of the new garden as an opportunity to repair the physical rift between the museum and Loring Park caused by Interstate 94. Rather than building yet another generic Minneapolis skybridge to join the two, the Walker commissioned artist Siah Armajani to design a pedestrian crossing. His 375-foot-long footbridge spans the yawning freeway chasm with an inverted pair of catenary arches, gaily painted pale blue and yellow. Minneapolis's necklace of parks and lakes is unparalleled as a local

amenity, and the Irene Hixon Whitney Bridge re-integrates the sculpture park as a link in this verdant chain.

Barnes suggests that "the big thing this design is doing is suddenly linking the Walker-Guthrie entrance in a city plan." Indeed, as one crosses over the bridge from Loring Park, the sculpture garden is seen as a grand new foreground for the Walker and Guthrie Theater complex.

The garden plan is classically simple, symmetrical, and commodious as a setting for sculpture. The central *parti* is a cross-axis that establishes four equal courts. These are balanced to the south by the blocks of the Walker and the Guthrie Theater and to the north by an open, rectangular meadow.

The axes are wide allées of compacted crushed limestone, lined with linden trees. Long, unimpeded vistas are the signature of the design, unifying the heroic scale of the site. The east-west allée is terminated on the west by the new conservatory and on the east by an apse that forms a classical sculpture niche.

Because of the block's isolation, it was obvious to Barnes that a strong site plan was needed to unite the garden with the museum and theater across the street. The formal garden plan resulted not so much from a desire for symmetry as from, as Barnes relates, the need for "something to rivet the axis of the lobby." So the strong north-south axis was drawn perpendicular to the Walker-Guthrie blocks. "Once you have a line like that, you find yourself into the whole system of axial planning. And I felt the need of a strong axis and a strong connection to cross on that line."

The heart of the sculpture garden plan is the four 100-foot-square grass courtyards, each framed by double-walled stone planters containing arborvitae. These plantings are still immature but in a few years' time will be clipped to resemble the crisp box hedges that outline traditional European parterre gardens.

Facing page, the conservatory and portion of the courtyards. Above, sculptures: 'Spoonbridge and Cherry' by Claes Oldenburg and Coosje van Bruggen (top) and Richard Stankiewicz's 'Grass.'

Seventeenth-century illustrations of the gardens of the Villa Medici present a striking parallel to the Walker's garden plan, particularly in its combination of box parterres with long rows of trees along the allées.

Barnes recalls that during his morning jogs through the Boboli Gardens in Florence he was struck by how "the different rooms in these gardens are completely cut off from each other by the height of the hedges. So I came back and talked to Martin about making rooms, and putting in the trees, so that in 10 years they would be really private rooms." To achieve this privacy, the arborvitae hedges surrounding the grass courts may be allowed to grow to a height of 15 feet.

Barnes stresses that it will take time for the plantings to "settle in" and for the powerful architectural form of the foliage to be fully realized. He anticipates that the garden will, in maturity, be a mysterious place, shadowy and romantic.

European parterre gardens were often completely enclosed, containing decorative plantings and patterns to be admired from outside the garden. Barnes instead created unembellished outdoor galleries to walk through. In this way, the minimal architecture of the Walker extends itself into the garden. The analogy to the Walker design is continued in the carefully planned openings in the court's hedges to frame views of sculptures within, an effect not unlike Barnes's placement of wide doorways between the Walker's galleries to give glimpses of the next floor. Noting the deliberate break Barnes made with the Olmsted-style naturalism of other Minneapolis parks, Friedman describes their shared goal of a "museum character" for the sculpture garden:

Photographs © Richard Payne, AIA

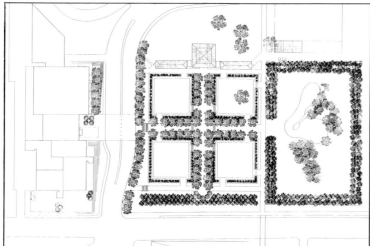

Hacker Books, Inc. New York 1979

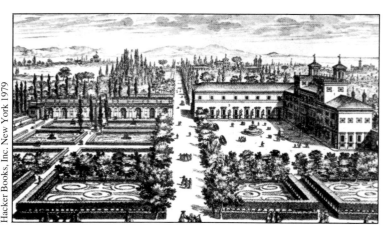

"There is an outside museum as well as an inside museum."

To provide this strong architectonic framework, Peter Rothschild selected trees such as the Glenleven Littleleaf linden, which would lend themselves to pruning. Rothschild and associate Claudia Thornton obtained no fewer than 875 arborvitae, 200 Black Hills spruce trees, and 70 linden trees. A constraint on the landscape architects was the stipulation that the garden have no floral displays, nothing to compete with the sculpture.

Extensive grading of the site was required to achieve the terracing of the courts, which step down to the north. The granite planters sharply define the grade. The same carnelian granite that paved the Walker's roof terraces is used for the garden's stairs and planter walls. In contrast to the predominantly European character of the garden, Rothschild found inspiration for the low stone walls in New England. The rustic effect of a split-faced stone appealed to him, as he explains, because "we were trying to create a marriage between what was very architectural and planned and a reality that was full of growing plants and grass and nature. The idea was to soften the effect of the walls by making them seem more like the kind of walls that a farmer in New England might have laid." The battered walls are self-supporting and laid with soil, not mortar, allowing for natural movement as the ground freezes and thaws.

The rectangular meadow at the garden's north end is defined

Facing page, the conservatory's facade opposite the gardens. This page, right, Gehry's fish sculpture is the centerpiece of the conservatory's main pavilion. Left, from top: Jackie Ferrara's 'Belvedere'; 'BLACKVAULTfalloffstone' by Peter Shelton; 'Prophecy of the Ancients' by Brower Hatcher. In drawings, left, Barnes's formal garden plan reflects 17th-century European designs; Medici Gardens above.

by double rows of Black Hills spruce trees. The focal point of this court is a colossal fountain sculpture, titled Spoonbridge and Cherry, by Claes Oldenburg and Coosje van Bruggen. Sited over an elongated pond, the sculpture slyly usurps the role of the traditional *isolotto* in Italian gardens. For Barnes, however, a key idea was to have water act as the terminus to the long view down the garden's central axis. "What can you put at the end of the vista any better than something that reflects the sky?" he says.

Barnes's partner Alistair Bevington's conservatory is a strong, yet exceptionally delicate, building. The most striking view of it is by night, as its softly glowing transparent volumes rise above the garden. Its spare elegance results from the strength of its cross-braced welded frame formed of six-inch-diameter structural steel tubing. Over this simple structure is laid a traditional light aluminum and clear glass greenhouse skin. The symmetry of the garden plan is reiterated in the conservatory's pair of low, 110-foot-long side wings that flank a 62-foot-high central pavilion. While the long houses are familiar greenhouse forms, the pavilion is an exercise in pure geometry, composed of elemental Barnesian prime forms.

The building's delicate appearance belies a heavy concrete foundation system with 80-foot-long piles, all necessitated by an unstable site. The land was a former lake bed, and, as the underlying layers of peat would compress under pressure, piles had to be driven down to bedrock. Bevington notes that much more of the building's weight is actually below ground than above.

The enormous expense of the foundation eclipsed earlier and more costly schemes for the greenhouse design. As it turned out, modesty is the virtue of the final plan. One early scheme featuring sheer side walls rising up into a counterpoint of shed roofs appeared too monumental, for both people outside and

plantings within. The reduced upper mass of the final pavilion design and the low eaves of its side wings keep it at a comfortably human scale. Bevington says, "We used a traditional form of glazing, and that rather conditioned the kind of house we got." Small details such as the lapped horizontal joints of the greenhouse skin give the building its charm and prevent it from being merely a cold, high-tech cage. A feature appreciated in the Minneapolis winter is an interior walkway through the building that keeps visitors warm on their way from a parking area west of the garden up to the Walker-Guthrie lobby.

Regarding their design for the conservatory's Regis Gardens, Michael Van Valkenburgh recalls that he and Barbara Solomon shared the idea of "repeating an element all the way down the long houses" and treating the central court as a stopping place. These repeated planar elements flank the through-axis that continues from the north entrance to the end of the south house. In the south house, Van Valkenburgh divided the interior with a series of hanging scrims that support a delicate tracery of clinging vines. Solomon's four topiary archways in the north wing amplify the formal link to the architectural character of the outdoor garden. Within the long houses are massed beds of intensely aromatic white gardenias and brilliant orange bird-of-paradise.

The most nontraditional of the glass enclosures, the tall house is conversely the setting for what Solomon calls "the classic palm court." The tranquil pool with water lilies encircled by palms could be a scene from a 19th-century winter garden. Yet what 19th-century glass house ever boasted Frank Gehry's Standing Glass Fish as a centerpiece? The translucent sculpture shimmers within a cage of palm tree trunks and the prismatic glass house. Solomon's comment that "the division between nature and art is invisible" sums up the design not only of the conservatory but of the sculpture garden as a whole. □

Giurgola in Canberra: Quiet Colossus

Avoiding anything overbearing. By Philip Drew

Being American is easier, somehow, than being Australian—at least, that is how many Australians see it. Americans seem to be intact, to have come out of the oven with a nice golden crust.

Australia, unlike America, remains something of a mystery. Any attempt to define it must seem like trying to spar around with a great shape. Eventually, you find yourself punching at clouds—it cannot be pinned down.

This, in part, was what faced Mitchell/Giurgola & Thorp when they decided to enter the international competition for the new Australian Parliament House at Canberra, 290 kilometers south of Sydney. Their design for a new complex to replace the temporary Parliament building that had been in use since May 1927 was unanimously and enthusiastically chosen from the second-stage submissions by the jury on June 26, 1980.

Seen from the lakeside, the newly completed Parliament House is much less imposing than might be expected. Beneath its green carapace of earth and lawn it is hidden from view except where the forecourt and silhouette of the great veranda push forward in front of Capital Hill. In front, between the new Parliament House and the lake, the old Parliament building, which has been retained, steals much of its thunder.

It is impossible to know what the Australian people expected of their new Parliament House, but one thing is apparent. It accords with the desire of many Australians to avoid anything overbearing or self-important. Australians are distrustful of bombast, ill at ease when confronted by formalism and pretention. In response, Romaldo Giurgola, FAIA, seems to have struck

the right note. If his building errs, it is in the direction of understatement.

Some buildings are outgoing, like some people. They come forward and inform you about themselves. The Parliament House is as elusive as its architect. Like the man, the building is quiet, inwardly reflective, and modest. At the same time, it infuriates because it is so self-contained and, in so many regards, inaccessible, if not evasive—a building far more complex than its appealing simplicity of plan suggests, whose meaning is not without contradictions.

From some angles, the new complex recalls the Cretan citadel of Mycenae. The landform is primary, as Australians perceive their identity to be closely bound up with their relationship to the land. Giurgola drew his inspiration from the landform and from the design of Canberra by Walter Burley Griffin, an American Prairie School architect who was once Frank Lloyd Wright's office manager. Giurgola derived his circular motif and the great swinging walls inscribed over his variation of the Renaissance cross-and-square centralized plan from an indication for Capital Hill in the 1911 rendered plan of the Australian Federal Capital made by Marion Mahony Griffin.

In effect, the Parliament House is a low-key St. Peter's in which the architect has disguised the formal classical character of the plan by cutting off the top of Capital Hill to make way for the building, then pulling part of the hill back over it to give the impression that it had been conserved, leaving four exposed terraces—three for buildings, and the fourth, on the north side facing Canberra, for the forecourt.

The great flag mast rising above the rounded profile of Capital Hill is visible from a considerable distance, an ungainly four-legged structure that gives much the same appearance as a

---

Overleaf, a view from the north with bowed entry screen wall at left. Photograph by John Gollings.

Aerial view at left shows Parliament House's fit into Walter Burley Griffin's plan for Canberra's Capital Hill. Ceremonial axis from Parliament House to Lake Burley Griffin is interrupted by the Provisional Parliament House of 1927, which is to be·made into a museum and orientation center. In site/ground floor plan above (oriented to match aerial), the round element at lower right is the ceremonial pool, which, in photo at right, reflects the entry screen wall. Australian coat of arms is centered above the wall.

newborn giraffe struggling for the first time to stand upright. Its awkwardness has been commented upon many times; one especially troublesome factor is the connection of the legs to the two curved walls.

When you drive around the Parliament House on State Circle, which forms an encircling roadway, the building alternately springs forward or pulls back into the hill in an unnerving fashion. One moment it is large as life, and the next moment it is gone, withdrawn into the hill. There, yet not there. This phenomenon also makes the building appear smaller than it really is. So much of it is tucked away or hidden from view, either under the hill itself or behind the Parliament offices that stand in front of the other buildings in their retreat into the hill, where they are framed and held in check by the grand gesture of the two great curved walls.

If any single element dominates, it is these walls, not the buildings as such or the House chambers, which can be distinguished by their red tile roofs—reminiscent of the tiled roofs of the Australian suburban bungalow. The curved walls attract more interest even than the vestigial hill. These two deft surgical incisions into the belly of Capital Hill—precise, subtle trajectories of gray granite—connect the the Parliament House with the grander geometry of the city manifested by Commonwealth and Kings avenues, which converge at the Parliament House site.

The curved walls invite comparison with Bernini's magnificent colonnades encircling St. Peter's Square. They establish scale and grandeur, a generosity of gesture that is in keeping with the site, and they act as a palliative to the inevitable monotony that attends so massive and extensive an architectural composition. The walls constantly change direction as they cross the hill, and this produces subtle variations in the modulation of the sunlight

that penetrates the regularly spaced openings in the walls' face. They are to the Parliament House what Griffin's lakes are to Canberra.

Reduced to its simplest terms, Canberra is organized around two axes—a land axis intersected by the secondary water axis. This classical axial arrangement is overlaid by a triangle joining the three civic nodes: Parliament House at the apex, with City Centre and the Australian American Memorial establishing the baseline. Both the principal axes are aligned with mountains: the north-south land axis with Mount Ainslie and the east-west water axis, intersecting the lake system, with Black Mountain.

Griffin's baroque scheme is overstretched in Canberra. The distances are too great and the terrain too uneven, so the city that has emerged in the late 20th century is a city lost in a park, a 19th-century garden city trying to come to terms with the grandeur of Le Nôtre. Canberra lacks strong focal monuments and urban tissue to flesh out its skeleton and give organic substance to Griffin's overextended plan.

In underplaying its own monumentality, at least on its exterior, Giurgola's Parliament House does little to tighten the formal composition of the city. The pierced screen of the great veranda, for instance, has been scaled to relate to the old Parliament House, with the result that it is far too weak when read in relation to the building's forecourt and the city. It is a matter of proportion. Yet, in a curious way the building does manage to hold the city together, if not in balance, more by its gesture than by its presence.

The forecourt is the front terrace, a broad, sloping plate of red stone with radial patterning. It is the place of arrival, where the visitor can take stock of the building or, turning around, can look out over Canberra across the lake and appreciate the build-

ing as the hub of the city. Spilling downhill toward the lakeshore, the forecourt has an island at its center, a drop of Aboriginal identity surrounded by ocean on all sides. It is meant to represent the red center of Australia, the empty heartland, the land of Ayers Rock. On the island is a mosaic based on Michael Nelson Tjakamarra's "sand painting," representing ceremonial gatherings of the Aboriginal tribes of the dingo, wallaby, and iguana ancestors. The composition is a roundel of concentric circles on which converge white snakelike squiggles and arrows. But the image cannot readily be appreciated, spread out as it is over the pavement; it is even less intelligible from the water's edge.

Because the city axes converge on the new Parliament House, the view is better looking out from the building than toward it. From the top of Capital Hill, visitors easily recognize that they are standing at the center of the city—the political center of Australia. From the forecourt the space spills out over the edges: this is the Campidoglio in reverse, with diverging sloping walls but without the accompanying palazzo to contain the space. Perhaps that is an Australian flaw—too much openness.

Two rows of flagpoles on either side struggle valiantly to contain the forecourt. But the stepped profiles of the granite walls above the instep of the hill are too distant to lend a hand. In the middle of the forecourt, water surges and splashes as it rushes down the inclined paving, adding movement and contrast to an otherwise empty space. The forecourt needs people to bring it to life. Crowds. Demonstrators. Waving banners. Shouting.

You enter the Parliament House through the great veranda, really a classical portico in disguise. It is different from a real veranda, which in the 19th century was a cool place that visually connected the house with the garden. In lieu of the traditional veranda canopy of light corrugated iron, Giurgola has inserted a series of V-shaped radial ridges of glazing that stretch outward from the foyer facade and grasp the freestanding screen wall. The curved line of this wall gathers the portico space in toward the center and sharpens the focus on the entry.

The rectangular openings in the portico screen are a little too routine, bland. The wall isolates rather than connects the building to the outside, an effect that is further accentuated by the entry into the foyer that seals off the interior.

The Parliament offices on the east and west sides of Capital Hill are severe concrete blocks punctuated in marching precision by regularly spaced vertical slashes serving as windows. The effect is deliberately simple. But Giurgola's serried groups of offices stand one behind the other and, instead of stepping up to catch the view, are arranged so that the outer row blocks the view of the offices behind them.

For all their dullness, these facades, the most exposed and public face of the Parliament House, do exhibit a certain primitive quality and precision that Giurgola has sought to enliven by adding sculptured porte cocheres attractively faced with red and gray stone. His aim was to draw attention to the entrances and contrast them with the flat office facades.

The Parliament House, like the city of Canberra, has two axes. The north-south ceremonial axis is aligned with Griffin's land axis and expresses the progressive experience of time from prehistory and Aboriginal habitation into the future. It is intersected by an east-west axis on which are situated the two legislative chambers, satellite centers on either side of the ceremonial axis, their accompanying support facilities, and the elected representatives' offices and suites. Imposed on these axes is a rectangular circulation route that circumnavigates the two legislative subcenters, rather in the manner of St. Peter's.

Facing page, courtyard with glassy link between the House of Representatives block (at left in photo) and the members' hall at dead center of plan behind curved wall. This page, clockwise from bottom left: the same courtyard from top of curved wall; sculpture of Australia's Olga Mountains in the executive courtyard; entrance to House of Representatives chamber on building's eastern periphery; pergolas in executive courtyard.

The great veranda leads to the foyer, which traces the path of the ceremonial axis and represents the 19th-century forest fastness that settlers encountered. The first impression is of regularly spaced, green, marble-clad columns, like tree trunks. Forty-eight in all, they rise in stately profusion from a glistening marble floor, patterned in elaborate square and circle designs, to about two-thirds the height of the gridded ceiling that comes down part of the way to meet them. Without question, the foyer is the most sumptuous space in the Parliament complex. It is a splendid gesture of welcome that makes people feel important. The space is cool and restful, especially after the red desert of the forecourt. But the green tree trunks seem unfinished, and there is something disconcerting about the cladding, which extends only two-thirds the way up. The intention, apparently, was to lower the apparent height of the space and make people feel more comfortable, but the white ceiling extending down increases rather than diminishes the height of the space.

It is in the foyer that one of the most significant dislocations in the building's conception occurs. The Parliament House was designed as a symmetrical composition of considerable richness and complexity about a central processional axis much like a cathedral with its nave. Yet, it remains a diagram, for the public is rarely, if ever, granted the privilege of experiencing this

space. Instead, visitors are redirected up the two grand staircases on either side of the foyer and led through the building on the second-floor level, from which they may look down on, but not enter, the members' hall. These two staircases with their exaggerated size and exquisite detailing are meant to tug attention away from the doors of the great hall, which are kept closed except on state occasions. The stairs are the dominant notes in this confused space; they pull the eye forward and sideways, never letting go for an instant. But it is a glorious confusion.

The great hall itself, for all its considerable refinement of detail and expensive timber paneling, is a great boxlike room for holding banquets and the like. It reminds one of nothing so much as an oversized multipurpose high school gymnasium. The set-out markings on the brown parquet flooring reinforce this impression. Giurgola attempts to make the size more digestible by introducing a human-scaled element in the form of door-sized panels—a module he carries around the walls. He opens up the ceiling to the sky by introducing a complicated central roof monitor, and, although this is an improvement, the great hall remains the most boring space in the Parliament House.

Following such mundane ordinariness, the members' hall is a dramatic climax to the ceremonial axis. A space intended for reflection, a place of silence, it is tall and square with a pyramid-shaped ceiling light towering high overhead astride the crossing of the two main axes at the precise center of the Parliament House. It replaces the domed crossing of the Renaissance plan, whose transepts have been shortened to accommodate the two Parliamentary chambers. The intricate layering of the high members' hall suggests, rather than reveals, the extent of the Parliament building spilling out across the leveled Capital Hill.

However, the members' hall is also a melancholy void. Except

for the elegant black reflecting pool cut out of the hall's paved floor, the space is empty. The circular latticed opening under Bernini's baldachin, which in St. Peter's in Rome allows a view into the crypt on the spot where St. Peter was martyred, has been replaced in the Parliament House by the reflecting pool. In it, weather permitting, you may glimpse the Australian flag on its giant mast above the skylight. The flag symbol seems a belated pop art image from the 1960s. The question arises whether it makes any sense at all to attempt to adapt the sacred symbolism of the Renaissance centralized church plan to convey something of the substance of the modern nation-state.

In many respects the Parliament House works extraordinarily well. It takes into full account the importance Giurgola's mentor Louis Kahn gave to daylight in architecture. Kahn is recorded as saying, "I realize that the daylight must come down from a high point where the light is at its zenith." That, in the more important working and ceremonial spaces of the Parliament House, is exactly what Giurgola has allowed to happen.

But there are also many unhappy moments in the House of Parliament. For one thing, the centralized plan is inflexible—it cannot be easily expanded. The centralized church was intended to be an image of perfection, something complete in itself that could neither be added to nor taken away from without destroying that perfection. It was never intended for change. But the Australian Parliament inevitably will grow in time. Even during construction the Parliament instructed the architects to provide additional offices for members of the House of Representatives.

Moreover, the principal architectural attraction in the two most important working spaces—the chambers of the House of Representatives and the Senate, located on either side of the members' hall—is, inappropriately, the ceilings. These are large,

oblong rooms, rather plain, which Giurgola has attempted to enliven by kicking out the corners and devising ceiling lights and lanterns of impressive complexity that focus all interest upward. In some ways the complexity of the lighting is self-defeating because it eludes comprehension. Also, in the House chamber the space spills out diagonally through a gap in paired columns. In the Senate chamber, on the west side of the Parliament House, a circular geometry has been introduced to distinguish this chamber from its larger brother. It has a similar diamond lantern at the center, but its skylight is simpler and much more effective. At night, when the House and Senate are in session, the lights will constitute a light sculpture marking the event.

The great size of the Parliament building sometimes defeats Giurgola. Thus, the mechanical repetition of so many identical elements results in monotony. It also has a human cost. Joan Child, the speaker for the House of Representatives, commented when interviewed that she could not maintain eye contact with members in the chamber. The House chamber is not scaled for intimate debate or attuned to the cut and thrust of exchanges on the floor. With provision for permanent seating of 170 members, the House chamber is also impersonal and dull. Like so much of the Parliament House, its design is tasteful and conservative, an interior that melts into the background. It lacks character.

The circular form and smaller size of the Senate chamber make it a more human and intimate room, which contributes to a greater sense of drama on the floor than is possible in the House chamber. The Senate's enclosing, inclusive geometry makes people a part of the interior.

The members' and senators' offices are uninspiring if roomy quarters that read all too clearly as standard barracks for politi-

Above, the Senate chamber lighted by clerestory slots in ellipti-cal drum; eight speaker clusters are suspended from ceiling. Fac-ing page, clockwise from top: the members' hall with screen wall supporting pyramidal skylight over square reflecting pool; the hypostyle foyer with columns partially clad in marble and strong floor patterns; and the square-plan House of Representatives chamber with lights on suspended track.

cians. Giurgola has insisted on a commendable Scandinavian restraint in the interiors and has avoided the more exuberant, funny, and at times outrageous color combinations of post-modernism. This limited palette of materials using a few natu-ral finishes and graduated shades of green and red results in a building that is sober and lacking in personality. Furniture also is tasteful and dull, though it probably anticipates the members' own tastes. The same is true of the Prime Minister's office.

Another problem is the absence of views. With so much of the building overlooking internal courts, people look into other offices. It is the bane of the Parliament House. The Prime Min-ister's office is not exempt. It overlooks a bare, granite-paved desert peopled by a group of bronze tors by Marea Gazzard.

The art program for the Parliament House was enlightened and ambitious and deserved to be successful. Unfortunately there was no real precedent. There are some wonderful successes, but overall the artworks are a disappointment. The fault was not Giurgola's. The Arthur Boyd tapestry in the great hall is a typi-cal example of what could and did happen. The idea for the tapestry was taken from a 19th-century painting by Tom Rob-erts of a forest scene at Sherbrook in Victoria. Boyd's painting lacked the necessary strength for translation to a larger scale. As a result, the 20x9-meter (66x30-foot) tapestry is a delight to

look at close up but a disaster in terms of its contribution to the architecture of the great hall. To make matters worse, a rectangle had to be cut from the tapestry for the doorway con-necting the great hall with the adjoining members' hall.

There have been many attempts to explain the meaning of the Parliament House, some of which, responding to its part-subterranean nature, have inferred that it signifies death and have likened it to a mortuary tomb. In some ways the Parliament House resembles Daedalus's labyrinth, an underground complex with a single entrance. From this viewpoint, it is not something that has grown from nature, no matter how much its design might give that impression. It is a work of art. This means that it is a human copy of something.

Giurgola chose to fly with Daedalus, but, unlike Jorn Utzøn, who flew with Icarus in designing his Sydney Opera House, and so suffered Icarus's fate, Giurgola stayed nearer to the ground so he could follow its established landmarks in finding his way across unknown territory. His wings, unlike Utzøn's, held together.

In its own fashion the Parliament House says something equally important about Australia and Australians, and it is not about death. Quite the opposite. A mixture of cave and hill, the build-ing is expressive of birth, of new life making its way into the world, forcing a passage for itself from under the earth. Like the Pitjantjatjara myth of the great creation spirits who emerged one by one from the depths of the earth, pushing the earth back as they came, so the Parliament House expresses the emergence of a new entity.

The form of the Parliament House suggests a country that is still emerging, a country as yet unfinished. It is the message of a country beginning to shape itself but, as yet, far from fully formed. □

ESSAYS
1980s

Essays by

Richard Guy Wilson • Joseph Esherick

Margaret McCurry • David Gebhard • Robert Frasca

Donn Logan • Glenn Robert Lym • Mark Simon

Frances Halsband • Samuel Mockbee • Peter Forbes

Robert Geddes • Doug Kelbaugh • Robert Ivy, Jr.

Assessing a Decade Whose Only Constant Has Been Change

A set of essays responding to the questions: 'How would you characterize the architecture of the '80s? Have you discerned any trends, the beginnings or endings of any significant movements? What individual works have been most representative of the period?

Richard Guy Wilson: 'Show biz made a pernicious impact.'

Already historians and political commentators have labeled the 1980s "The Reagan Imperium," and for those interested in the arts or architecture a question arises as to the possible connections. Political epithets applied to architecture are not unknown—the terms Georgian and Victorian were originally political, and in this country we use "WPA Moderne" and "General Grant" as stylistic identifications. The Grant label is not flattering since it implies a connection between the nation's most corrupt (until recently?) Presidential Administration and the bloated, mansard-roofed behemoths that came to symbolize political machines, graft, and payoffs. Sadly, we have not yet identified either a "Camelot" style or a "Tricky Dick" idiom though, perhaps unwittingly, the Kennedy Center and the Watergate complex in Washington, D.C., serve the purpose for the respective Administrations.

The Reagan Reign in architecture in the 1980s has meant a flashy, show biz, surface-deep glamour along with an open worship of $$$ and conspicuous consumption. In 1980s America, flash and greed are not sins—they have replaced modesty and service as virtues. American architecture in the 1980s adopted the slogan "more is more" in the strangest display of overscaled ornament, oddly placed temples, pediments, Roman thermae windows, and columns that any historical period has ever seen. Glitz and shine are everywhere: there are now at least 20 different types of marble to compete with all the gold-plated, chrome, and brass fixtures. Certainly not all of this has been bad. A return of some sensuousness to architecture compared with the roughness of hammer-bashed concrete is to be welcomed, but there is an overly plump quality to much of American architecture—too many flocked finials and anodized pediments that need Dr. Mies's 10-day guide to slim thighs.

Historic preservation continued in the 1980s; though, in trying to meet the "real world" of real estate and developers, it found itself like the virgin in the back seat of a car: an innocent flirtation leads to deeper problems. Architects who earlier had viewed preservation with suspicion now found it a money-maker and embraced it. But while preservation was adopted it scarcely made a dent in the grittier issues of the built environment.

Increasingly the city and indeed the entire environment are privatized: we are in danger of having all our social functions taken over by the shopping center.

Show biz made a great and pernicious impact upon architecture. Instead of being known for good work, just being known became the goal of some figures in the architectural and art worlds. Andy Warhol, a relic of the 1960s, became the archetypal '80s artist—empty of meaning, but known. Architects became celebrities, or superstars; being published in glitzy magazines or gossip sheets was the highest accolade. On a more positive note, in the 1980s architecture moved into the public eye in television programs, specialized bookstores, and exhibits of architectural drawings, artifacts, photographs, and furniture. Museums actively collected and tried to interpret architecture to an ever more sheeplike public. With all this attention came a possible problem: is architecture just one more collectible, a disposable commodity?

The style of the 1980s is pomo. Postmodernism, which began years earlier as a critical inquiry concerning history and modernism, became a style—pomo. This is a well known path; movements always lose their intellectual substance and become styles taken up by lesser hands—the spec builder, the shopping center developer, the design studio critic. Now this is not to say that everything has been awful. Some real masterpieces have been created—Michael Graves's San Juan Capistrano Library is one—and there have been some quality designs, such as Kliment & Halsband's Columbia University computer center and Hardy Holzman Pfeiffer Associates' Best Products headquarters. At a much lesser level, shopping centers may not be any better, but at least they have entrances.

The other significant development has been the re-appearance and the serious discussion of straitlaced revivalism, "neotrad" (neotraditionalism), or perhaps better termed "retread." The political connections are obvious: the new intellectual respectability of conservatism and also the neoconservatives, or those old-line liberals who found new and great virtue in far-right polemics, have their equivalents in the former architectural modernists who converted to neotrad. Of course revivalism, especially in the form of the colonial, never really disappeared; it survived very well in the hands of the contractor and (what we euphemistically call) provincial architects such as Philip Shutze and Jimmy Means down in Georgia. But now in the 1980s traditionalism in architecture has an intellectual respectability not present since the 1920s. In this re-appraisal of history I might point not immodestly to the role of historians in re-evaluating the past. Also, I do not mean to accuse all of the neotraditionalists of conservative politics, since in many cases their responses were derived from context and quite appropriate. By this I mean work such as Hartman-Cox's addition to the commerce school at the University of Virginia or Kevin Roche's announced scheme for the Jewish Museum addition.

Certainly an aspect of both neotrad and pomo has been the revived interest in classicism, which has ranged from straightforward revivals to more abstract open trusses and cylinders. Art deco has found appeal as a classically based modernism. Classicism as the true academic system, in that it has a heritage of written *texts* (a favorite word of the '80s), found a haven in the schools; and there has appeared a new classicist personality, similar to Jerry Falwell in its proclivity for strict interpretation with about the same depth. The hope of some classicists for a development similar to that of the Beaux-Arts or the American renaissance at the turn of the century is already doomed. The problem of the postmodern mind, which includes all of us, is that we know too much—we realize there are alternatives and the clock cannot be turned back to a time that never existed.

Already a new wind is blowing, and, while historians are not astrologers, it does not take much to sense that molded stone dentils are but one answer. The problems are too diverse to allow for single solutions. As in politics, polemics are a subterfuge for facing issues. Have the '80s been an

interlude? A time of avoiding reality? Is architecture simply window dressing? Or does it speak to deeper—cultural and social—concerns? Yes, we have had our fads; decon (deconstructivism) arrived and left within four months, though we now have to work our way out of "exploded" or "caved in" buildings for a few years. But we are living in a modern world and, while old-line modernism is certainly out, the fast-approaching millennium will bring a retrospective sensitivity and a quest for a new approach. Recently I have heard several architects openly say, "I am a modernist, not a . . . ," words unthinkable two years ago. The buildings of the 1980s that will be remembered will be some of those noted above and those that seem to escape immediate concerns and assume the air of timelessness, such as Fay Jones's little chapels (below, Thorncrown) down in the woods of northern Arkansas.

Illustration by Brian McCall

Joseph Esherick: 'No movement has had sticking power.'

The architecture of the 1980s could be characterized by a notable increase in variety of building types and approaches to design. Some of the variety has been movement-directed. While some of the movements may appear to have had initial significance, none seems to have had significant staying power. Some, postmodernism for example, have attacked what was claimed to be one style with another style. A result has been a proliferation of acceptable forms that identify the movement; the speed with which the movements marketed these forms and thereby arrived at an apparent stability is remarkable.

Some branches of some movements have

invoked history, but what history and whose history is not easy to say. History as we have known it appears to have given way to instant, invented history, invested for the particular project. It must make historians cringe.

Some movements—for example, "energy-responsive design" and "contextualism"—struggling along with modest success, probably suffer from the awkwardness of their identifying names. As movements they have had a more notable effect legislatively or administratively, but their influence pervades much of what is done. Thus, energy issues, because they now are embedded in codes and regulations, become an underlying current that goes through all work. Contextualism is less formally mandated but has become an administrative tool of planning bodies and community action groups.

What didn't happen in the '80s is perhaps more interesting than what did happen. The promise of new building forms based on a greater sensitivity and responsiveness to energy issues hardly appears to have been met in spite of impressive demonstrations of the previous decade—for example, the various "demonstration" buildings built by the State of California—nor does responsiveness to human issues seem to pervade the work of the '80s. Housing that might be available to any but the relatively well-to-do has all but disappeared, and the individual architect-designed house, the proving ground for so many young architects in the past, is now a rarity.

European architectural forms have had a broad impact, but, curiously, European building technology, indeed even Canadian building technology, seems to have had relatively little impact on the work in this country.

In any attempt to characterize the '80s, one needs to look not just at the resulting phenomena and the movements but also at the forces influencing, if not driving, the whole process. Projects such as the suburban office park and regional and subregional shopping centers founded on the use of the private automobile, and the related sharply zoned residential areas of apartment houses, town houses, and single-family residences, each Zipatoned to its own specific area, are development-driven, and the client structure is entirely different from what obtains with the private client or most public-body clients.

We are beginning to see a new "patron" structure with a symbiotic relationship between the developer and the press, galleries, and the media generally. The developer and publisher alike need notably identifiable products. The architecture of utility or of quiet domestic pleasure—of the ordinary world—is probably too dull and too stable to satisfy the developers or the media's need to sell. Both require a significant difference and some kind of uniqueness, some sort of thematic, perceptible image that fits with an explanation (and in the hands of skilled performers it may be hard to tell which came first, the image or the explanation, or which is the architecture and which is the description of the architecture).

I sympathize with the journals and the museums—how can one, in a limited space or on the flat plane of a page, describe even so simple a piece of architecture as a house or a workshop and what it is like to live in it or work in it? In the effort to produce significant differences there is a paradoxical driving out of diversity. As hard as the image-making forces try to establish new directions, they do not seem to be able, perhaps from their remoteness from the heart of the matter, to do more than reinforce new orthodoxies.

With luck, we may see in the '90s a broadening of the disclosure. Certainly it ought to be becoming apparent to the managers of some of the movements, with their emphasis on acceptable form described in a private language, that the results are not broad cultural integration but Balkanization. What I think we need is an open and understandable discourse, especially one that can include so many who have been left out (or have opted out) of the discussion.

Margaret McCurry: 'The seeds were planted in the '70s.'

What has characterized this decade of the 1980s is the condition that all the leading players were on stage or in the wings in the '70s. In fact, their most original work was conceived in the previous decade; it was executed in infinite permutations throughout the '80s and, inevitably, at the conclusion, has become mimetic.

Pluralism, the umbrella "ism" of the past two decades, is still extant, but beneath this firmament other isms have waxed and waned. The most controversial, least codifiable ism of the 1970s—post-modernism—was a sincere, romantic search for historical roots on the part of its creators. Its penultimate chapter was written in the late '70s with Michael Graves's design for the Fargo-Moorehead Cultural Center Bridge. In the '80s the movement has degenerated into a style that lost its vitality as it filtered down through the grass roots and languished in the hands of less talented sycophants. That postmodernism has lingered through the '80s and will continue to limp into the '90s is a testimony to its usefulness as a style. Historicism, its most comprehensible component, is after all the embodiment of the laical sensibility.

What has been significant about post-modernism—and its offshoots of vernacularism, contextualism, and regionalism—is that it reconnected architecture

Illustrations by Brian McCall

with mass culture and re-established the roots that modernism so willfully pruned. What will remain of it are these roots, from which new movements inevitably will grow.

This decade began with the publication of Frank Gehry's Santa Monica house (above)—the precursor of the much maligned and little understood deconstructivist movement. But it is significant that this influential work was not the outgrowth of applied literary theory but rather of artistic intuition.

Attempts to deconstruct a building literally as one would an architectural text have met largely with frustration. By definition architecture is the art of three-dimensional spatial construction, and no two-dimensional language—no matter how it is structured—can span between these two constructs. An architectural construction can certainly have a "text," it can certainly be "read" (often through many layers of meaning and memory), and its totality can even be partially deconstructed into three-dimensional components (witness Gehry's Loyola law school). However, to attempt to totally deconstruct a building is by definition to disunite its structure and thus to destroy its significance as architecture. That the revolutionary spirit of deconstructivism, too, is waning was signaled by the show last summer at the Museum of Modern Art, which, as it legitimized the movement, assured its acceptance as a style, thus prey to the dilutions of stylists.

The 1980s will end with a lot of sound and a little fury, but not without signifying something. The diverse isms of the decade will propagate and nourish new movements as architects, with their usual irreverence for prominence and insatiability for recreation, continue to embrace new attitudes. As these movements unfold, America will at best continue to revere and restore the monuments of its past while remaining optimistic with respect to the creation of significant new forms in its future that respond to new ideas and technologies.

The question for the 1990s is whether these new forms will be original or will retain traces of their former selves reassembled, reconstituted, or reformed—and, as such, will there be scars?

David Gebhard: 'A replay of the egocentric 1920s.'

While no moment can ever fully re-enact an episode of the past, there are nonetheless periods of time that do share points of similarity. The Reagan years we have just lived through share many salient points with the 1920s, so revealingly summed up in F. Scott Fitzgerald's *The Great Gatsby*. Both the decade of the 1920s and that of the 1980s represent an age that has sought to serve egocentric individuals' needs, particularly expressed through material aggrandizement. During the first decades of our century there was a shared feeling that those who controlled wealth had express obligations to use that wealth to help solve pressing social and economic problems. Not so in the '20s, nor in the '80s; the new rich in both decades made it plain (with a few exceptions) that their obligations were singular, to themselves.

As in the '20s, the architecture of the '80s tended to be a plaything of the rich. Modesty and reticence seemingly disappeared from the scene. Architects and their products participated in this scene, and, as Ruskin, Sullivan, and others had observed, the buildings of the period tellingly sum it all up. Again, in the early years of the century, those involved in business were often the principal supporters of the City Beautiful movement, of housing for the working class, and of the garden suburb and city. What is the legacy of the 1980s business community? With the fewest of exceptions, those involved in building within our major urban centers have left us very little. When a public space—a plaza or a spot of greenery—has been provided, it has generally been the result of public and government pressure, not of a private expression of obligation.

The urban buildings themselves, especially the high rise, openly declare through their excessive bulk and height that it was the financial ledger that prompted them, and little else. And in upper-middle-class suburbia, the accumulation of wealth has been expressed through oversized houses too large for their sites.

The fashion of postmodernism, similar in certain ways to period revivalism in the '20s, has provided both architect and client with a wide variety of possible images to select from. The classic postmodern image of pediments, columns, and piers, of hipped or gabled roofs, shares a remarkable number of similarities with the rage for the art deco style at the end of the 1920s and on into the early 1930s. Both of these images could be (and were) seen by the public as being up to date and modern and at the same time somewhat traditional. Both were looked upon by the public (and quite rightly so) as transitory occurrences of fashion. Each of these modes quickly developed a limited set of recognizable design elements, which could be seized upon by any architect who wished to produce an up-to-date image.

Side by side with the classical postmodernist imagery has been the increased urge to return to one or another of the historic styles—whether to the "heroic" phase of the International Style of the 1920s or to the French Norman château. This sally into the past has been vividly reflected, in everything from high-rise buildings to our 6,000- and 7,000-square-foot modest little suburban homes.

The '20s, too, expressed a similar catholic taste, but what that decade produced seems far more satisfactory than what we have brought forth. Why is this? The answer, I suspect, lies partially within the whole realm of beliefs held by society, but it also resides specifically in the architectural profession itself. In the 1980s the architecture of high seriousness proceeds from the world of the High Art object; the architects of the 1920s zeroed in on episodes of the past, which they sought to instill in their own buildings.

A governing principle of these Beaux-Arts-educated architects of the '20s was an obligation to produce objects of beauty and romance. One can search diligently through the buildings of the 1980s, many of strong character and of forceful ideological content, and not discover one considered beautiful. While a few of our major architectural practitioners have sought out and expressed a sense of romance, this has not become a governing quality of the decade.

In a remarkably perceptive manner the architect Louis La Beaume observed in the pages of the September 1928 issue of the *Journal of the American Institute of Architects* (in response to a plea for the modernist cause by Lewis Mumford), "It is all very well to hold an esthetic theory, but to let it loose at the wrong time may prove calamitous." In looking back at the 1980s, we too might ask whether the heavy pretensions of postmodernist theory have in fact produced a decade of architecture that later we will look back upon with great love and fondness. A guess would be that the visual evidence of the buildings may well be overshadowed by the intellectual world of theories, let loose (perhaps) at the wrong time. La Beaume had argued that in the '20s the task of the architect was not to mirror the "sordidness, the seriousness, the steadying business of life"; rather, it was to provide a means of "escape from the real world, which, though chaotic, we do not regard as picturesque, into a world of dreams." Perhaps this then is the essential difference between the architecture of the two decades: in the '20s we had a loving, childlike escape to fairyland; in the '80s, a carrying on of the modernist principle of expressing (in this instance) the sordidness of the age.

Robert Frasca: 'The profession is market-driven.'

The past 10 years have reminded us that style in itself has little to do with making beautiful rooms and places. Before 1980, the thinking in my professional lifetime had been confined to a single style, and, although modernism seemed inert, the alternatives to it were confined mostly to paper. In the '60s, we had been retaught to admire our heritage but we hadn't been able to develop a new vocabulary that had the flexibility to satisfy our society's diverging values. Suddenly there was an alternative. Postmodernism burst on the scene like an African sunrise, and it probably seems more vivid to me because it started in my hometown with the Portland Building. The movement quickly popularized architecture because it had struck a respondent chord in the consumer, something the other variants of modernism hadn't accomplished.

Because much of the profession is market-driven, before the decade was half over the jury was in and the results were mixed. The originators, such as Venturi, Graves, and Moore, had for the most part built well, but some of the most skilled practitioners of modernism who coerced themselves into trying their hand at it often ended with disastrous results. Postmodernism had in part changed the way we thought about buildings, but we saw some wretched results in the name of the "context." The style was as easily corrupted as modernism in serving the purposes of the most heinous client. It caused us to remember that what we admired about historic styles was not that they were intrinsically beautiful (although ugly buildings, like ruthless men, gain dignity with time) but that they had been built carefully and thoughtfully. Being stylistically ambitious was not a substitute for building well. Postmodernism reminded us also that

nature has always been niggardly when it comes to human talent and that beauty and ugliness come in all styles.

In evaluating what produced the best of the decade nothing has changed. As always, the best architects recognized what the problem offered and then went beyond it. It required sometimes a powerful vision, such as Romaldo Giurgola's wonderfully heroic capitol at Canberra, and other times a modesty of purpose, as in Kallmann, McKinnell & Wood's carefully crafted American Academy in Cambridge, Mass. In some cases, these architects really had not involved themselves in the polemics of the decade. For example, Fumihiko Maki and Richard Meier, at opposite ends of the planet, continued to build beautifully and consistently. The National Museum of Modern Art in Kyoto and the High Museum in Atlanta (below) are both products of a dedication to principles developed over a long time. In other cases, exceptional buildings go beyond their own site boundaries. Arata Isozaki's MOCA in Los Angeles enlivened an otherwise deadly renewal area while building beautiful rooms for viewing art. Exceptional buildings dignify that which is around them, as does James Stirling's fine museum in Stuttgart.

These high points (not coincidentally) are not building types that deal with the problems typical of our cities, but that doesn't make this decade especially conspicuous in the history of our art. We continue to celebrate beautiful objects mostly because the artistic opportunities presented by more fundamental problems are modest. The important issue of the next 10 years is the same as it was for the past 10: that is, one of healing an urban environment that has been almost terminally wounded from half a century of bad judgment and indifference.

If the last decade began with the precepts of Robert Venturi, the next begins with the sensibilities of Frank Gehry. It is because the more everything becomes the same, the more we want to celebrate that which makes us unique, and Frank Gehry is first and foremost a regionalist (some

would say a microregionalist whose work thrives only in areas with high levels of carbon monoxide). As much as I appreciate his work and the "guerrilla" architects fighting in the margins of the Southern California megalopolis, their work has little to do with the aspirations of, for instance, Kansas City, Mo., or Portland, Ore. (facing page, the Portland Building). Our thinking should be directed even more so to the particulars of place, and no one's style will travel well. I am optimistic that good things will continue to happen when I see examples such as Tony Predock's museum at Arizona State University and Scogin Elam & Bray's Clayton County Library in Georgia. I don't see a confused or dismal future, and I've never expected an immaculate one.

Donn Logan: 'Most work has been of the 'look at me' variety.'

Did much happen in architecture in the '80s? The period being still upon us, it is hard to say. However, I feel as if something has happened whose impact will be clearer in retrospect, or something is about to happen. The mid-'70s and early '80s might be characterized as the time when modern architecture lost its way. In reaction to the banalities of its lowest common denominators as seen in the majority of private and institutional buildings, and the poverty of its urbanistic ideas, we turned away and sought to re-approach history and its many lessons about buildings and cities that had been misplaced. This was good. As with any reaction, however, the pendulum was inclined to swing too far. The result was a lot of bad buildings— buildings without content. Being facile was confused with being truthful. A few practitioners (Moore, Graves, Beeby, etc.) could deal with mannerist and neoclassical themes and pull it off better than others by virtue of talent and originality. But most of the so-called postmodern work was just as dreary and empty as the worst results of catalogue modernism.

What is the legacy of this period? What have we learned? For one thing, we have relearned history; there were many valid concepts of architectural space and urban space before the period chronicled by Sigfried Giedeon that are still appropriate, but they are not necessarily appropriate when applied casually, thoughtlessly, irreverently, or out of context. We don't need empty classicism any more than we need empty modernism.

Perhaps we have learned that pioneer modernism had a compelling ethical and intellectual thrust to it that, even though lost, could not be replaced by the subsequent "post" and "neo" movements. Modernism at its best was not a style, nor even a technological movement, but rather a fundamental search for an architecture that expressed its time, in reaction to the perceived phoniness of what had gone on before.

Perhaps we are at a point in history similar to that of the early modernists. What has gone on recently in architecture is not a true or sufficient expression of our time. There is evidence, however, in some of the experiments that are going on now, that a search for a truer, more valid, and more profound expression is being sought, and with some success. In the work of Maki, Predock, Holl, and others, one can glimpse the eventual emergence of a renewed modernism—one that accepts history, accepts the vernacular, is less straitlaced than earlier modernism, but is still true to means and purposes. In an earlier essay in the pages of this journal, I called this direction "expressive modernism." This is still an appropriate term, I think, but not sufficient to completely describe the direction. The most important aspect of the emerging direction is, I believe, the rekindled concern for content. We are once again interested in an architecture of ideas, not just one of appearances.

Urbanism is another topic worth speculating about. The modern movement did not do much good for us here. Except perhaps in the area of transportation planning, the precepts of CIAM were largely disastrous for cities. The Team 10, Archigram, and Metabolist concepts of the '60s, with their preoccupation with megastructures and interchangeable parts, were heady but lacked any connection to our culture or politics. The various "back to Europe" movements, such as the townscape school, the neorationalists (Krier, et al.), likewise have little to do with American cities.

How can the alleys, squares, and piazzas of Europe have any value for the American grid city that was laid out to facilitate movement and land speculation and did not grow organically from the Middle Ages? Clearly the urbanistic power of New York, Chicago, and San Francisco demonstrates the value of native prototypes. Already in the '80s we are seeing beginnings of an interest in American urbanism. The case of Battery Park City (Cooper, Eckstut, et al.) demonstrates that we can build upon our own paradigms.

Finally, there is the relationship between buildings and cities. Modernism and postmodernism both put emphasis on the building as an object. In spite of much rhetoric about context, most work of the past decade has been of the "look at me" variety. The term context has been used as a stylistic device rather than a true expression of concern for neighborhood. Perhaps in the '90s we can get back to exploiting the immense power of buildings to accomplish and even to lead urban design. Our cities will be better when the status system of the profession rewards ensemble values as well as solo works.

Glenn Lym: 'Every generation sends a hero up the charts.'

Architectural style wars are exciting to watch. They give us a sense of architecture advancing in our time. In the past 10 years, we have seen postmodernism attempt to overthrow modernism only to lose ground and be seen as a bit dated in comparison with fresh deconstructivism. What we are witnessing today recalls what I remember from my adolescence in the late '50s and '60s when Mies van der Rohe's work was pushed aside in the architectural limelight for the more sculptural work of a younger generation of what Jencks has called late-modern architects. It must be a re-enactment of an eternal passing— "Every generation sends a hero up the pop charts," as Paul Simon's song says.

But, as composer Brian Eno has argued, art does not develop linearly from style to style nor from seminal practitioner to seminal practitioner. Eno noted that music has many styles, which are all developing simultaneously. At any given time, a musician selects from a particular cross section of musics to create something that is vivid for that moment or that context. The same may characterize architecture as we build for our own collections of special, compromised contexts. Style wars distract us or, perhaps to put it better, keep us going in the face of fundamental changes in the nature of work we are asked to do. Style wars give us a sense of spacious adventure while we attend to the more fundamental and grueling problems of working in a time of more limited economic means and aspirations.

Up through the early 1970s, our national sense of unlimited power and wealth led to grand design with grand aspirations. Yet, as we have seen, many of those designs were ultimately crude and lacking in architectural and social qualities necessary to create genuine urban fabric. The large urban renewal and transportation efforts in all our major cities have stopped. We no longer have the wealth, power, or will to execute them. Today we no longer think architecturally from a clean-slate, large-scale perspective. We are forced in our commissions to look from more sensitive and intimate points of view. We must build relatively inexpensively while conserving energy and providing accessibility for the handicapped. We must fit our projects into complex, existing sites, as land is in short supply. In short, we are asked by our time to accept and conserve our environment.

Late in his life, Charles Eames lectured on the role of strong constraint in evoking the richest of designs. So perhaps postmodernism inadvertently helped answer the problem of what to do with walls in an era in which increasing energy costs have led to the demise of the curtain wall. And perhaps it is the mark of our era that we have stylistic advances in projects that also genuinely respect their complex contexts while giving new qualities to them—as do Gehry's Norton house and Kohn Pedersen Fox's Frankfurt office complex.

When I was a student, I was fascinated by early-'50s psychological investigations of the attitudes of psychotherapists as a function of their ideological bent (for example, Freudian, Jungian, Behaviorist) versus the number of years they had practiced. These studies showed that the longer therapists practiced the more similar their attitudes about patient treatment became. Ideology gave way to knowledge gained from working directly with people. In American architecture, our stylistic ideologies continue to be engaging and divisive. Yet, just maybe, the work is beginning to indicate that we are learning from our relatively short experience of building cities.

Illustration by Brian McCall

Mark Simon: 'A nonstop cycle of invention, critique.'

I have looked at the moon and wished I didn't know it was a sphere circling the earth. It would be magical, a glowing talisman with a different shape each day trying to tell me something very important.

Twentieth-century architecture has marched on through the last decade in a parade of styles beating their drums. It has become a spectacle of variety. Down the street come modernists, postmodernists, the latest in deconstructivists, with reborn classicists close behind. A few of our bands, fifing sweet little tunes, would be happy to avoid the attention of the crowds and get lost on the side streets. Others would like to lead the parade or, better still, be loud enough to drown out all the rest. I am sorry they feel that way. The variety doesn't bother me; as long as the playing is good, I'm willing to listen.

Nonetheless, some of the frozen music hasn't been so hot (or should I say cool?). With the acceptance of postmodernism, memory has been trivialized. Architecture by formula now has a mawkish arch for every window and no irony, wit, or soul. This has led to a dread of sentiment and an understandable eagerness to get the hell out of Candyland to do something honest. With sharp edges. Now don't get me wrong—I adore sharp edges (as I do the marching bands) if they're *good* sharp edges. But I assume that, when Honesty trickles down, instead of walking through a paper Palladio into my favorite pizza parlor, I will run a gauntlet of broken glass as inappropriate as the arches.

Great strides have been made in the last decade—from reborn urbanism to newly respected materials. But even in talented hands the progress means little without the patience to listen to clients, to look at sites, and to respond to them no matter what the agony. No pain, no gain. Our poetics are pompous when they're selfish.

Architecture is that rare discipline that requires using both sides of the brain—the rational and intuitive in quick turns—a nonstop cycle of invention and critique. Change is how we work. And, like the moon's phases or marching bands, there's magic and delight in it—we need not fear it. But, with respect to the last decade, my plea is that we not depend on it.

Frances Halsband: 'Defining four streams of current thought.'

Yes, there is change in the air. Is it the end of a decade, or the approaching end of a millennium, or just a surfeit of prose and photography?

We are just beginning to emerge from the warm bath of the genteel battle of the styles. This battle, fought first at the expense of rich people and their houses, and now at the houses of the corporations, concerns whether the past is ironic or serious, whether the past is incorporated through quotation or through spirit, whether the classical language is the only true language for architecture, whether our age is expressed through modern materials, which are understood to be steel and glass, or whether it is best expressed through reinterpreting the works of modern European masters of 60 years ago.

I believe that we are tiring of this battle, not because of the quality of work that has been produced in the last 10 years, which has been very high, but because the issue of style seems too narrow to contain all our interests. We are told what not to do: don't use steel and glass, don't use the classical, don't make boxes. Some architects are starting to look for something positive to do. Dogma, or, to use a more polite word, polemic, is beginning to be replaced with a new theory of design.

Four streams of current thought may well be the basis for this new synthesis: a theory of place based upon landscape; a theory of preservation that embraces history and design; a theory of craft; and a theory of civic design that encourages new programming.

A theory of place: We are all familiar with the wonderful work of Christian Norberg-Schulz and also Charles Moore and Donlyn Lyndon on the theory of place. We are now seeing an extension of that theory, not a renunciation. We are beginning to see the possibility of landscape as the basis for a new esthetic in architecture. We can learn from landscape as context, as we have learned from cities as context. Landscape is, of course, itself derived from natural context. Downing said, if you want to know what color to paint a house, pick up a handful of earth at the site. This also suggests the erasing of the figure-ground relationship of architecture and landscape. The influence of landscape brings also the task of integrating ecology into design.

New theories frequently develop outside of the limits of practice. The Architectural League of New York sponsored the "Cold Spring Conference on Architecture and Landscape" in 1985, and an exhibition entitled "The Inhabited Landscape" in 1987. Last fall, the Museum of Modern Art in New York held a conference entitled

"Landscape and Architecture in the Twentieth Century." All were attempts to develop a new understanding of the relationship between the two arts.

The work of Emilio Ambasz in San Antonio, the work of Fay Jones, and Mitchell/Giurgola's Parliament House in Canberra (above) can be interpreted as erasing the figure-ground relationship between architecture and landscape and creating, instead, reciprocal contexts.

A theory of preservation: A great deal of work has been done on the "scientific" history of architecture—"what really happened when"—and scientific work has been done in the field of historic preservation by paint scratchers and dirt scratchers. Missing is a critical theory for determination of excellence, standards for what to save and how. Preservation cannot be a tool for some other agenda. The fuzzy-headed and sentimental view that "old is good" is no longer good enough.

We need to understand more deeply how to integrate our history into the present. In New York in the '80s we have witnessed the creation of a new building type: the skyscraper perched on top of a landmark. How are we to judge these efforts? How are we to design them? What are we saving when we save an old building? We have an obligation to develop an intellectual basis for a theory of preservation.

A theory of craft: We have a rich heritage from the postmodern movement, in its return to interest in how things are made. "Postmodern" began with painted wallboard but ended with the re-introduction of a wide range of materials that had not been used for a long time. We have 20 kinds of marble and granite intermixed, wood paneling with inlays of gold and mother-of-pearl. "Modern" has also increased the palette significantly. We have Gehry's chain link, we have copper, we

have mill-finished stainless steel and shattered glass. A new respect and love for the craft of making things has emerged. There is a new interest in detailing; not in ornament, which suggests that old battle of the styles—but in detailing and in the techniques of construction.

In the '90s, we may see this interest in craft extend beyond detail, into engineering as a source for form.

A theory of civic design: This is a concern that is not yet visible as an esthetic but may be more important than all the rest. We are beginning to see a new call for civic responsibility, a return to large-scale planning to solve large-scale problems.

The increasing privatization of the environment no longer can obscure the necessity for a civic public spirit. We no longer are content with soap company skyscrapers as our cathedrals and shopping center malls as our public spaces. Too many citizens are excluded from these so-called public places. We need a real civic architecture, and real city planning—public works provided by the public authorities for the benefit of the public.

New program types are needed to address the growing concern for civicness: airports and highways as gates to the city, public spaces for public celebrations, schools that are centers of community activity, housing for the homeless. Le Corbusier said, "To design well you need talent; to program well you need genius."

We are coming to the end of a cycle of community control. Started as an antidote to mindless large-scale planning, community control has become an institutionalized system that prevents growth and change. We need a large-scale civic vision of our future. We are ready to contribute to a collective plan to improve our individual experience.

Samuel Mockbee: 'An infatuation with fashion.'

If the last decade can be described as 10 years of cultural stasis, it certainly seems fair to say that architecture has suffered symptoms of the same malaise: a state of inertia marked by reflections of a mythical past transformed by nostalgia and by an inability to address the challenge of the future.

Fortunately, however, a new framework seems to be emerging, one that can develop into a commitment to an architecture engaged with the essential characteristics that shape our culture. As Kenneth Frampton urged in his essay *Towards a Critical Regionalism: Six Points for an Architecture of Resistance,* "the primary principle of architectural autonomy resides in the *tectonic* rather than the *scenographic.*" A coherent and articulate architecture can be achieved through a commitment to the tectonics that create our buildings. This, along with a design extracted from the idiosyncratic attributes of context, site, and climate, can invoke an appropriate cultural expression. Through "maintaining a high level of critical self-consciousness" in utilizing these contextual and tectonic qualities, architectural design can achieve exceptional results. The best architecture produced during the past few years has conscientiously responded to Frampton's concerns.

But what of the less desirable aspects of the past decade? Much of the body of work presented to the public reflected a languishing posture of nonadvancement due to three factors.

First, much of the work of the past 10 years betrays an infatuation with fashion. As evidenced in the popular media, the public was never more attuned to embracing architects as trend-setters and architecture as a consumable product. Sadly, architects acquiesced, producing glib artifacts without lasting value, elevating planned obsolescence to the grand scale.

As polemicists controverted over the year's fashion, architects declined to engage a design committed to maintaining a framework of meaning. Fundamental issues were obfuscated by a pursuit of the stylistic. The deficit was principally pursued through a design based on antecedent. This dependence on sentimentality seems now to be waning.

Second, the inability to move forward was due largely to a lack of criteria for judging the merit of the architect's intent. (Even the freedom associated with pluralism is not value-free.) Without such criteria, architecture seemed incapable of viable interconnection; content has been unintelligible, our cultural artifacts fragmented.

Third, fragmentation was amplified by the rejection of the modernist's optimism rooted in the idea of technological progress. Since the mid-'60s, we've been hindered by this manifest lack of faith in progress. The consequence is an abundance of eminently unprofound designs that can only be described as gratuitous representations.

Considering the technology that shapes our present environment, architecture of the past 20 years or so has been left behind. While increasingly sophisticated technological advances have developed, architects have not appropriated those advances. Seemingly unwilling to grasp that (for better or for worse) technology is a logical and ongoing product of our cultural evolution, we have not weaned ourselves from obsolescent technological equipage. With some notable exceptions, the inability or unwillingness to articulate the technological component of our society has precluded architects from participating actively in the tectonics that shape the very buildings we design.

For architecture of the coming years to perform as a meaningful simulacrum of society's foremost ideals and characteristics, it has to reject the pursuit of ephemeral stylization. To avoid in the future labels that quickly expire through overuse and misappropriation, architects of the next decade should aspire to produce a body of work unshackled by the lexicon of fashion. In developing an architecture that relates to cultural experience, an earnest engagement with that experience is necessary. Beyond that, criteria of critical evaluation need to be employed to adjudicate that engagement. An architecture that cogently utilizes its technological and contextual locus can produce a built environment that responds to our social responsibility.

Peter Forbes: 'Pulling stylistic rabbits out of a hat.'

In the two years since our last analysis in these pages, there has been every indication of an incredible acceleration in the stylistic paroxysms of architecture. I am piqued with excitement and trepidation to see what happens in the next two, let alone 10 years as we hurtle toward the millennium.

Sadly, architecture continues to be involved almost exclusively with style—in Mies's words with "inventing a new architecture every Monday." That imperative, to keep pulling stylistic rabbits out of a hat, is a difficult exercise, and the results have not been particularly successful: postmodernism, happily, seems to have collapsed, proving that structural sheetrock can support only so much literary allusion, and seems to be flourishing only in north Jersey strip development and, of course, Disney World.

Historicism, of which Boston has been a particularly sad victim, continues to wallow along in its ¾-inch-thick "rusticated" stone; suspended, weightless brick; instant shingle style; and colonial windows with snap-in mullions: fin-de-siècle nostalgia for a simpler time with all the modern conveniences of a consumer society discreetly hidden behind false fronts. In Boston they even prop up *old* fronts, emasculated remnants of once-honorable buildings, and hide whole high rises behind them in an ostrichlike hope that the new building, if not seen at street level, will somehow not truly exist.

Deconstructivism, the most recent of polemical statements, is suddenly in vogue and threatens to be built, probably much to the surprise of its philosophical originators. There is a curious dichotomy between built space that houses functions and people (remember people?) and a theoretical position that self-consciously proclaims an "architecture against itself" and champions "madness and play over careful management." However delightful and exciting it is to work within this style, there is an unsettling dervish quality to its constructs as it whirls across the land in a celebration of self-destruction. One has the sense of being in a Goddard movie, impotently observing an impending auto wreck.

And what of poor old modernism? It is still kicked around by each successive wave of stylists, still accused of being sterile and unresponsive, of pandering to the lowest common denominator (although postmodernism is invading that market). And, although as a discipline and intellectual construct modernism has much that remains valid, or else there would be nothing to kick around, as a *style* modernism has all the faults of other styles. That is, all these styles of the '80s are hollow expressions of fashion's whim. Will the buildings for the spring collections have hemlines three inches or six inches above the knee?

For the most part, architecture of the past decade has continued to be either, as I said in 1987, a nearly total philosophical void or, more recently, the product of a philosophy of hermetically isolated vacuity. Viewed from outside the profession, or even from outside the United States, our architecture's posturing and indecision must be both perplexing and disturbing. Clearly the oscillations of style are exceeding any notion of valuable "stylistic breadth" or "architecture of inclusion." Rather, we are confronted with apparently random gropings, massaged by both a jaded market and an architectural press panting for the next stylistic titillation. Ironically, the paper architecture of the impoverished '70s, which was created only for publication as a substitute for reality in built form, has been replaced by constructed buildings that only achieve "reality" when they are photographed, published, and pigeonholed in the appropriate stylistic niche—a crazed extrapolation of Descartes' tree falling, unheard, in the forest.

What we are witnessing is a profound confusion in architectural values and in the societal values that inevitably shape them. If there is a definable spirit of the age, it is anxiety. And, God knows, there is plenty to be anxious about: a very dicey economic situation, rampant social ills, impending ecological disaster, etc., etc. However, rather than these identifiable sources of anxiety, the fundamental cause of nervousness seems to be concern about our unknown future. Not only are we approaching a new century, a new millennium, but we are in the middle of enormous structural changes in our society and its institutions. Shifts to an unprecedented global interdependence, incredible scalar changes in economic disparities, sheer quantities of people, information, *things,* and, by inversion, sheer scarcities of space, resources, arable land, and, most of all, *time* are inducing fundamental shifts in our perception of reality.

For the first time in history we are, if not comfortable, at least conversant with the notion of infinity. Even young children, with the initiates' tolerant amusement at the special effects in "Star Wars," are informed about light-years, black holes, supernovas, and the like. We are about to launch a telescope into space that can "see" 12 billion light-years, and we know space continues beyond that. Maybe forever. At the same time, and also for the first time in history, there is *widespread* capability to totally destroy life on this planet. Maybe forever.

We live in this magnetic field between infinite continuity and instantaneous oblivion. It is a highly charged atmosphere that

tends to induce selfishness, a run-for-the-lifeboats mentality that, among other manifestations, I believe is in no small measure a cause of the unbridled greed characteristic of our society through the past decade. It is a difficult moment in which to focus attention on problems outside the individual, such as someone else's homelessness, some other country's debt.

Nor is it an atmosphere conducive to thoughtful introspection. There is a pervasive sense of nervous impatience that precludes analysis of who we are at this moment in time, what our values have been and might be, what our institutions are that give us definition. Is anyone at this time really looking for "volume zero," as Louis Kahn did, or, for that matter, truly asking about the meaning of a wall or what a building wants to be?

In 1985 the late Italian author Italo Calvino was to give the Charles Eliot Norton lectures at Harvard University. Calvino died on the eve of his departure for the United States, but the lectures he was to have given have recently been published as "Six Memos for the Next Millennium." In the published texts Calvino propounds fundamental precepts for literature—values, qualities, and peculiarities—that he believes are essential if literature is to continue to be a meaningful component of our lives in the next millennium. The lectures are clearly the product of just the sort of thoughtful introspection that is so rare in our time. In his lecture "Multiplicity" Calvino says, "Literature remains alive only if we set ourselves immeasurable goals, far beyond all hope of achievement. Only if poets and writers set themselves tasks that no one else dares imagine will literature continue to have a function . . . the grand challenge . . . is to be capable of weaving together the various branches of knowledge, the various 'codes,' into a manifold and multifaceted vision of the world."

In every instance where Calvino uses the words literature, writer, or poet in this excerpt and, almost equally, throughout "Six Memos," I believe the word architecture or architect could be substituted.

In 1964 Aldo van Eyke wrote in the "Team Ten Primer" that, unless there was a substantial change in the preoccupations of architects, we would become "true specialists in the art of organizing the meager." How prophetic he was, and, if architects continue to refuse to address the excruciatingly difficult task of genuine introspection, of attempting to deduce a larger order from humanity's needs, institutions, hopes, fears, and beliefs, we will continue to involve ourselves merely with Style. We will be environmental beauticians.

Robert Geddes: 'Diametrically opposed metropolitan trends.'

In the 1980s, two diametrically opposed trends have radically changed the form and character of the American metropolis. One trend strengthens architecture's role in building cities. The other threatens to destroy it.

Consider the potentially destructive trend first. Over the past decade a new component of metropolis has emerged— the regional growth corridor. It is a disjointed conglomeration of discrete structures for businesses, industries, and residences strung helter-skelter around a transportation route. This new settlement can hardly be called a city in any conventional sense. It has no core. Nor can it accurately be called a suburb, for there is no "urb" to which it is a "sub."

What is it then? Even the U.S. Census Bureau will have trouble with its definition of metropolis and its classifications of places as urban or rural. The New York *Times* reported on a new place name, "countrified city." While the term itself may not last, it does express the hybrid nature of the beast, urban in economy and scale, rural in myth and location, fragments scattered on the landscape.

In a sense, this strange new hybrid represents the triumph of 20th-century zoning principles. Originally developed to protect people from having factories in their backyards, suburban zoning ordinances have kept all functions neatly apart from each other. As the logical extension of this approach, the growth corridor separates offices, industries, shopping, and residences each into their own private domains. They don't interfere with each other. But they don't interact with each other either; they are separate areas, not parts of any groups or wholes. They don't connect.

On the other hand, an encouraging trend has developed in our nation's downtowns. There, the whole has become stronger then ever, thanks to a re-affirmation of the traditional city fabric. The important elements that tie a downtown together—most significantly, the street and the sidewalk— are once again recognized as the keys to urbanity.

Indeed, two of the most significant architectural achievements of the past decade are related to this trend. They are not buildings but documents—the downtown plans for San Francisco and for Philadelphia. These two plans will guide the building and the shape of their respective cities in ways that are radically different from the postwar concepts of city-building. For example, Philadelphia now is working on an innovative zoning code, including a new classification of interior space, "the public room," akin to a Nolli map. The code will ensure that the plan will succeed as a blueprint for directing growth without destroying the city's character.

The impact of these documents extends beyond San Francisco and Philadelphia. Other cities will feel their influence. While the documents themselves reflect the idiosyncratic character of the cities for which they were drafted, their underlying theme is universal. Both recognize that a city's greatness depends on its streets, not its individual buildings. If the streets and sidewalks of a city are designed to encourage life and activity, then architecture, in its public role as a street wall, will flourish as well.

The sad paradox of this decade remains. American downtowns, after decades of mistakes and false starts, seem to have learned their lesson, recognizing that a great city is not a loose conglomeration of high-profile buildings but a densely woven fabric in which buildings are part of the whole. Streets, sidewalks, and public spaces, both exterior and interior, are all crucial to the health and vitality of the downtown. But this seems to be a lesson unheeded in the new outlying component of metropolis. In growth corridors, streets and sidewalks don't connect. Architecture is reduced to a box in a parking lot. Buildings tend to be blank and mute. From the highway they might be seen as graphic images, but they are signs that don't truly communicate any indication of purpose or value.

The metropolis has changed. It is better downtown and worse in the countryside. There, architects must weave a fabric where none exists and find ways to link the fragments. These formless settlements demand a reunion of architecture and landscape architecture.

Doug Kelbaugh:
'A sense of limits. . . from the last decade'

More than anything else, a sense of limits is what I take from the last decade into the next. Limits manifested themselves in several architectural ways: regionalism challenged internationalism, figuration challenged abstraction, convention challenged invention, and typology and precedent challenged originality and functionalism. And the not-in-my-backyard syndrome challenged growth.

In the 1960s, advocacy planning and community design placed a new social and political imperative on architecture. There was a conviction that part of the population was simply not being served by the profession and that architects should voluntarily intervene on their behalf.

Then the energy crisis in the 1970s promoted an architecture more sympathetic to the environment. Natural resources were seen as finite, as was the planet's ability to absorb our wastes and support our consumption. This ecological view encouraged us to use such passive design strategies as natural heating, cooling, lighting, and ventilation. More important, it compelled us to make our designs more site-specific, i.e., tailored to the local climate, terrain, building materials, and practices. It was not only a question of saving BTUs but also of heeding a theoretical position that posited a more humble view of humanity's place in the natural world and a more modest planetary allotment for our national and our individual needs. There seemed to be a fundamental connection between Modernism and the exploitation of natural resources and the deterioration of the environment.

One of the major changes of the 1980s seemed to be a shift from treating both architectural space and natural resources as infinite and open-ended toward treating them as finite and bounded. This shift represented a rare convergence of environmental and postmodern thinking—a positive note, given the divergence in contemporary architectural theories. The idea of finitude offered promise of intellectual agreement between these two schools of thought. The Modern Movement's conception of architectural space—gridded, universal, and continuous—gave way to a particular, local, finite, and static conception. (Whether Deconstructivism will overturn this change remains to be seen.)

There has also been a shift from treating architectural form and space as abstract and asymmetrical toward treating them as positive and figural. It had seemed that the city might become little more than a World's Fair, with each building screaming for attention louder than the next and

with little concern for civic hierarchy. In the 1980s, buildings gained their presence from symmetrical composition and figuration of the facade rather than from the irregular footprints, gymnastic sections, and abstract elevations that often characterize modernist buildings.

Background buildings came to be appreciated as much as "object," or monumental, buildings. (The realization that coherent cities must have many quiet background buildings for every monumental foreground building was probably the single most important revelation of the decade for me. As a teacher, I now find myself constantly beseeching students to save their grand gestures for important civic buildings and not to waste them on every building they design. This is a far cry from my student days in the 1960s, when it was an unspoken rule that *all* designs had to be bold and inventive.)

Site specificity—perhaps the passive solar movement's greatest architectural legacy—aroused a sense of regional specificity in the 1980s. Regionalism elevated local culture, history, and mythology, as well as environmental concerns, to be prime determinants of form. This more complete set of limits attempted to inform an authentic, local, rooted architecture that resisted mass culture and operated on the margins of the corporate world and big government. Regionalism attempted to satisfy our need for the particular, while an interest in building typology replaced mass production and standardization in our search for the universal.

Typology—the language of building types—revived a traditional way of looking at function and re-established precedent as a point of departure for designing a building. In the 1980s, typologically minded architects began to study building types that have evolved over time rather than following the mandate of the Modern Movement to discover new forms latent in the program, site, or technology. (In archi-

tectural education, typology brought me to see our discipline as a traditional language rather than a scientific/technical field in which invention is valued more than convention.)

Over the last 10 years, typology has shifted the scale at which invention occurs. Instead of feeling compelled to make a creative, original statement at the building scale—a hallmark of the Modern Movement—the architect of the 1980s sometimes seemed content to let Type determine the overall building configuration. This in turn let the designer concentrate more attention on the room, as opposed to circulation or structure, which often drove modernist design. Related to this re-emerging interest in discrete rooms, as opposed to infinite or flexible space, was greater design emphasis on fixed components, such as the door, window, moldings, and so forth.

The scale of attention also shifted to the street and the square. Public space took on an importance equal to if not greater than that of the buildings that configure it. We learned to treat spaces as a hierarchy of outdoor rooms that are smaller, better defined, and more figural than the broad streets and heroic, but inhuman, plazas of the Modern Period. Postmodernism reversed the figure/ground relationship of our cities, trading the figural buildings of the modern city for the figural public spaces of the classical city. This fundamental change may prove to be its greatest contribution to urban design.

Lastly, a major sense of limits began to emerge in suburbia. Of the millions of new households that were formed in America during the 1980s, it has been estimated that only 25 percent contained married couples. This statistic represents an astonishing demographic shift. Not only do the suburbs lack the social mix and vitality of cities, but the traditional nuclear family, for whom suburbia was conceived, now represents barely one out of four new

households. But "we are still building World War II suburbs as if families were large and had only one breadwinner, as if jobs were all downtown, as if land and energy were endless, and as if another lane on the freeway would end traffic congestion," to quote *The Pedestrian Pocket Book*. The AIA Vision 2000 report recently listed the urbanization of suburbia as one of the most important trends of upcoming decades.

If the 1980s began to see the application of better urban design principles, this next decade must develop new architectural models and social ideals for suburban design. Strategies for limiting and ordering suburban sprawl are imperative. Designing sustainable and liveable communities—ones that don't tax the environment too heavily, that celebrate regional differences with recognizable vernacular and monumental building types, that mix people of different ages, ethnicities and incomes and that have a sense of public place—would be a great agenda for the 1990s. Otherwise, many of this last decade's gains will, in my opinion, have been in vain.

Robert A. Ivy Jr.: 'A dominance of corporate confidence.'

When seen from a distance, the architecture of the 1980s resembles an abstractly patterned patchwork quilt. Its framework has been the hegemony of the American urban, corporate culture; the pieces of the pattern, a growing respect for uniqueness of place, of time, or of motive.

An architecture of particularity, as stylistically diverse as the 50 states, is replacing the ironic historicism of early postmodernism. It is more than regional, yet tied to specific place; it is authentic, responsive to landscape, climate, or context, sometimes self-confidently up from the culture. Many of these terms could be applied to Predock's Fuller house, Esherick's Monterey Aquarium, or scores of other buildings.

As Michael Graves's San Juan Capistrano Library appropriates local idiom, it endows its new home with scale and resonance that reinforce archetype with a new California twist. Frank Gehry's Norton residence arises from and enriches a different California culture—eclectic Venice. There is much more work in these projects than good taste, something beyond style, yet the operative is something different from the 19th-Century romantic ideal of isolated, brave new buildings in an endless landscape. All joyfully appropriate this nation's cultural variety.

Appreciation of America's rich building legacy has continued from the '60s and '70s, sometimes in conjunction with new construction (Church Court condominiums by Graham Gund, FAIA), sometimes for the sake of the older building. Among the most splendid work of the last decade have been the restorations of the Tennessee and California state capitols, the New York Public library, and Washington's Union Station. Throughout the '80s, new and renewed individual works of architecture, like embroidered swatches, have come to rest in the borders of a solidly American urban framework. Despite increasing internationalism and strong personal statements, the '80s reflect a dominance of corporate confidence and a spreading embrace of the continent by urban influence.

Concentric rings of interstate highways now circle almost every major city, spreading abstract glass towers of urban-initiated development into the landscape. "Edge cities," such as Dallas's Las Colinas or Atlanta's Perimeter Center (actually clusters of office towers, shopping centers, or condominiums metastasized from original city stock), rise like sand castles along major highways. The word "area" grows in importance: "Where are you from?" no longer elicits Park Slope/Seventh Avenue, but rather, "the New York area." The Big Apple, like other metropolitan sources of capital formation and development ideas, exhibited its own strength during the '80s, accepting bold additions (Battery Park City) and a renewed waterfront.

Beacons from New York skyscrapers and Los Angeles hills have spread the design media's messages throughout the country. During the '80s both print and broadcast media reached deep into the heartland and provoked informed cocktail debate in Rapid City about San Francisco's building prohibitions or the additions to Washington's Vietnam Memorial. Atlanta's Scogin Elam & Bray summed up the pervasive media influence in a library in one small Georgia town, where a satellite dish serves as both chandelier and metaphor for our country's shrinking borders.

At its best the urban reach into the landscape blends structure, whether Wrightian, high-tech, International Style, or funky, with the natural order. Fortunately, institutions and corporations have built with increasing sophistication and sensitivity to the landscape. Kallmann, McKinnell & Woods's Becton Dickenson headquarters and American Academy evoke idealized garden landscapes that are a civilized foretaste of a more mature nation.

Both maturity and creativity, urban development and the architecture of particularity, converge in the decade's model project, which is not a building but a plan. At Seaside, Fla., Andres Duany and Elizabeth Plater-Zyberk, together with urban theorist Leon Krier and client Robert Davis, brainstormed the new small town. They jointly produced a master plan that encourages diversity, seeks the occasional idiosyncratic gesture, demands an architecture of respect, while fostering the individual statement.

While Seaside is both a rational and sensitive Utopian model, it is a consciously limited one, a resort community born of a single organizing vision rather than commercial or social imperative. Even with the utmost sensitivity to place, even with an eye to variety of experience, the town is creating its own time signature. It ultimately will lack the authentic patina that accretion brings to our cities.

As developers fill in the remaining canvas of this continent's manifest destiny, many are examining Seaside's approach as a case study. How well the planning method for one small resort community can be translated into edge city, suburban, or commercial applications is not clear.

Yet Seaside is an encouraging model for the future and an appropriate paradigm for the past 10 years of American architecture. Despite its stylistic conformity and its flaws, Seaside responds to basic human desire; no one who has rambled its paths or sat on its porches leaves unmoved. The trick in the '90s will be to dream dreams that are as memorable, that sensitively consider not just individual buildings but relationships, that grasp the essence of the zeitgeist and transform a new era's motives into fresh, valid patterns of enterprise and art. □

Mr. Wilson is a professor of architectural history at the University of Virginia. Mr. Esherick is AIA's 1989 gold medalist. Ms. McCurry is a principal in the firm of Tigerman McCurry Architects. Mr. Gebhard is a professor of architectural history at the University of California, Santa Barbara. Mr. Frasca is a partner in the Zimmer Gunsel Frasca Partnership. Mr. Logan is a partner in ELS/Elbasani & Logan Architects. Mr. Lym practices in San Francisco. Mr. Simon is a principal in Center-brook Architects. Ms. Halsband is a principal in R.M. Kliment & Frances Halsband Architects. Mr. Mockbee wrote in collaboration with his partners L. Coleman Coker, AIA, and Thomas S. Howarth, AIA. Mr. Forbes practices in Boston. Mr. Geddes is a principal in Geddes Brecher Qualls Cunningham. Mr. Kelbaugh is professor and chairman of the department of architecture, University of Washington, Seattle. Mr. Ivy is proprietor of Ivy Architects.